An East Asian Challenge to Western Neoliberalism

Analysts generally agree that, in the long term, the biggest challenge to American hegemony is not military but rather China's economic rise. This perception is spread in no small measure because Xi Jinping has – in the face of patent military inferiority – conducted himself much more boldly on the world stage than Hu Jintao. Meanwhile, China has also begun conjuring up an alternative vision for global leadership, now widely termed as the 'China Model'.

This book therefore offers a critical and comprehensive explanation of the China Model and its origins. Using a range of case studies, covering varying historical and geographical approaches, it debates whether the Chinese experience in the last three decades of economic reform should be interpreted as an answer to the reigning hegemony of neoliberalism or rather a further reinforcement of it. To answer these questions, it provides an investigation into what China may have learned from its East Asian neighbours' earlier economic successes. It also examines how it is responding to and might even reconfigure the world political-economic system as it develops fresh and potentially more powerful regulatory capacities.

Providing a multi-dimensional analysis of the China Model, the book will be of interest to students and scholars of Chinese Economics, Economic Geography and Chinese Studies.

Niv Horesh is a professorial visiting fellow at the School of Government and International Affairs at Durham University.

Kean Fan Lim is an assistant professor in economic geography in the School of Geography at the University of Nottingham.

Routledge Studies on Comparative Asian Politics

Books in this series will cover such areas as political institutions and systems, political economy, political culture, political thought, political psychology, public administration, law, and political histories of Asia. The studies may deal with Asia as a whole, a single country, or a group of countries in Asia. Those studies that have a clear comparative edge are especially welcome.

The series is edited by Shiping Hua, the Calvin and Helen Lang Distinguished Chair in Asian Studies, Director of the Asian Studies Program and Professor of Political Science at the University of Louisville, USA.

The Authoritarian Public Sphere
Legitimation and Autocratic Power in North Korea, Burma, and China
Alexander Dukalskis

An East Asian Challenge to Western Neoliberalism
Critical Perspectives on the 'China Model'
Niv Horesh and Kean Fan Lim

An East Asian Challenge to Western Neoliberalism

Critical Perspectives on the 'China Model'

Niv Horesh and Kean Fan Lim

Routledge
Taylor & Francis Group

LONDON AND NEW YORK

First published 2018 by Routledge

2 Park Square, Milton Park, Abingdon, Oxfordshire OX14 4RN

52 Vanderbilt Avenue, New York, NY 10017

Routledge is an imprint of the Taylor & Francis Group, an informa business

First issued in paperback 2018

British Library Cataloguing-in-Publication Data
A catalogue record for this book is available from the British Library

Library of Congress Cataloging-in-Publication Data
Names: Horesh, Niv, author. | Lim, Kean Fan, author.
Title: An East Asian challenge to western neoliberalism: critical perspectives on the 'China model' / Niv Horesh and Kean Fan Lim.
Description: 1 Edition. | New York : Routledge, 2018. | Series: Routledge studies on comparative Asian politics | Includes bibliographical references and index.
Identifiers: LCCN 2017011197 | ISBN 9781138926745 (hardback) | ISBN 9781315683041 (ebook)
Subjects: LCSH: China—Economic policy—1976–2000. | China— Economic policy—2000– | China—Economic conditions—1976–2000. | China—Economic conditions—2000– | China—Foreign economic relations.
Classification: LCC HC427.92 .H673 2018 | DDC 330.951—dc23
LC record available at https://lccn.loc.gov/2017011197

ISBN: 978-1-138-92674-5 (hbk)
ISBN: 978-0-367-18994-5 (pbk)

Typeset in Times New Roman
by Apex CoVantage, LLC

Contents

Illustrations

Figures

Tables

Box

Acknowledgements

The need for a book such as this was identified during a casual introductory meeting between the authors one summer afternoon in 2014 in the Aspire Café at the University of Nottingham's Jubilee Campus. At the time, the Jubilee Campus was a lively scholarly hub of Chinese studies, bringing together researchers from different disciplines on a collegial basis. Hailing, as the authors do, from different fields (history, geography) was not unusual, in that sense. Nevertheless, that the project could come to fruition in concrete terms in the face of mounting administrative pressures and funding cutbacks is particularly gratifying. It is a reminder to us that the job of scholars is to produce original scholarship and provide quality education to students before anything else. All the rest is merely 'white noise'.

What ensued from that meeting at the Aspire Café was therefore a stimulating and rewarding intellectual journey. It has been made possible through the faith, guidance, generosity and patience of numerous colleagues and friends both at Nottingham and beyond.

We would first like to thank Professor Shiping Hua, the Series Editor for his belief in our work. Following the commissioning of the book project, the editorial team at Routledge – Stephanie Rogers, Georgina Bishop and Rebecca Lawrence – provided excellent support during each stage of the publication process.

Some of the findings and discussions in this book are an elaboration on joint work published in academic journals in leaner form – these research outputs are listed under the authors' surnames in the bibliography. Engagement with journal editors and referees subsequently helped in tightening up our arguments in the book and making it a more holistic study. We would like to express our gratitude to the following editors for their guidance in that regard: Professor Chris Bramall (*The China Quarterly*), Professor Shaun Breslin (*The Pacific Review*), Professor Leong Liew (*Journal of the Asia Pacific Economy*) and Professor Yongnian Zheng (*China: An International Journal*).

Niv Horesh would like to broadly acknowledge generous scholarly feedback on his work on China over the past few years from Professor Emeritus Mark Elvin (Oxford University); Professor Richard Burdekin (CMC); Professor Valerie Hanson (Yale); Professor Emeritus Yitzhak Shichor (HUJI); Professor Yuri Pines (HUJI); Professor Anoushiravan Ehteshami (Durham); and Dr Sara Hsu (SUNY New Paltz).

On a more personal note, Niv would like to express special thanks to all his extended family in the UK for making his four-year stay there so congenial, and to the lovely Donna Brown for her wisdom, affection and introduction to the best-kept secrets of Derbyshire.

Kean Fan Lim would like to acknowledge funding support from the University of Nottingham's School of Geography Research Capacity and Networking Award. This support made fieldwork possible in Guangdong in 2015, which contributed in part to the materials developed for this book.

On a more personal note, Kean would like to thank his wife, Stephanie Lim, for her unwavering support and constant encouragement during the course of this project. He would like to share the book with Stephanie and their wonderful new addition to the family – Ethan Lim.

1 Introduction

East Asia as an alternative modernity?

Complaints about the political apathy of many of today's' reality TV and social-media-ridden students are not uncommon amongst baby-boom professors. Recently, eminent historian Mark Lilla of Columbia University deplored, in an article for *Die Zeit*, that very apathy, diagnosing it as one that affects not just American students but nowadays even Chinese students born after 1989. For Lilla, to animate the heady ideological battle of the Cold War in the classroom felt, at present, like a "poet singing of the Lost Atlantis". He therefore ridiculed the Western impulse to prescribe "individual freedoms" as a quick fix to all the world's post-1989 problems.[1]

Lilla may be exaggerating the ideological vacuum left by communism's downfall. For, as David Brooks recently suggested in *The New York Times*, the kind of "democratic complacency" that followed the Soviet Union's disintegration is now being quickly filled by global wonderment at the East Asian developmental state model. Brooks argued that authoritarian countries like Singapore, as just one example, seem "more successful right now" in view of the economic and political malaise afflicting Washington since the 2008 Global Financial Crisis.[2]

Following the fall of the Berlin Wall, Francis Fukuyama famously and quite sanguinely pronounced the triumph of American ideology as the "End of History".[3] It was perhaps one of the classic cases of a social scientist lending oneself to what Butterfield dubbed as "Whig" historiographical teleology, presenting the past as a linear progression towards liberal democracy around the world.[4]

Fukuyama's 1990s sanguinary is now assailed on several fronts, not least by Vladimir Putin's second-term attempts at reincarnating Russian global influence in defiance of Washington, or the spectre of the so-called Islamic State (ISIS) sweeping to power in the Middle East on the back of two controversial American military interventions. There are emergent signs that Xi Jinping, the current leader of the ruling Communist Party of China (CPC), might opt, towards the end of his tenure, to more closely align with Putin by way of tempering American global hegemony.[5]

And here is the crux of the matter: in the long term, the biggest challenge to American hegemony is scarcely military; most analysts agree instead that America's military cannot be surpassed any time before 2050. Rather, East Asia's success in general, and China's *economic* rise, in particular, are seen by more and more analysts as incrementally undermining American global leadership, even if it will take many more decades for Chinese per-capita income to reach developed-world levels. This perception is spread in no small measure because Xi Jinping has – in the face of patent military inferiority – conducted himself much more boldly on the world stage than Hu Jintao, stepping up China's assertive handling of the territorial disputes with Japan over the Senkaku/Diaoyu Islets and with Vietnam and the Philippines over the South China Sea atolls. Concomitantly, under Xi, China has begun conjuring up an alternative vision for global leadership now widely termed as the 'China Model'.[6]

This nascent narrative is still riddled with internal contradiction, however. At the rhetorical level, it skirts between a "great awakening" (*weida fuxing*) and "dreams" (*meng*) of the Chinese people – an obvious oxymoron. On substance, political economists remain uncertain whether the Chinese experience of the last three decades of economic reform should be interpreted as an antidote or fillip to the reigning hegemony of neoliberalism.[7] And as prominent economist Richard Burdekin has observed, China's efforts at turning the renminbi (RMB) into a veritable global reserve currency like the US$ or pound sterling are far from complete:[8]

> Although a growing array of bilateral currency swaps and offshore renminbi centers have expanded RMB usage as far as Europe, Africa and South America, the most long-established offshore RMB market remains Hong Kong.

It would thus be helpful to evaluate the supposed exceptionalism of the Chinese developmental experience and the remit of China's global ambition on the premise that historical objectivity is always open to (re)evaluation.[9]

The basic goal of this book is to examine the historical framing of the China Model discourse compared with perceptions of the broader East Asian and Western trajectories. It proceeds from two angles. First, we seek to problematise the historical *basis* of what many in the advanced 'First World', particularly in America, used to see as their superior model of governance. Second, we posit the alternative 'China Model' as similarly problematic upon re-examining its historical record.[10]

This double complication circumvents the question whether this recently much-discussed regulatory prototype can be abstracted and empirically concretised. Addressing this question presupposes the existence of an internally coherent and objective template, from which deviations or alignments can be ascertained, whilst in reality, the postulation of putatively superior models and their (by implication inferior) alternatives more accurately reflect wishful thinking and psychological needs on the part of their proponents. In the final analysis, the current enthusiasm, in some quarters, of the international media (particularly in western Europe and North America) about the 'China Model' may have nothing to do with China *per se*, but more to do with the decline of self-celebrated models that are in and of themselves ideal-typical abstractions rather than historically grounded entities. Similarly, triumphant portrayals of Chinese exceptionalism by China-based scholars have been predicated on a troubled Mao-era legacy, the implications of which remain unclear for understanding the increasingly fragmented and globally involved Chinese political economy today.

Emerging insecurity about neoliberal superiority

Commentator Joshua Ramo has famously lumped various threads of that narrative under the rubric 'Beijing Consensus'. Subsequently, that narrative took on new dimensions, both in China and the abroad, countervailing along the way the International Monetary Fund (IMF) and World Bank as the organs behind globalising Anglo-American neoliberal discourse ('Washington Consensus').[11] Why then has Beijing's narrative attracted so much attention if the Chinese experience is, in reality, so hard to define? Mainly, it would appear, because of an emergent insecurity amongst policymakers and the intelligentsia in western Europe and North America about the validity of their *own* social and political values, and the salubrity of their *own* societies.

Evidence to that effect can be found beyond Brook's litanies about the loss of American dynamism and the bumbling of the Barack Obama administration. More importantly, a growing body of academic literature has built up over the last few years to underscore how grossly unequally distributed income has become in the West. Many economists, not just on the far left, now indict the Ronald Reagan–Margaret Thatcher project of neoliberalism for reversing the great post-war baby-boom march towards equal opportunity. Inequality seers like Paul Krugman, Joseph Stiglitz, Thomas Picketty or Luigi Zingales may not necessarily agree about the salubrity of the Chinese economy *per se*, but they certainly share a platform when it comes to inveighing against the godfathers of financial deregulation, which they see as underlying America's post-2008 recession.[12]

To be sure, there has always been critical interest in American academe in the failings of the 'system', and in democratic 'optimisation' of economic outcomes. Buchanan and Tullock's pioneering 1962 work on public choice is a case in point. They sought a free market-friendly mathematical formula that would curb the ability of vested-interest groups to bypass the will of the silent majority through, for example, 'pork-barrelling' swing voters or 'lobbying' career politicians. However, in the 1960s, even studies such as Buchanan and Tullock's were informed by the "genius" of America's founding fathers and its 1787 Constitution,[13] whereas today many commentators of different partisan persuasions see the Constitution itself, if not the Union's whole political architecture, as anachronistic and unfit for purpose in that they paralyse decision-making in Washington.[14]

In search of new answers, the previously mentioned insecurity has resurrected interest in once-marginalised, "heterodox" economic theories, ranging from Mancur Olson, through Hyman Minsky through Wolf Ladejinsky, and Karl Polanyi to John K. Galbraith. All heterodox thinkers shared, in their time, deep-seated suspicion of the ability of free markets, or representative democracy for that matter, to pre-empt resource misallocation. In other words, they rejected in one way or another neoclassical economic theory. As has been argued elsewhere, this disillusionment with neoclassical diktat has also led to renewed interest in the lessons economic history, economic sociology and new institutional economics might offer, thus revitalising these three disciplines.[15]

Recent historically informed work by economists is now almost *de rigueur*, going well beyond left-leaning circles. Taking issue with the root causes of the 2008 Global Financial Crisis, such work – ranging from Reinhart and Rogoff's right-leaning *This Time is Different*, to Acemoglu and Robinson's more centrist *Why Nations Fail* – hankers back in its temporal scope several centuries earlier. At the same time, older work by contrarian economic historians and economists that has been somewhat neglected in 1980s, when neoliberalism was at its height, is now finding new readers amongst conventionally trained economists – from Paul Bairoch through Chalmers Johnston to Alice Amsden. Outside academe too, authors like Joe Studwell draw on that once-neglected work and converge on the view that the East Asian experience belies neoliberalism and exposes the small government biases thereof.[16]

Freshly published, path-breaking and quantitatively compelling research in economic history is further validating Studwell's insights. Ha-Joon Chang, Robert Allen, Michael Lind and others have respectively shown, for example, that *un*free-market, industrial espionage and big-government designs not only typified the East Asian path to industrialisation. In fact, such grand design could also be attributed to England's take-off well *before* the Industrial Revolution and to America's global rise later in the early 19th century. Baldly put, Chang, Allen, Lind and others argue that wealthier countries start preaching to poorer countries about the need for free trade (read: reduce tariffs designed to protect nascent industries) and the need to reduce government size (read: allow foreigners to buy up vital sectors of the national economy) only after they themselves had completed industrialisation on the back of very protectionist measures.[17]

For these reasons, the human rights discourse in the modern developed world is critiqued by scholars like Naomi Klein, Noam Chomsky, Daniel A. Bell and Martin Jacques as a value-laden, ahistorical sugar-coating of what is in essence crude economic interest. Much like "free markets" in neoclassical parlance, human rights are conceived of as bringing about immediate betterment of the human condition irrespective of time and place, whereas in the Chinese narrative "individual" rights and "markets" are both viewed as contingent on "collective will" and on evolutionary social reform.

Yet, as Stiglitz alluded to, the wealthier "collectivist" China becomes, the harder it is to shrug off its affinity with the "individualistic" US. Whilst, on the right, some Western critics still cling to the democracy-vs.-tyranny binary, and on the left, some critics starkly posit American neo-imperialism vs. China's "peaceful rise", both contending powers are in fact experiencing flagrantly unequal wealth distribution; they are both big polluters, big military spenders and capital-punishment enthusiasts; they also both incarcerate large segments of their population. [18] In short, not only are their logics of socioeconomic regulation increasingly more similar to each other, China and the USA are now more economically *inter*dependent than at any other point in history.[19]

Much of the self-doubt in America, as well as the newfound interest in institutional economics, after all have to do with the fact that the "one man, one vote" system proved incapable of stalling that reversal of the post-war social contract in the West, which had in turn nipped in the bud the spread of communism. Ironically, as Picketty poignantly shows, once the spectre of communism had diminished, inequality exploded.[20]

Peerenboom and Whyte's recent work is very important in this context because it shows – based on independently gathered polling data – that the absence of "one man, one vote" in China is not yet costing the CPC much popular support. Peerenboom, in particular, does much to dispel the fairly common Western notion that the peoples of the developing world would prefer a greater degree of democracy and social equality to rising living standards in absolute terms.[21] The argument, to be sure, might hold well beyond China. It specifically brings to mind Latin America: whilst that part of the world democratised relatively recently, in some cases following decades of oppressive dictatorship, most Latin Americans still seem to prize economic performance over universal suffrage. Moreover, a few democratically elected Latin American governments have arguably taken social inequality well beyond the norm under their dictatorial predecessors.[22]

US-based academics like Minxin Pei and Huang Yasheng often invoke India by way of inspiration for the developing world that is alternative to the "China Model"; one that is more democratic and therefore one that would prove more economically compelling in the long run.[23] After all, India is the biggest and one of the longest-running democracies in Asia. However, as Drèze and Sen's work indicates, the fact that the Gini coefficient for supposedly communist China may now be higher than that of India conceals the tough everyday realities that the overwhelmingly rural populations of either country face. For Drèze and Sen, perhaps more instructive is the fact that Chinese economic reforms of the last three decades did not whittle away at arable land distribution. In India, by way of contrast, arable land distribution remains badly skewed, despite Nehru's socialist legacy.[24] What this points to, then, is the need for any transfers of concrete policies and regulatory ideologies – in particular that of the supposedly superior neoliberal reason – to be contextually – and historically grounded.

There has been, however, another dimension of CPC legitimation that is urban in nature, constituting a break with the Mao era, but at the same time defying Seymour Lispset's prediction that the emergence of a powerful capitalist middle class would facilitate democratic transition.[25] At the Fifth Plenum of the fifteenth Central Committee in 2000, the CPC committed itself to "the healthy development of the self-employed and privately owned businesses", thereby suggesting a parity between officials running state-owned enterprises and entrepreneurs. On 1 July 2001, then Party Secretary Jiang Zemin recommended that entrepreneurs be allowed once again to become CPC members, after a long ban that had been in effect since the 1989 Tiananmen student demonstrations. In 2002, during the sixteenth CPC Congress, the Party's constitution was formally amended to that effect, and the new spirit of entrepreneurial co-optation – known as the "Three Represents" – was touted until it became the definitive legacy of the Jiang Zemin era (1993–2003). Although Hu Jintao's (2002–2012) subsequent decade in power saw greater preoccupation with social-justice slogans and a rhetorical pursuit of greater income equality, in reality it was not only the case that entrepreneurs continued to be welcomed into Party ranks, but *also* the case that many Party members were encouraged to enrich themselves by taking the plunge into the "sea" of private business (*xiahai*).[26]

Seeking answers to Mao's troubled legacy

Contrary to China-based social scientists in the 1980s, the academic authors of China's emergent narrative of leadership are typically well-travelled and acutely aware of the kind of transnational comparative data that foreign scholars like Drèze and Sen tend to invoke. Though these Chinese authors' vision for the future is far from uniform, they all reject not merely the "Washington Consensus", but also the sanctity of the "one man, one vote" principle as ill-suited for China, if not for the developing world as a whole.[27] The most strident example is perhaps that of economist and visionary Hu Angang. In a recent analysis, Hu has gone so far as damning the entire American discourse on China as deriving from a "psyche of arrogance" (*zigao zida zheng*), which he unfavourably compared with what he saw as a Chinese cultural preference for "modesty". In the same breath, Hu diagnosed American society as suffering from irreversible "decline" (*zhujian shuiluo de guocheng*).[28] Hu's analysis is notable for more than just his triumphalist tenor and overt anti-Americanism, of which other China visionaries are more cautious. Rather, what is remarkable about the analysis from a scholarly point of view is his reading of Mao Zedong's era (1949–1976) into the 'China Model' discourse. Until recently, that discourse had been largely confined to the economic-reform era (1979–present), if not explicitly directed *against* the guiding principles of Maoism. On this point, Hu therefore dangerously overturns studies by other prominent economists who contribute to China's emerging leadership narrative, e.g., Justin Lin, Li Daokui, Zhou Tianyong or Ding Xueliang.

In essence, Hu asserts that net economic growth under Mao was significantly positive on balance, and the rate of growth then did not, on average, fall much behind the growth rate in the reform era. Other Chinese economists may occasionally argue for Chinese cultural or historical exceptionalism in other contexts, but their observations about the Mao era are much cooler, to say the least. In particular, Zhou and Ding also point to the *exceptionally* high social price that economic growth in China across both eras exacted, in terms of environmental degradation and suppression of independent trade unions.[29]

Yet, precisely because Western economists like Bramall as well as the aforementioned Drèze and Sen buck the Western trend by valorising the durability of Mao's land reforms, his universalisation of healthcare, his effective promotion of literacy and the relevance of Maoism to China's current achievements cannot be dismissed offhand.[30] Moreover, amongst the New Left circles, one can still find residual admiration for Mao, decades after the catastrophic upshot of his utopianism and megalomania have been uncovered.[31]

Here, one can identify an increasingly boisterous divergence in the scholarly literature. On the other end of the spectrum, Susan Shirk has observed, for example, that Mao's policies actually benefited foreign proletarians, not Chinese ones; Mao in other words ". . . did the workers of the world a favour by keeping hundreds of millions of Chinese labourers out of the global economy until 1978".[32] When it came to alleviating poverty for the masses of peasants in China's countryside, in whose name the CPC had come to power, Zhao Ziyang did – in Shirk's judgement – much more that Mao by disbanding collective farms and sanctioning the House-hold Responsibility System.[33]

And if present-day China as portrayed by, for example, Stiglitz is not that removed from the kind of China that Hu invokes, then in the realm of history, Mao's legacy certainly remains evermore polarising. Notably, scholarly echoes for Hu's favour-able standpoint on Mao can perhaps also be found in a detailed study of land reform in Wuxi in the early 1950s published by James Kung as recently as 2008. Kung found that the CPC had successfully "preserved the rich peasant economy" there, whilst redistributing land to the poor in a way that increased overall productivity.[34]

To be sure, the conventional wisdom in the West about Mao's economic legacy is still the one penned by Naughton. Before 1978, China according to Naugh-ton had been a badly inefficient command economy, much like the USSR; only that China was far more malnourished and poorer as a direct result of Mao's Great Leap Forward (1958–61) and Cultural Revolution (1966–71). Moreover, barriers to rural migration that Mao had put in place in the mid-1950s meant that China became less urbanised than the USSR. Chinese peasants, in turn, were badly discriminated against in terms of resource allocation, compared with urban-ites. China's relatively small industrial base was still more diffuse and decentral-ised compared with that of the USSR. In sum, China languished behind other communist-bloc countries; it remained an overwhelmingly agrarian polity, yet could barely feed itself.[35]

As already mentioned, the scholarly Mao cleavage has grown substantially over the last year. If ever there was some agreement between Western and Chi-nese economists on Mao's economic-policy credentials – rather than on his many faults – it invariably concerned his land reform. But the conclusions scholars like James Kung drew not so long ago have now come to be assiduously challenged by Dikötter's 2013 opus, *The Tragedy of Liberation*.

To a great extent, the verdict handed down by Dikötter on Mao has been fore-shadowed by Mark Selden and his co-authors, Edward Friedman and Paul Picko-wicz, back in 2007. In their *Revolution, Resistance and Reform in Village China*, Selden *et al* highlighted violent resistance by Hebei villagers to Mao's disastrous Great Leap Forward in the 1960s. But their primary sources were mostly inter-views, and they had not delved much into the CPC seminal experience with land reforms earlier on. Li Huaiyin's otherwise exemplary study of the Chinese coun-tryside under Maoist socialism was similarly constrained by the same regionally delimited scope and absence of archival evidence on the 1950s.[36]

Taking advantage of discrete documents that have recently (and somewhat selectively) been released by Chinese provincial archives, Dikötter casts his net right across the entirety of the country, powerfully arguing that Mao's land reforms in the 1950s had, *in toto*, bordered on genocide. He marshals various data to argue that – far from judiciously "preserving the rich peasant economy" as Kung might suggest – the CPC issued random death quotas that saw up to 2 million middle-income landowners executed and devastated the productive fabric of rural society.[37] Interestingly, this important work lends support to proponents of Chinese historical *continuity*: without the transformative and hard-handed policies instituted during the Mao era, the platform would not be established for Deng Xiaoping to unleash market-like dynamics, while keeping in place the regulatory structure of the party-state apparatus.[38] What requires further exploration, then, is how this legacy morphed as subsequent regimes launched place-specific institutional reforms and deepened China's engagement with the global economy.

Argument and structure

The anti-communist bent of much of Dikötter's work to date does not detract from the validity of *some* his observations.[39] For better or worse, he sets a high evidentiary benchmark for anyone attempting to parcel the Mao era up with China's twenty-first century exuberance in too facile a manner. In that sense, 'China Model' visionaries like Hu still have a lot to answer for, even if their prognosis of American decline is accepted in some Western quarters. Arguably, the emergent Chinese scholarly narrative of leadership would have rung more compelling outside China if, in the absence of democratic ideals, it entailed at the very least more sober, open evaluation of socioeconomic policies instituted during the Mao era.

One might forgive Xi Jinping – whose own father, much like Zhao Ziyang's, had been tormented by Mao – for invoking the Great Helmsman by way of affirming the historical legitimacy of CPC rule.[40] But for the Chinese party-state to muster soft power anywhere near that of the USA, one might expect a greater degree of candour and introspection in Chinese academe. Soft power matters here because, as argued earlier, both militarily and in terms of per-capita income, China will not catch up with the USA anytime soon. Pending such evidence-based introspection, and in full view of Hu's triumphalism, claims that the China Model constitutes a challenge to the prevailing global neoliberal order may well come across as deficient.

Yet, as Cartledge reminds us in distinct ways, historical understanding of the evolution of democracy in Euro-American contexts, and of the protections from power abuses it might provide, can be at times just as partial.[41] Unwittingly influenced by Shelley's romantic poetry, the glorification of the "ancient" Greek origins of Western governance systems often leads us to overlook the very narrow (and short-lived) franchise of democracy in times past: the persistence of slavery in ancient Greece and in antebellum America being two obvious cases in point. This democratic teleology is pernicious because, to borrow David Runciman's argument, it breeds complacency and understates the fragility of and enormous challenges facing the deepening of democracy worldwide.[42] That Byzantium shaped Greek heritage no less than Pericles' Athens is an apt reminder: Byzantium turned out to be a much longer-lasting polity that was hardly characterised by "one man, one vote". An assessment of emergent portrayals of the China Model within a broader East Asian multi-layered framework might perhaps yield some interesting findings about East Asia as an alternative economic modernity.

This book will therefore provide a critical and comprehensive explanation of the China Model and its origins, examining the issues that are critical to our understanding of the significance of China's rise. We are primarily concerned here with what China might have learned from its East Asian neighbours' earlier economic successes, and the ways in which China is responding to and might, in turn, reconfigure the world system we now live in as it develops fresh and potentially more powerful regulatory capacities. In that sense, we are attuned to both Chinese grand perceptions of the US and Japan, and self-perceptions of China; at the same time, we aim to critique these perceptions – along with the Chinese aspirational meta-narrative as a whole – with concrete and timely economic-policy analysis, both at the local and national level. And in doing so, we are otherwise informed not just by economic *history*, but also by China's *future* plans for monetary saliency, as explained, for example, by the aforementioned work of economists Burdekin and Tao.[43]

Following this Introduction, Chapter 2 construes the profundity of China's challenge to Western liberal democracy from a distinctly longer-term historical perspective. We shall start by examining the emergent historical rationale for a Chinese re-ordering of international system architecture, and question the extent to which actual Chinese foreign policy is consistent with that rationale. The second section in that chapter will then explore why the Tang era (CE 618–907) is so frequently evoked as a blueprint of China's aspirational narrative of global leadership by contemporary authors, with particular emphasis on the interplay between state and religion. The third section will revisit the tension between egalitarianism, racial tolerance and meritocracy in their re-enactment as cardinal historical tropes of the contemporary Chinese narrative. Finally, we will aim to examine the validity of linkages drawn between premodern Chinese statecraft and its contemporary socioeconomic transformation.

Chapter 3 attempts to shed a sidelight on the degree to which the Chinese themselves see their country as an alternative to the US-led neoliberal world order. It juxtaposes two of the most influential yet under-studied America watchers within the top echelon of the CPC, Wang Huning and Zheng Bijian. To be sure, the two have indelibly shaped CPC attitudes, yet surprisingly enough, although Zheng has been written about extensively in the English language, Wang has hitherto largely remained outside academics' purview. This chapter also aims, in passing, to explore linkages between the ideas of Wang and Zheng and those of other well-known America watchers like Liu Mingfu and Yan Xuetong. It is hoped that this comparison will offer clues about the extent to which the current advisory shaping CPC thinking on the US differs from the previous generation, and whether CPC thinking is un-American or anti-American in essence. The conclusions will tie the study together by speculating, based on Wang and Zheng's views, about the degree to which New Confucianism, as opposed to neoliberalism, might shape Chinese society in the future.

Chapter 4 spells out how the 'Singapore Model' has constituted the only second explicit attempt by the CPC to learn from a foreign country following Mao Zedong's pledge to contour 'China's tomorrow' on the Soviet Union experience during the early 1950s. This chapter critically evaluates policy transfers from Singapore to China in the post-Mao era. It re-examines how this Sino-Singaporean regulatory engagement came about historically following Deng Xiaoping's visit to Singapore in 1978 and offers a careful re-reading of the degree to which actual policy borrowing by China could transcend different state ideologies, abstract ideas and subjective attitudes. Particular focus is placed on the effects of CPC cadre training in Singapore universities and policy mutation within two government-to-government projects, namely the Suzhou Industrial Park and the Tianjin Eco-City. The chapter concludes that the 'Singapore Model', as applied in post-Mao China, casts institutional reforms as an open-ended process of policy experimentation and adaptation that is fraught with tension and resistance.

Chapter 5 shows that the Chinese political economy is a dynamic entity constituted by multiple developmental trajectories. Recent debates on two seemingly divergent 'models' in Chongqing and Guangdong help foreground the potential contradictions of this dynamism. Whilst existing research has attempted to evaluate these trajectories as outcomes of elite politics or ideological incommensurability, an overlooked, but no less important aspect is the connections between these trajectories, Mao-era regulatory policies and the post-1978 system of reciprocal accountability. Synthesising empirical materials from policy documents, academic commentaries, statistical data and interviews with planners from China, this chapter provides a critical evaluation of these connections.

Finally, Chapter 6 explores China's post-Mao development trajectory through a comparative perspective encompassing the Japanese South Korean and Taiwanese experiences, with references to the perceived economic falling behind of India and Latin America. It places the shifting logics of socioeconomic regulation in China in relation to the global neoliberal hegemony since the 1980s and the concomitant shifts in regulatory approaches across East Asia. In so doing, the chapter demonstrates that China has creatively adapted and repurposed regulatory logics from the Washington Consensus and other East Asian developmental state policies to consolidate its own version of state-led development. That development pattern has now turned China into a country that is about half urbanised, whereas it was overwhelmingly rural on the eve of reform in 1979.

In our Conclusions, we will speculate about the degree to which the Chinese trajectory may be of use to smaller, poorer and predominantly rural countries elsewhere and the degree to which it might intellectually reinforce the East Asian developmental state model on the whole as a credible alternative to neoliberalism.

Notes

1 www.zeit.de/2014/37/ideologie-freiheit-westen
2 www.nytimes.com/2014/05/20/opinion/brooks-the-big-debate.html; for a similar streak of wonderment at East Asian achievements and anxiety about America's future, see also Roger Cohen's recent *New York Times* columns, e.g.:- www.nytimes.com/2014/12/04/opinion/roger-cohen-feeling-uneasy-about-the-future.html?_r=0
3 Fukuyama (1992).
4 Butterfield (1931).
5 Rozman (2013).
6 For a discussion of these developments, see e.g. Horesh *et al* (2013).
7 Liew (2005); Dirlik (2006); Lim (2014).

8 Burdekin and Tao (forthcoming).
9 Duara (1995); Dirlik (1996); Callahan (2012).
10 For a more detailed discussion of continuities between imperial and modern China see e.g. Zheng (2009).
11 Ramo (2004); see also Kennedy's powerful critique (2010) of Ramo's arguments .
12 www.nytimes.com/2013/07/19/opinion/krugman-hitting-chinas-wall.html?_r=0; www.vanityfair.com/business/2015/01/china-worlds-largest-economy; www.haaretz. com/israel-news/.premium-1.560536; www.ft.com/cms/s/0/7ca6cfc2-1b39-11e5-a130-2e7db721f996.html
13 Buchanan and Tullock (1962).
14 See for example Fareed Zakaria: – http://globalpublicsquare.blogs.cnn.com/2011/06/20/is-it-time-to-update-the-u-s-constitution-2/
15 See, e.g., Horesh (2009); Peck (2010); Block and Somers (2014).
16 Studwell (2014).
17 Chang (2002); Allen (2011); Lind (2013).
18 www.vanityfair.com/business/2015/01/china-worlds-largest-economy
19 Ferguson (2008); Lim (2010).
20 Picketty (2014).
21 Peerenboom (2007); Whyte and Dong-kyun Im (2014).
22 Peerenboom (2007), pp. 254–255.
23 https://casi.sas.upenn.edu/iit/pei; Huang and Khanna (2003).
24 Drèze and Sen (2002), Ch. 4.
25 Lipset (1959).
26 Dickson (2008), pp. 40–41.
27 Notable critics of Western democratic values in Chinese academe include centrist Pan Wei (sociology), leftist Wang Hui (literature) and nationalist Yan Xuetong (international relations).
28 www.zhongdaonet.com/Newsinfo.aspx?id=10898
29 Zhou (2013); Ding (2011).
30 Bramall (2008).
31 Gao (2008).
32 Shirk (2008), p. 22.
33 Shirk (2008), p. 34. Interestingly, Zhao's wealthy father was a Henan landlord killed by the CPC during the land reforms of the late 1940s.
34 Kung (2008).
35 Naughton (1995), pp. 38–55.
36 Friedman *et al* (2007); Li (2009).
37 Dikötter (2013).
38 See, for instance, Bramall (2007); Kueh (2008).
39 For a sobering critique of Dikötter (2013) see Wemheuer (2014).
40 www.nytimes.com/2015/01/05/world/chinas-maoists-are-revived-as-thought-police.html?partner=rss&emc=rss
41 See Cartledge (2011), pp. 124–133.
42 Runciman (2013).
43 Burdekin and Tao (forthcoming). See also Burdekin (2008).

2 Restoring Tang splendour?

A critical historical assessment of China's new aspirational narrative of global leadership

In this chapter, we examine the extent to which China's post-1989 rise, and its more recent emerging narrative of global leadership, might dent Western-style liberal democracy as teleology of progress. Explicit in our focus is the argument that China poses not just the most serious economic challenge to the US in the post-Cold War era, but also a much more comprehensive, serious and historically grounded ideational challenge to the US than is commonly acknowledged.[1] Foregrounding China as *the* challenge is, however, not self-explanatory. In fact, up until Hu Jintao's tenure (2002–2012) as General Secretary of the CPC, China's rise had been perceived by most Western scholars as a fillip to Francis Fukuyama's notion of triumphant liberal democracy. Indeed, much of Jiang Zemin's decade in power (1989–2002) had been portrayed as a period when China would increasingly converge with Western market and international-citizenship norms.

By now, of course, China has been given a modestly larger say on the world stage. It wields enormous foreign-currency reserves and economic interest that straddle the entire planet. What China is sorely lacking, apart from long-range military equivalence, are better public relations. The CPC is acutely aware of this shortfall, and its functionaries are therefore engaged – by now, quite openly – in crafting an alternative ethical narrative to the one promoted by the US. The Chinese aspirational narrative draws much more on the country's illustrious pre-modern history than on Mao Zedong's radical thought. In essence, the Chinese narrative conjures up a more harmonious world, in which diverse religions, cultures, values and lifestyles can coexist peacefully and where big countries do not meddle in their smaller neighbours' affairs. Imperial China is cast as such a sophisticated tolerant polity that was administered by peace-loving, selfless sage bureaucrats; a polity where both ethnic minorities could reach high office on merit; and a polity whose emperors always welcomed trade missions from Korea and Japan but, unlike European or Japanese empire builders, never sought to subjugate other Asian peoples in the name of trade profit.[2]

The following three sections construe the profundity of China's challenge to Western liberal democracy from a distinctly longer-term historical perspective. We will start by examining the emergent historical rationale for a Chinese re-ordering of the international system architecture and question the extent to which actual Chinese foreign policy is consistent with that rationale. The second section will then explore why the Tang era (CE 618–907) is so frequently evoked as a blue-print by the contemporary authors of China's aspirational narrative of global lead-ership, with particular emphasis on the interplay between state and religion. The third section will revisit the tension between egalitarianism, racial tolerance and meritocracy in their re-enactment as cardinal historical tropes of the contempo-rary Chinese narrative. Our conclusions will finally aim at examining the validity of linkages drawn between premodern Chinese statecraft and its contemporary socioeconomic transformation.

Is China's geopolitical posture exceptional?

In 2000, influential international-relations thinker Aaron Friedberg predicted that Europe's early twentieth century, where Britain, France and Germany vied for supremacy, "will become Asia's Future".[3] Therein, Friedberg warned enthusi-asts of Asian multilateralism of exaggerating the "pacifying" effects of growing cross-border regional trade. Rather, Friedberg cautiously predicted that the more South Korea and China become economically powerful, the more they will seek to undermine Japan's regional status and eventually confront the US, even as the economies of all three East Asian countries become intertwined. In that sense, the risks of geo-strategic instability in the region looked greater to Friedberg than the prospect of forming an EU-like mechanism that would bind the region politically closer. The watershed here by way of analogy was of course World War Two: it took much devastation in Europe for states to prefer cooperation over competition for power.

One might nowadays object by suggesting that the three East Asian giants – China, Japan and South Korea – can learn from the European experience and decide to skip the confrontational stage right onto economic if not political inte-gration. However, Friedberg argued, in turn, that the dynamics of great power competition often overrode what *prima facie* might appear like a sensible stra-tegic choice for conflict avoidance and mutually beneficial peaceful economic prosperity. Indeed, compositionally, the three East Asian giants resemble today early twentieth century European powers in one important way: none has yet been substantively reconfigured by post-war immigration or the discourse of multi-culturalism, as is the case in the West.

China, Japan and Korea's sense of cohesion therefore relies on ethnicity to a greater extent, and their sense of historical insularity is often purposefully height-ened by ruling elites. By contrast, in much of the European Union and North America, the nation-state is moving slowly – in the face of an isolationist backlash – towards *de facto* multicultural and multi-ethnic societies with a high degree of population mobility. China, to be sure, has 55 recognised ethnic minorities, yet its "nation-state" project is still a work in progress, as up to 30% of all Chinese can-not yet properly speak Mandarin, the official language.[4] Efforts at conjuring up a shared sense of Chinese history and citizenry are far from complete. Thus, even as some are promoting China as a unique "civilizational state" that transcends ethnic tension and is inherently averse to territorial expansion, China is in fact investing heavily in nurturing a collective identity, at much the same time as the West has come to question, if not wholly disown, its colonial expansionist heritage.[5]

The crucial question is whether, precisely because of China's identity insecurities, the magnitude of its nation-state project and the reach of its economic achievements might beget claims to an alternative world order. Or is it the case, as Foot and Walter suggest, that whilst China may be on occasion emitting anti-US rhetoric, it is in fact a rising power uninterested in setting new international norms, but is one that is being "normalised" into the existing US-led neoliberal world order?[6] Indeed, more recently, China's enthusiastic acceptance of the Basel banking reforms following the global financial crisis of 2008, its contribution to the Vienna accords resolving Iran's nuclear question and its critical role in forging the 2015 Paris Agreement on the reduction of greenhouse gases are pieces of evidence that can be easily adduced in favour of "normalisation".[7]

Yet, critics of China in the West are quick to point to its recent build-up of an aircraft carrier fleet, its dredging of islets for airstrips in far-flung and disputed corners of the South China Sea and the recent announcement of its intension to build a naval facility in Djibouti.[8] When coupled with China's establishment of the multi-billion dollar Asia Infrastructure and Investment Bank (AIIB), there are clear signs – critics allege – that China's claims to "peaceful development" are insincere. The AIIB is cast in that context as a direct threat to the US-designed geopolitical architecture, as manifest in institutions like the IMF and World Bank or the 1951 San Francisco hub-and-spoke treaties with Japan. And Xi Jinping's "One Belt, One Road" initiative is similarly portrayed as an attempt to drive the US out of Eurasia.[9]

Granted, the mystique of the premodern overland and maritime Silk Road is being enthusiastically harped on by China in its new advancement of the AIIB, whilst its "nation-building" project at home over the past decade or so has been subsumed by a historically hued discourse of New Confucianism. The continuity and longevity of Chinese civilisation is a rhetorical marvel, even as the precise dating of Chinese antiquity compared with Western civilisation is in dispute amongst Chinese and Western archaeologists. Political correctness in China itself collocates a history that is 5,000-years long. But Western experts, by and large, still treat the veracity of the seminal Xia dynasty (c. BCE 2070–1600), which their Chinese counterparts have advanced as a starting point, with much suspicion.[10]

The range of New Confucian thought is at any rate broad, and not all of its constituents enjoy state backing, even if overall the rekindling of interest in the sage is actively promoted from earlier. Mainland-based New Confucians do lend, at least provisional, support to the CPC quite naturally, but a few oppose it on ethical grounds; some want to reconcile Confucianism with Western democratic ideas, whilst others see Confucianism as providing an alternative to Western liberal democracy; and some look at Confucianism as a possible repository of universal values, whilst others are primarily interested in filling in the cultural void in China itself.[11]

An anathema during the Mao era (1949–1976), the ancient aura of Confucius (c. BCE 551–479) has at any rate come to play a leading role in revitalizing and re-legitimizing CPC rule during the Hu and Xi eras. Originally a variant of the

Lee Kuan Yew Asian Values discourse of the 1990s, pitting collective rights over individual rights, New Confucianism is now openly promoted by Xi to amplify China's "dream" of re-surging on the world stage. At a popular level, although not within internal Party elite thought, universalist Marxism has similarly given way to Chinese cultural particularities, including a carefully monitored revival of Buddhism in Chinese society.[12]

Advocates of New Confucianism often cast it as universalist, non-Western and non-interventionist approach to international relations. However, critics of New Confucianism describe it as an apologia for one-party rule in the guise of engendering a more "harmonious society"; a vacuous portmanteau with which to, for example, inculcate "Patriotic Education" to Hong Kong residents that lionises the CPC's "united front" politics as opposed to America's 'dysfunctional' two-party democracy-cum-plutocracy.[13]

***

What, then, is China's overall strategy at a time nation-states in the West may be demographically transformed? It seems Zbigniew Brzezinski was right in predicting, over a decade ago, that China was unlikely to align with Japan, by way of challenging US Pacific hegemony, even though the two are avowedly nation-states that share "Asian values". Brzezinski suggested, in turn, that for the US – as non-Eurasian power – to remain a world hegemon, it must ensure no great contender emerges through a new alliance system across the great bulk of humanity, i.e., Eurasia. In practical terms, that means, above all, keeping China and Russia apart.[14]

Another more specific prediction from a few years ago by the prominent strategist, Edward Luttwak, seems to be partly shaping up on the ground already. Luttwak suggested that South Korea would gradually slip out of a US system of alliances to orbit China. But he also concluded that despite its spectacular economic success and growing military power, all of China's immediate neighbours were averse to what the 'China Model' of capitalist authoritarianism conveyed. Luttwak therefore predicted that Australia, Japan and Mongolia, as well as much of Southeast Asia, would gang up on China with US backing to deny China undisputed regional hegemon status.[15] Notably, even non-democratic Vietnam remains mistrustful of China, despite its dependence on Chinese imports. And in the Middle East, where anti-Americanism is at least as fierce as in China – there has been little enthusiasm for the kind of secularist pragmatism that China is identified with, although there is by and large great awe at its economic achievements.[16] Tensions between Xi and Abe mean Sino-Japanese relations remain fraught, even though both sides have gone out of their way in recent months to de-escalate maritime collisions around the Senkaku/Diaoyu Islets in the East China Sea.[17]

***

China watchers in the West are divided about the degree to which China is 'normalising' into the US-led world order, not least because within Chinese academe there has been a vigorous debate about whether or not China should continue toeing a low profile internationally. Prominent experts Wang Yizhou (Chinese

Academy of Social Sciences) and Wang Jisi (Peking University) have argued passionately, for example, that China needs to continue enmeshing itself within the *existing* international order rather than re-inventing it, whereas the more hawkish academic, Yan Xuetong, of Tsinghua University has hinted at the exigency for China to align more closely with Putin in confronting America by way of eradicating Westphalian conventions.[18]

Against the backdrop of vigorous debate within China itself, influential commentators outside of China, like Zheng Yongnian, have recently warned Beijing of declaring an all-out ideological war on liberal democracy.[19] Here, we argue nevertheless that a careful perusal of the ideas emanating from the CPC-endorsed wing of New Confucians does cohere into a narrative that can be read as alternative to liberal democracy, at least in the developing world, a narrative that entertains profound if as-yet internationally lesser-known historical and ethical dimensions. In that sense, we believe we are meaningfully expanding on earlier accounts, which tended to study Chinese responses to neoliberalism mostly in the domestic context of state-owned enterprise reform, as well as the clash between perceived free-marketeers like Premier Zhu Rongji (in office 1998–2003) and his followers and the Chinese New Left.[20] And we suggest, in the same breath, that vindication for this research agenda may be found in Xi Jinping's recent brief, yet explicit, warning to Chinese proponents of Western neoliberalism not to use his supply-side reform agenda to promote their cause.[21]

Based on extensive interviews, Scobell and Harold find in fact that China's higher-profile approach began in 2008, well before Xi formally took the reins in 2013, and was driven by two contradictory factors: on the one hand, a sense in Beijing that the US was becoming more deferential to China's interests, and less committed to East Asia, as it was licking the wounds from the global financial crisis. And at the same time, Chinese leaders' hypersensitivity to popular nationalism, fears of the spread of the Arab Spring and poor bureaucratic coordination amongst an expanding number of foreign policy actors bred a pre-emptive militancy of sorts.[22] As the gravity of the global financial crisis became apparent, a pro-Tibetan demonstration in Paris disrupted the relay of the Olympic Torch ahead of the 2008 Beijing Games, a scene that was repeated on smaller scales in other venues around the world where the Torch passed. This caused an upsurge of Chinese nationalist counter-protests both in China and overseas, galvanising, if not forcing, the CPC to take a visibly bolder anti-Western stance with claims of intentionally lax security arrangements designed to blemish Chinese pride.[23]

Despite these contradictory thrusts, Chinese domestic media savvy has increased by leaps and bounds since 2008, as has Chinese outward direct investment. If propaganda in Mao's era was deeply invasive through radio, street billboard and workplace mass-line campaigns – the CPC today is relying on a softer breed of online and satellite TV infotainment both at home and overseas. In addition, Confucius Institutes advance the new breed of state-endorsed Confucianism in lieu of aloof Maoist sloganeering.[24]

China is currently advancing an image of itself as an older and more sage world power; therefore, they are a more moderate and less violence-prone world power compared with the US. But to what extent historical analysis bears out that Chinese society in premodern times was less violent than elsewhere is moot. Ter Haar suggested, for example, that whilst the elite ethos *after* the Tang era came to frown on the use of physical force in the private domain, that attitude did not necessarily extend to the public domain or foreign policy.[25]

Residual non-interventionist and non-alignment tropes from the Mao era – when China was in reality much more internationally belligerent[26] – have come to blend in CPC rhetoric with more traditional portrayals of the splendour, tolerance and cosmopolitanism of the Tang dynasty (CE 618–907) as a blueprint for the future. Note, for example, the lavish Tang-style reception laid out for Indian Prime Minister Narendra Modi when he visited Xi'an in May 2015.[27]

In that sense, the authors of China's aspirational narrative of global leadership nowadays posit their country as globally central, much like the ancient Tang capital of Chang'an – perceived as the entry point of the Silk Road to Europe – that was known to all, far and near. The Tang "prosperous age" (*shengshi*) is somewhat wishfully cast as one more cosmopolitanism, peace-loving and magnanimous than was found in coeval empires elsewhere in the word or other dynastic empires in Chinese history; open to the world, yet more confident on the world stage; and tolerant, yet more battle-savvy, if not more 'virile' than later dynasties. The Tang ethnic melting pot is subtly contrasted with mass racially-grounded slavery,[28] war-proneness and colonialism pursued by later European powers. Concomitantly, this Tang template is also made to contrast with the Japanese historical trajectory, which is perceived as invariably expansionist and war-prone.[29]

In many ways, the Tang template can serve as a trope with which to inveigh against the US or even the Westphalian notion of sovereignty informing Western international-relations theory. The Chinese historically hued counterpoint to these is *tianxia*, literally translated as "all under heaven". In the Chinese mindset, the term connotes Chinese emperors' sense of suzerainty, one that symbolically extends to all of humanity but is, out of convenience and frugality, not exercised in practical terms outside of Sinosphere, broadly defined.[30] In other words, *tianxia* conjures up an old-new world order that entails an expectation for universal recognition of China's cultural superiority through the presentation of tribute (*chaogong*), in return for promised minimalist meddling in other people's affairs and the bestowal of asymmetric economic benefits on foreign countries' leaders and peoples (*houwang baolai*).[31]

Such benefits can be augmented by showing grace in admitting foreigners into the Chinese realm through educational co-optation, marriage and ultimately cultural assimilation (*heqin*). Timeless China is projected in that sense as a benevolent empire that has never been interested in subduing foreign people as cheap labour, captive markets or extracting their mineral wealth. To the contrary, it is a power that did and would once again treat the rest of the world with value-free, non-judgemental magnanimity; it would allow smaller stakeholders freer rein (*jimi*) than is the case under the US-led world order. That world order is depicted, by contrast, as grounded in US naked economic exploitation of poorer countries and their mineral wealth. Whilst the US pays lip service to the sanctity of other countries' sovereignty and preaches cultural equivalence, it is cast as spreading a demeaning and value-laden discourse.[32]

Restoring Tang splendour?

It is one thing to be deconstructing the Tang-hued blueprint on historical grounds, quite another to speculate about the extent to which the CPC or, for that matter, the average Chinese are genuinely internalising it. The blueprint for the future seems bold, but, as indicated at the outset, what lies beneath is, in no small measure, identity insecurities arising from an unfinished nation-state project, not to mention epistemological tensions within the gamut of New Confucian thought.

As indicated earlier, the CPC has derived much vitality from the 2008 financial crisis in the West. The ensuing Western crisis of self-confidence that writers like David Brooks have blamed on the Obama presidency are grist to Chinese meal.[33] In China, responses to Barack Obama's election cut to the heart of the matter because they contrast with the multicultural, multi-ethnic complexity of contemporary Western society, where the wrongs of Western colonialism in times past are fading from memory. Here, the CPC message seems to have by and large won the day, domestically at least: though a few liberal-minded Chinese intellectuals joined in the chorus of global enthusiasm over President Obama's election in 2009 as America's first black president, surveys suggest most Chinese remained indifferent.[34]

At the heart of the matter are enduring Chinese notions of benevolence towards ethnic minorities that are, on the one hand, assuming superiority, but on the other hand, eschew overt racism or Darwinian connotations of the early twenty-century Western streak. In the Chinese contemporary narrative, China is in fact cast as historically disinterested in foreigners' (no to be confused with *foreign*) affairs. To borrow Pan Wei's imagery, most Chinese leaders to this day, distinguish between a Sinophone (*Hua*) sphere of influence and an alien (*Yi*) sphere, where non-interventionism is to be practised even if that sphere includes a sizeable Chinese ethnic minority.[35]

The sub-text of the narrative is that racial discrimination has always been a non-issue in China, hence China does not need to partake in the West's contrived enthusiasm at the election of America's first black President. However, a historically informed reading of the narrative might suggest that Americans and Chinese have, in a sense, one major common pedigree: both American and Chinese modern nationalisms have, to a large extent, been cast in the mould of the anti-colonial struggle against Britain. One might point to defeat at the hands of Japan in 1895, rather than to British victory in the 1839–1842 Opium War, as the epiphany of Chinese modern nationalists, yet anti-Japanese sentiments in the USA have also boiled over at times in the past 150 years. On the other hand, anti-colonial baggage did not preclude the formation of a common interest-based "special relationship" between the US and Britain in the early 20th century, nor did it stop the CPC from teaming up with Britain, largely behind America's back, in the mid-1940s when overriding interests were at stake: Britain feared that a strong, US-backed

Kuomintang (KMT), or the Nationalist Party, emerging out of World War II would threaten its hold on Hong Kong much more than a victorious CPC would.[36]

The shared anti-British cause between China and the USA should not be overstated, at least not historically. Barack Obama might have described America as a nation built out of ". . . revolution against the [British] empire" in his famous 2009 Cairo speech,[37] but, as Eric Kaufmann has shown in his pioneering book, by the nineteenth century, American school textbooks lauded their country folk as "distilled Englishmen", and England itself – despite being a "less free" monarchic polity – was nevertheless perceived by American elites at the time as second only to the US in harbouring "Anglo-Saxon genius". In that sense, American identity, much like English identity, was forged racially and religiously against the image of the "papist" French and Spanish who had settled in North America.[38]

Arguably, differences today lie in that American world view is still driven by a kind of *manifest destiny* that militates towards spreading American values world-wide, whilst the Chinese have not, so far, shown any real "missionary impulse" to spread their version of authoritarian capitalism, even if Confucianism is beginning to be promoted softly outside of China too.[39] In the words of Cold War historian Odd Arne Wested, the United States was from its inception ". . . an interventionist power that based its foreign policy on territorial expansion", even if it has always exuded disdain for 'old-school' European imperialism as a result of its formative struggle against British rule. The American notion of liberty could not exist without the sanctity of free enterprise and private property. Even Thomas Jefferson, who glorified the early nineteenth century self-sufficient smallholding white protestant farmer as the ideal American, recognised enthusiasm for free global trade and commerce as built into the American character.[40]

***

Tang splendour, though not necessarily familiar to Westerner audiences yet, does strike a chord with overseas Chinese. Celebrated American-Chinese legal scholar and "tiger mum", Amy Chua, has, for example, essentialised Tang as a historical paragon of empire-building that owed much to tolerance of enterprising minorities and sufficient cultural cohesion. By comparison, Chua casts the earlier Han empire (BCE 206–CE 220) as less dynamic. This is because, unlike coeval Rome, the Han, whilst sprawling over bigger territory, did not, in Chua's view, fuse and build on foreign influences to the same extent.[41]

Early Tang elites were made up of many ethnic minorities. The Tang royal house was itself of quasi-native extraction. It employed many non-Chinese generals and bureaucrats and welcomed expatriate trading communities from all over Eurasia within its midst. However, as Marc S. Abramson has shown in his detailed study, that precise interpenetration could trigger xenophobic backlashes at times. On balance, Abramson concludes that although anti-Buddhist sentiments degenerated at times into negative physical stereotyping of Indians and steppe people, Tang elite thinkers, by and large, did accept that Chinese-ness was a *taught* cultural trait rather than an *innate* racial one. In fact, cases of positive stereotyping of steppe and South Asian people are not unknown in Tang discourse. By extension, Tang society as a whole was more tolerant of ethnic differences than the Song (CE 960–1279), Ming (CE 1368–1644) or arguably even Qing (CE 1644–1912) societies.[42]

How much of the early Tang legacy carries over to modern China, where the standing committee of the CPC politburo does not incorporate any women or ethnic minorities? If anything, a few Western experts on PRC ethnic relations ascribe the country's formative policies to outdated divisive ploys borrowed from the Soviet Union in the 1950s rather than to any notions of tolerance carrying over from China's imperial past.[43] So to what extent can the authors of China's leadership narrative, at present, credibly arrogate Tang tolerance to PRC everyday realities?

Quite to the contrary, William Callahan has recently built on Frank Dikötter's provocative work to suggest that, in fact, racism historically constituted a much bigger problem in China than CPC rhetoric might acknowledge. The People's Republic's version of multiculturalism casts the country as the domain of the *Zhonghua* nation, which is made up of the Han and 55 prescribed minorities, who all share distinctive features and provenance. Yet, as Callahan observes, the *Zhonghua* trope inevitably understates the broadly accepted theory about the African origins of all *Homo sapiens*.[44]

Callahan therefore concludes that the Tang trope is vacuous. Moreover, according to Callahan, many Chinese have nowadays come to interpret the concept of modern nation-statehood as racially grounded statehood, much like in Japan before World War II. In other words, one might infer, Chinese modernity has not moved on, as Western multicultural societies have (post-war Japanese multiculturalism is a non-sequitur).

More generally, Dikötter's claims – which Callahan evokes – about the emphatic premodern (i.e., non-European) mainsprings of today's Chinese racialist attitudes have been partially, yet fairly effectively, challenged in studies by Yuri Pines and Don. J. Wyatt.[45] On his part, Pan Wei also insists that the dichotomy in Chinese eyes between Chinese and non-Chinese ('Barbarians') in premodern times was culturally rather than ethnically derived. According to Pan, it is this cultural derivation that has been informing up to the present an intrinsic – if subterranean – Chinese abhorrence of meddling in other peoples'/nations' affairs (*Hua bu zhi Yi*). Consequently, Pan argues that China will remain, by and large, disinclined to police other parts of the world or to remake them in its own mould. It is not preaching its 'Model' to the rest of the world, but other countries are of course free to 'borrow' from its culture, if they so wish.[46]

This is also consistent with the CPC view that the Western democratic ideal of "one man, one vote" is not only alien to the Chinese way of life but also a sham designed to conceal the nefarious degree to which the West is in reality controlled by plutocratic vested interests. Who is nominally elected president, it is argued, matters much less: he or she cannot change the rigged system.

Yu Ying-shih, a scholar who resided in the US for much of his adult life, is arguably the best known critic of the historicity of such CPC claims. He contends that the Chinese scholar-philosopher Huang Zongxi (CE 1610–1695) actually came close to cogitating an early Chinese variant of democracy and human rights in his famous essay *Mingyi daifanglu*. There, drawing on the Mencian concept of *minben*, which loosely translates to "the welfare of common people comes first", Huang railed at the tyrannical excesses of late-Ming emperors and their eunuch abettors and called for the curbing of imperial power by righteous, meritocratically selected ministers with the imperial bureaucracy.[47]

Yet, students of premodern Chinese history might note that *minben* had nothing to do with "one man, one vote" in the Confucian tradition. Moreover, China's first meaningful experiments with constitutional monarchism and parliamentary democracy in 1905 and 1912, respectively, were both very short-lived and tumultuous: they did not leave a lasting societal imprint and are not widely celebrated today.[48]

On the other hand, scholars used to believe that the earliest and most radical articulations of meritocracy in China went beyond strict Confucian teachings, hankering right back into the pre-imperial past, not long after Confucius himself died. Namely, it is well known that during the Warring States (BCE 453–221) era ancient thinkers like Mozi (BCE 476–390, cf. Confucius BCE 551–479) preached anti-hereditary sentiments, asserting that virtuous rulers must by definition cede power to the most *competent*, not necessarily to their next-of-kin. However, analysis of the recently deciphered *Gudian* bamboo slips increasingly suggests that, inspired by the Yao and Shun legend, many of Mozi's Confucian near-contemporaries also warmed to idea of non-hereditary cession of power. Several might have even called for outright abdication in favour of worthy commoners of humble upbringing. Albeit bold and widespread at the time, such sentiments do not quite amount to advocacy of popular vote in the Athenian sense, leaving, for the most part, selection and elevation at the discretion of the incumbent. In any event, these sentiments receded from the fourth century BCE onward, fading into the margins of statecraft discourse by the end of the Tang era.[49] Whilst infrequent voluntary and involuntary abdications (read: throne usurpation) did later occur in China, the abdicators never elevated commoners in their stead.

Rather than through popular peaceful protest, unrighteous emperors would in the Chinese meta-narrative simply lose their "mandate of heaven" (*tianming*) through popular revolt and be deserted by the bureaucratic elites. Whilst reigning, emperors were not to be agitated against directly. Instead, the cycle of nature would almost perforce bring decadent, immoral and *fin-de-siecle* dynasties to an end. Confucius himself, after all, had postulated that a benevolent person ought to stand one's ground but never engage in factionalism (*qun er bu dang*).[50]

Though, in reality, bureaucratic factional fighting within the imperial bureaucracy often turned endemic and bloody during the Tang and Song eras, it was seen as a side-effect of weak emperors' indecision and a sign of impending dynastic collapse. Li Deyu (CE 787–850) and Ouyang Xiu (CE 1007–1072), some of the most prominent premodern Chine thinkers, considered, in theory at least, horizontal alliances between like-minded officials as subversion of the principle of vertical loyalty to the emperor.[51] In a treatise entitled like Li's (*pengdang lun*), even Ouyang Xiu tempered his enthusiasm for factions by suggesting that the only true criterion for dynastic legitimacy is the ability to unify "all under heaven".[52]

Ultimately, Ouyang's position was quashed in another eponymous treatise by no other than the Yongzheng Emperor (r. 1723–36) himself, and it is that less tolerant outlook that became emblematic of the late-imperial era as a whole:[53]

> sometimes people's minds harbour several interests so that they are unable to accept the ruler's preferences, and as a result the sentiments of superiors and inferiors become opposed and the distinction between noble and base is subverted. This is what always comes of the habit of forming cliques and factions.

***

Be that as it may, the argument advanced here is that the "one man, one vote" pre-occupation in a Chinese historical context may distract from an equally important factor underlying Chinese notions of exceptionalism at present, namely, the role of religion in legitimating or challenging imperial power. Crudely put, the crux of the matter here is that in the West, secular and church authorities were mutually reinforcing but, at times, caught up in bloody contestation of power. The Roman legal code, however, pre-dated the enshrinement of Christianity as a state religion and, in that sense, foreshadowed a more distinct separation of powers than in the Chinese trajectory. To put it more precisely, it is commonly believed that because secular authority and religious one became more pronounced in early modern Europe compared with the rest of the world, the modern separation of judicial, legislative and executive powers could emerge there.[54]

The flipside of this crude generalisation is that, in the Chinese contemporary narrative, we often find a self-perceived historical pattern of moderation com-pared with the bloody faith wars raging in Europe and the Levant. Zhao Tingyang, for example, draws on Daoist, Confucian and Marxist precepts so as to cast Chi-nese political thought as devoid of imagined irredeemable polar enemies (read: subalterns) or the transcendent religious or ethnic absolutism, more generally. For Zhao, that holistic thought entertains much latent universalism that can, if extended, potentially remedy conflicts in today's globalised and increasingly mul-ticultural societies much better than the United Nations, since the latter is blem-ished by the narrow logic of the nation-state.[55]

But, if anything, the gradual subjugation of organized religion to the state was a hallmark of late-imperial China (c. tenth century to 1911). In the early-imperial era, we can arguably find more frequent episodes of religious persecution of Bud-dhists and Daoists, as well as power-broking between state and religion. In fact, Buddhist monastic institutions had acquired something of political autonomy in fourth century China, not unlike the power the Catholic Church wielded in Euro-pean medieval times. Indeed, as Erik Zürcher reminds us, Huiyuan (CE 334–416) famously mustered the courage to declare: Buddhist clergy do not owe allegiance to political authority (*Shamen bu jing wang*).[56]

Rendall Collins suggested that premodern China constituted a more ideologi-cally and territorially cohesive polity than was the case either in Europe or India at that time. Though Buddhism first entered China during the later Han era, it was not until the Tang era that the import of Indian Buddhism could reach its zenith with some adjustments. Despite episodic state persecution, several Tang emperors actually became enthusiastic patrons of particular Buddhist sects, whilst in premodern India, state rulers much more rarely intervened in sect endorsement. However, after the tenth century, as Buddhism in India itself was being eclipsed by *bhakti* forms of devotional popular Hinduism – Buddhism would ironically come to exert a lasting intellectual impact on its rival school of Chinese neo-Confucianism in China.[57]

As much as Buddhism transformed early-imperial Chinese society, it was thereafter transformed by Chinese societal conventions. Buddhist sects were codified, regimented and made more amenable to state diktat; Chinese Buddhism, as a whole, came to embrace in the late-imperial era the Confucian precept of filial piety, and its pantheon of *arhats* fused with Daoist and local popular deities. Unlike its Indian iteration, where, for example, agricultural work could be frowned on at times for fear it might cause harm to insects, Chinese Buddhism by and large accepted this worldly quotidian menial labour as one vehicle for ascetic introspection. Moreover, following the Tang era, Chinese Buddhists no longer considered India as the centre of their intellectual universe, and abandoned *famen* self-mutilation as a form of Buddha-relic worship because it contrasted with Confucian sensitivities.[58]

The upshot was that organized religion in late-imperial China became politically and economically *less* autonomous from the state apparatus compared with Western Christendom, South Asia and, arguably, even when compared with the Levant. At the grassroots, disparate expressions of spirituality were almost all subtly subsumed by an overarching imperial cult, which often invested local deities with the aura of afterlife state officials. Whilst tolerant of Buddhism and Daoism, the late-imperial bureaucracy enshrined neo-Confucianism; the Board of Rites in the Qing era went as far as organizing lectures for the peasantry on the importance of filial piety in small rustic settings (*xiang yue*) by way of instilling loyalty to the ultimate patriarch, the emperor.[59]

As Goossaert and Palmer explain:[60]

> This system integrated traditions of individual salvation, such as self-cultivation through meditation and body techniques, moral living, and spirit possession techniques, including spirit writing; kinship-based rites, such as life-cycle rituals and ancestor worship; and communal religion, such as cults to local saints and deities – all of which were only partly framed within the three institutionalised teachings of Confucianism, Daoism and Buddhism. Islam and Christianity were later arrivals; owing to their exclusive claims of truth, they did not become fully integrated into the system, even though they gradually became thoroughly sinicised . . . In late-imperial times and well into the 20th century, only clerics and a small number of devout laypersons would identify themselves as Buddhist or Daoist, but most people at least occasionally engaged in rituals officiated by Buddhist or Daoist priests. A state doctrine of the coexistence of the Three Teachings reinforced increased overlap and

mutual influence between them after centuries of interaction and universal acceptance among the populace, although functional differences remained, with Confucians monopolising statecraft and playing a privileged role in kin-based worship; Daoist liturgy often structuring communal festivals; and Buddhist priests often being the preferred choice for conducting funerals.

This unique trajectory seems to feed into the Chinese self-perception of relative secularism and this-worldliness nowadays, whereby the clergy cannot wield its power beyond the faithful's private domain; whereby the metaphysical encroaches far less on the political realm than vice versa.[61] Thus, for example, the CPC has begun pragmatically drawing on Buddhist tropes as a pan-Asian bridgehead over which to mend diplomatic fences with India. Note, for example, China's endorsement of Indian and Singaporean efforts to revive the Nalanda Academy in Bihar where several Tang-era monks have studied.[62]

***

Perhaps the most pertinent European emperor to provide a counterpoint to the Chinese trajectory is Barbarossa (CE 1120–1190), who at the height of his reign as Emperor of the Holy Roman Empire, prevailed *only* for a short time upon papal authority. Famously enough, a century earlier, Henry IV had submitted to Pope Gregory VII at Canossa.[63] To our mind, Barbarossa's exploits epitomise the deep-seated interdependence between state and religion in the premodern Western European context: an interdependence that is derived from and heightened alternative sources of political legitimacy, and one that is conspicuously missing from the late-imperial Chinese trajectory. Indeed, the Chinese modern composite term for "pope" (*jiaohuang*), which roughly translates as "Emperor of the Faith", would have been virtually inconceivable in the Chinese late-imperial setting, as would the saying spuriously attributed to Huguenot-born Henry IV, King of France (r. 1589–1610) about rule in Paris being "well worth the Mass".[64]

Instead, as Romeyn Taylor explained, there had been in late-imperial China a liturgical division whereby the imperial cult (read: official religion) – mostly administered by high-ranking Confucian officials – was framed as genuinely dedicated to the common good (*gong*). Propitiating good harvest, the core dynastic worship of Heaven and Earth was confined to the capital, yet it was hierarchically transmitted to all administrative levels, including remote communities, through smaller-scale local soil and grain rituals (*sheji*). Popular religion, on the other hand, was seen as tainted by idiosyncrasy and commoners' liturgical reward seeking (*si*). At the same time, official religion constantly aimed to co-opt popular deities into the sanctioned pantheon to contain the development of heterodoxy, sometimes through semi-official Buddhist or Daoist proxy clergy. Though emperors were cast as final arbiters in all religious matters, they were ". . . not a priest in the sense that the pope is a priest who has been trained and ordained in the princely vocation".[65]

What needs to be remembered in that context is that, despite episodic persecution, Buddhism and Daoism had, on balance, played a much bigger role earlier in the legitimation of Tang (and to a lesser extent Northern Song) rule. In that sense, the Tang template might be pitched as a pluralistic boilerplate for contemporary audiences. For example, though Daoist and Buddhist themes occasionally crept into the imperial examinations in the late-imperial era, questions specifically deriving from the Daoist canon featured more regularly in Tang examinations.[66]

Tension between egalitarianism, freedom and meritocracy in economic policy

The Italian city-states that Barbarossa tried to conquer whilst consolidating his power also underscore a modality of independence and political separateness that does not really exist in the late-imperial Chinese contexts, where city-kingdoms were virtually unknown. Yet, the authors of the Chinese narrative might note that China, by the same token, did not really experience the kind of religious fervency that swept through Europe at the time in the form of Crusades. That note does have perhaps a leg to stand on: Jonathan Israel's work might suggest that the legitimation of secularist, anti-papal, 'Radical Enlightenment' ideas in Western Europe from Issac Vossius (1618–1689) onward drew, to some extent, on contemporaries' admiration from afar of Chinese civilisation. The Jesuits who were acknowledged as having first-hand knowledge of China were nevertheless accused by those Enlightenment radicals of concealing Spinoza's secular thought when proselytising there.[67] And as is well known, even the French physiocrat François Quesnay (1694–1774), who served the *ancien regime*, turned to Confucius for inspiration.[68]

Neither did China experience anything similar to the later sacking of Rome and the imprisonment of Pope Clement VII by Holy Roman Emperor Charles V (CE 1500–1558) that famously led to England's breaking away from the Catholic world. Nor could an early-medieval 'European-style' warrior class or late-medieval plutocratic families wield quite so much political (and religious) power in late-imperial China as did the Medicis or Fuggars in Europe.[69] Ironically, the sweeping claims that China Model thinkers like Liu Mingfu make today – and are to be discussed later in the book – concerning the paucity of a martial spirit in contemporary China echo depreciative observations made in the sixteenth century by the first Catholic missionaries to China depicting locals as "far behind . . . in their valiantness and courage".[70]

Though not warriors, mention of the Medicis is apt here because, apart from religious zeal, they epitomise the confluence of wealth and political power in the European context. In the Chinese contemporary narrative, we often find a self-perceived contrasting historical pattern of not just non-belligerence, war aversion and relative secularism but also resentment of powerful hereditary nobility. Concomitantly, the Chinese narrative, at least in rhetoric, rejects neoliberalism or the wholesale privatisation of state assets advocated by institutions like the IMF as deepening inequalities in society; "collective" values like poverty alleviation and universal education are cast as more important than "individual" values like free speech, even as inequalities in China, measured in real terms by the Gini

coefficient, sky-rocket.[71] Interestingly, one might find echoes of premodern residual Chinese egalitarianism not just in what was otherwise a fairly elitist body of
Confucian classics,[72] but also in the *contemporary* narrative in the face of everyday
neoliberal-like praxis. Fan Peng, for example, a political scientist with the Chinese
Academy of Social Sciences, argues that China's future should be shaped by ideals and policies that have historically resonated strongly in the country rather than
Western recipes for development. For Fan, what definitively differentiates China
from the West in terms of social evolution is what he sees as a historically much
more equal distribution of land and a much stronger imperial centre.[73]

Nonetheless, the problem with powerful hereditary nobility is not so much in
the narration of perpetual inequality into European history as in the fact that under
Mao the entirety of Chinese imperial history, including of course the Tang era,
was tarred as "feudalism".[74] Herein, the New Confucian-hued rhetoric of the CPC
in the twentieth century contrasts sharply with the PRC ethos until 1979, which
championed the creation of a New China (*xin Hua*, *xin Zhongguo*) on the ruins
the old "feudal society".[75]

If under Mao the CPC cast itself as innovator, it is now promising to restore
China's illustrious past. Whereas under Deng Xiaoping and Jiang Zemin Chinese
economic reform, for example, was explained in terms of scaling down central planning, it is nowadays explained to Chinese and foreign audiences with passing references not just to Western textbooks but to premodern Chinese economic thought.

Former World Bank Vice President Justin Yifu Lin is the best marker of this
somewhat discombobulating trend: as a graduate of the University of Chicago,
he is at once a strong advocate of adherence to free market principles in Chinese
policymaking, but he often posits that his sense of good governance is equally
inspired by figures like Chinese engineering maestro Li Bing (c. third century
BCE). Similarly, Lin ascribes his enthusiasm for free enterprise and individual
choice to figures like disciplinarian Ming and general-turned-philosopher Wang
Yangming (CE 1472–1529).[76] Yet elsewhere, Lin averred that China's Confucian
ethos later prevented the onset of an English-style industrial revolution, because
China's exam-based imperial bureaucracy prized the memorisation of the classics
over the imparting of practical skill like math and engineering.[77]

Though Lin himself baulks at labelling premodern China as "feudal", the all-
too-common use of the term (*fengjian*) in the Mao era has masked, to this day,
far-reaching differences between early- and late-imperial China. The later period
can hardly be dubbed feudal in the European sense of decentralised economic,
military and territorial control. In fact, from the Song dynasty (CE 960) onwards,
Chinese society experienced the gradual diminution, if not complete disappear-
ance, of landed hereditary aristocracy, as well as of slavery, and the rise of the
gentry (*shi*), partly through very same civil-service examination system that Justin Lin denounces in another context.[78]

Notably, in his pioneering *Pattern of the Chinese Past*, Mark Elvin speculated
that mass manumission of slaves had begun in China as of the eighth century and that
many slave descendants ended up as serfs or tenants later on. But he also observed

that early Tang attempts at equitable agricultural land distribution were less far-reaching than those of the ethnic Tuoba Northern Wei dynasty, which ruled North-west China between CE 386–534. For example, slave owners were ordinarily allocated more land under the Tang system, and exemptions were made to dependents of the court. It was only after the breakdown of the Tang equitable-field distribution system, with its many exemptions and exceptions, that the court ". . . had to turn to the development of a centrally controlled system of civil service examinations in order to exert comparable control over the elite".[79]

Arguably, the last reign to contemplate extensive – as opposed to symbolic or peripheral – revival of the *fengjian* system was that of the Tang emperor Taizong (r. CE 626–649).[80] Yet as indicated earlier, the Tang later turned out a centralising polity in Chinese history in other ways. To be sure, right up until the collapse of the imperial order in 1911, authoritative emperors might be criticised in ahistorical fashion as resurrecting a commandery administrative system (*junxian*) reminiscent of the tyrannical, short-lived Qin empire (BCE 221–206).[81] Yet, beyond self-interested factional rhetoric, the Qin marked, in fact, an aberration in the early-imperial trajectory. The Maoist historical narrative was only partly correct to the extent that between BCE 1,000 and the Tang era, the Chinese polity had been intermittently administered as a loose confederation of semi-autonomous prefectures known as the *fengjian* system. Nevertheless, that system was not a cognate of European feudalism, not least because it entailed, by and large, a much stronger sense of empire-wide coordinated taxation and military conscription.[82]

Since the last millennium of imperial Chinese history (i.e., the millennium prior to 1911) saw on balance the attenuation of the *fengjian* legacy, gentry critics of 'big government' rhetorically pined for it by lionising pre-Tang antiquity. The Qin dynasty (BCE 221–206) served as the most hated trope in the eyes of late-imperial advocates of greater local gentry autonomy like Gu Yanwu (CE 1613–1682). Yet, whilst it was an easy target to assail in the distant past, even the Qin retained precisely the kind of hereditary nobility that would all but disappear in the late-imperial era. In other words, in post-Tang discourse – and particularly from the thirteenth century onwards – *fengjian*, far from connoting advocacy of hereditary privilege or territorial fragmentation, increasingly came to signify support for a leaner central bureaucracy, lower taxes and local gentry empowerment.[83] On the other hand, the famous Tang literatus Liu Zongyuan (CE 773–819), for example, praised in his famous essay *Fengjian lun* the stability and prosperity of his times, which he saw as departing from the *fengjian* mould. For Liu that prosperity was the result of the Tang's establishment of an exam-based, central civil service, which he compared favourably with the arbitrary state powers of Qin.[84]

Neither can China be timelessly and neatly pigeonholed along the *junxian-fengjian* spectrum in economic-policy terms. Tang economic policy is hard to capture as *laissez-faire* or *dirigiste* in modern Western terms. To be sure, in its later stage, the Tang dynasty came to enforce state monopolies on mining, salt and alcohol at times much more strictly than late-imperial polities, but at the outset, the dynasty had been much more oriented towards free enterprise.[85] By and large, later on in imperial history, the Qing dynasty enforced a more extensive poverty and famine alleviation through their ever-normal granary system (*changping cang*).[86]

Popularly, the Tang era is known as one when great financial innovations came to the fore. Tax farming and excise apart, the Tang state departs from the Western political economy in that it did not borrow much from its merchants but often competed with them in financial markets. In fact, the abstraction of "public debt" (e.g., in the form of government bonds) remained exceedingly marginal in China until the Republican era (1912–1949), even though the central state tax rate imposed on peasants was comparatively low. Similarly, state revenue and expenditure in the late-imperial era constituted a miniscule portion of the economy as a whole. Yet, it was beneath Chinese emperors to turn to private capital for help, whereas borrowing by European sovereigns from families like the Medicis or, later on, the Rothschilds, was a definitive feature of Western finance.[87]

This might invite analogies with China in its post-1979 iteration where, until recently, public and foreign debt have been largely eschewed. By the same token, as late as 2009, Chinese central government budget was smaller than that of France or Germany. Could it be that that facet of economic minimalism of the imperial legacy might have surreptitiously carried over into the contemporary China Model? If ever there was such resonance, it has been invalidated by the Chinese government's 2008 stimulus package that was designed to stave off the impact of the Global Financial Crisis through massive infrastructural build-up funded by provincial-government debt. Today, some analysts estimate composite private, provincial and central government indebtedness in China at a staggering 250% of annual GDP, i.e., a ratio not dissimilar to the US economy.[88]

The narrative analogy between past and present resonates slightly more persuasively in the realm of land ownership as a means of poverty alleviation. Apart from the Northern Song era (CE 960–1127), land tax provided for the great bulk of Chinese imperial revenue through cadastral, collective or individual (*baojia*) exaction.[89] In some ways, land-tax-framed statecraft was more salient in imperial China than in other parts of the world but, equally, Confucian filial piety translated into generous tax exemptions for charitable clan estates (*yizhuang*) and temple-based ancestral trusts (*tang*).[90]

The flipside of that system was nominal imperial ownership of "all land under heaven" (*pu tiaxia zhi di mofei wangtu*), which ensured that every peasant family had to pay a fairly low percentage of the value of its crop to the state. The principle of universal imperial land ownership had first been postulated in the Classic of Songs (*Shijing*, c. eleventh to seventh century BCE), and it is seen as still hardwired into the Chinese popular mindset, even today.[91] By the late-imperial era, however, a lively informal market for agrarian and urban land evolved in China. Transactions in that market typically entailed private-domain signed deeds (*baiqi*), whereby imperial stamp-duty represented by vermillion insignia (*hongqi*) would be dodged.[92] That duality, again, might invite narrative analogies with post-1979 reform China, where rural land remains collectively or government owned, but where provincial government often dislocates peasants with meagre compensation in favour of well-heeled property developers as a quick means of raising local revenue.[93] Whether the abolition of collective land ownership might alleviate or exacerbate societal inequalities is a moot point.

***

Is China appropriating the past rhetorically, whilst in fact embracing Western neoliberalism and acquiescing in the sheer inequality it begets? Or will it endeavour to offer, not just a narrative but also, substantive riposte to the dominant discourse of neoliberalism in the image of an East Asian developmental state? Following decades of retreat form *danwei* ('work unit') free housing, education and health-care, many urban Chinese might nowadays privately express admiration for the Scandinavian welfare states. Yet, it would be a mistake to deem China's New Confucian discourse as aiming at that. Instead of wealth distribution, that discourse promises genuine meritocracy, or more wealth to those genuinely more talented and worthy, where Singapore, rather than Scandinavia, is the endpoint.[94]

In that sense, the Tang is lionised as the progenitor of the modern civil service, where exams rather than connections are putatively the means for selecting the worthy. Where governments are paramount, entering officialdom ultimately means enhanced social status. Since talent and worthiness are not always inheritable, big government and strict civil-service exams are seen as a timeless, albeit admittedly elitist, pathway towards wealth redistribution and greater social mobility. Moreover, the authors of the Chinese aspirational narrative of global leadership claim that that Tang innovation later inspired the establishment of the Prussian and British modern civil services, and therefore, the CPC is nowadays in fact building its thrust towards meritocracy on a historically rich terrain.[95] Empirical evidence concerning the practise and prospects of meritocracy without more meaningful representative democracy and free press in China are still mixed at best. Shih, Adolph and Liu reject, for example, the suggestion that members of the Party Central Committee who superintend solid economic growth in their jurisdiction get promoted faster. Instead, they see factional ties, patronage, educational qualifications and revenue collection as more important in the larger scheme of one's career.[96] Zeng Jinghan, who studied the smaller but higher-tier Politburo Standing Committee membership, concluded that age and institutional rules mattered for appointment most, but patronage and family ties did not always boost candidates' success rate.[97]

Max Weber had once considered Confucianism as the antidote to innovation, and Justin Lin might still share the sentiment to some extent even today – yet scholars like Ho and Woodside respectively cast Confucianism as cementing the civil-service ethos and social mobility in the Chinese late-imperial polity. For Ho and Woodside, this was a feat of hyper-modernity in pre-modernity that was unparalleled globally, notwithstanding the fact that it was downplayed earlier by scholars such as Weber.[98]

To be sure, more detailed Western studies of the Chinese late-imperial civil-service exam system by and large accept that, at least in the Ming times (1368–1644), the system enhanced social mobility and equity. However, they also seem to indicate that that mobility at other times only pertained to 10% of the population, i.e., only male gentry could benefit therefrom, purely through mastering the Confucian classics. During the Tang era itself, the exam system had initially been characterised, as P.A. Herbert showed, by the same establishment families through extensive recommendation of family candidates and privileged access to state colleges in the capital Chang'an, where the Confucian classics were taught specifically in preparation for the classical version (*mingjing*) of the exam. The families' power base, nonetheless, gradually shifted from birth rights to progeny office holding. Indeed, after he managed to climb the ladder of success, high-ranking official Zhang Jiuling (CE 678–740) famously became a critic of the Tang system from within, because he believed it discriminated against candidates like himself, who had had *scholarly* background but no access to state schools, forcing them to take the harder literary version (*jinshi*) of the exam.[99]

Zhang Jiuling's scholarly family background aside, Ho suggested there had *also* been many cases in late-imperial Chinese history of *peasants* who mastered the classics whilst tilling the land (*gengdu*) to later pass the exam and reach fame and fortune. Certainly, the Chinese contemporary aspirational narrative posits Chinese exceptionalism as partly deriving from that fabled higher degree of social mobility historically, starting right from Emperor Yao's abdication over his son in favour of Shun: from Shun's similar abdication to Yu or Bai Lixi's elevation from poverty to the premiership in antiquity, and more so after the Tang reverted to promotion through exams. The late-imperial configuration of *gengdu* and equal land ownership are thus portrayed as inhibiting the rise of an enduring Western-style aristocracy. For that reason, so the argument runs, what might help the CPC move the country forward are *not* Western-style evolutionary models of representative democracy, but a reversion to time-honoured Chinese-style principles of egalitarianism. Rather than an obsession with pleasing mercurial public opinion (*minyi*), the government is encouraged to pursue the longer-term interest of the populace (*minxin*) with economic growth and grain security at heart.[100]

However, Elman's later study cast doubts on the feasibility of such peasant-to-riches concurrence in late-imperial China, arguing that much family wealth was needed to sustain teenagers as they were being groomed for officialdom.[101] Much like the precise dating of the Xia dynasty, the question of just how ubiquitous *gengdu* rags-to-riches individuals were is likely to remain in scholarly dispute for many years to come. They inevitably under-script the robustness of the contemporary Chinese aspirational narrative insofar as Confucian-hued claims to greater social mobility in the future are concerned.

Yu Ying-shih observed in that context that the linkage between exam scores, relational office holding and social esteem remained in effect during the Ming era, even though more and more gentry became alienated from what they perceived as autocratic Ming rule. Confucian self-validation amongst the *shi* thereby increasingly turned inwards, whilst social intermingling between merchants and scholars became more common. In the end, many Ming gentry sought rectitude within rather than through service in the exam-based imperial bureaucracy. Their longing for a sage emperor who would heed their advice and restore Confucian propriety (*dejun xingdao*) transmuted into a belief in the redemptive power of Confucianisation through popular education in the countryside (*juemin xingdao*).[102]

What is equally clear, at any rate, is that the discourse on meritocracy in China dates back a long way indeed, and the Tang exam system, however imperfect, marked a turning point much earlier than in the West. For, as Ha-Joon Chang reminds us, a "spoils" system, whereby public offices were allocated to loyalists of the ruling party rather than to prodigious examinees, typified Western democracies to one degree or another right until the end of the nineteenth century. Ironically, even after the passing of the 1883 Pendleton Act, only 10% of civil-service jobs in the US were subject to competitive recruitment, roughly the same ratio as in ninth-century China.[103] But all this is far from bearing out the meritocratic superiority of twenty-first century China over the twenty-first century West, if only because China specialists in Western academe are still divided as to whether advancement on the CPC leadership ladder is more determined by 'red' family pedigree, client-patron ties and factional affiliation or by education qualifications and previous job performance.

Conclusion

In her path-breaking study, Linda Colley observed that British modern identity was forged on the back of anti-papist rhetoric, Francophobia and enthusiasm for imperial expansion. In other words, British economic integration and the Industrial Revolution were necessary, but not sufficient, nation-building feats. England's formal acts of union with Wales in 1536 and with Scotland in 1707 were the start, rather than endpoint, of that identity formation.[104]

What might then be the commensurate milestones in the formation of modern Chinese grand identity? Following the establishment of the People's Republic in 1949, one might naturally speculate that Hong Kong's handover to Chinese sovereignty in 1997 mattered, as might some accommodation with Taiwan, if it ever were to occur. Similarly, in narrative terms, cynics might speculate that Mao's anti-capitalist principles would be replaced by Japan-phobia and a milder version of neo-authoritarian discourse with Confucian tenor stressing justice, equality and meritocracy, as well as perhaps a revival of *tianxia* symbolism, war aversion and non-interference in international relations.

Yet, whilst it is ideologically at fault through Chinese eyes, in some ways the US – the arbiter of the international system today – and China are becoming alike, not least in actual levels of social inequality and their enthusiasm for freewheeling entrepreneurship. The most important transformation of the CPC in the post-Mao era had to do with Jiang Zemin's "Three Represents" policy, which, as introduced in Chapter One, saw some of China's most talented businesspeople join Party ranks, even though the Party itself still nominally enshrines Marxism-Leninism-Maoism in its constitution. In other words, both Americans and Chinese have come to subscribe, in equal measure, to the notion that wealth should be a function of one's talents and can therefore never be equally distributed.[105]

Where the US and China remain at loggerheads in historical narrative terms, and where they emit contending blueprints for the future, is in their configuration of the relations between the state, society and organized religion. China's relative secularism is self-perceived as a modernising force, whilst faith in God is still hardwired into American (if not European) psyche. Arguably, CPC sensitivities to religious autonomy in the public sphere is informed by its own experience in colluding with secret societies before 1949 by way of undermining KMT authority; as well as perhaps by suspicion of alternative sources of legitimation carried over from the late-imperial era.[106]

In the Chinese blueprint, at any rate, *government* is a much bigger and more intrusive construct than it had ever been in the late-imperial era, yet there is professed aversion to exporting this model overseas that still arguably bespeaks minimalism. Americans are still infatuated by an ethos of small government, which they are determined to promote internationally. Both blueprints, at the same time, hanker after minimal social welfare and are in effect compatible with global neoliberalism in its current iteration. In other words, these blueprints seem to be equidistant from Scandinavian social democracy.

Whereas Mao's China strove to erect a communistic uber-utopia by breaking with the Chinese "feudal" past, the CPC at present is at pains to resurrect that very same past, at least rhetorically. This chapter has argued throughout that the new aspirational leadership narrative that is shaping up in Beijing is replete with internal tensions but, contrary to the prevailing view in the West, is a serious, intellectually complex long-term undertaking. It is already offering many counterpoints to the US narrative in profound ways. The authors of the narrative therefore deserve careful study rather than complacent scorn from their Western intellectual peers.

The vehicle with which to push this narrative through is a kind of new Confucian (not to be confused with late-imperial neo-Confucian) ethos, in which real or perceived Tang splendour, meritocracy and cosmopolitanism loom large. Though relatively moderate and secular in essence, because it downplays individual freedoms, that ethos is unlikely to win over the hearts and minds of people in the developed world, insofar as it is not sufficiently differentiated from neoliberalism. Whether the developing world might rally in years to come to this alternative blueprint will depend, in no small measure, on China's ability to translate *houwang baolai* rhetorical magnanimity into larger and more effectively managed overseas aid development compared with the US, Europe and Japan.[107] As part of this tributary rationale, what is probably expected in return for far-flung *houwang baolai* magnanimity in the Chinese narrative is insistence on neighbourly acceptance of China's 'natural superiority' in the developing world, as well as in its own backyard, namely, the East and South China Seas.

Notes

1   For the more common dismissive view in the West see e.g., Shambaugh (2013). For the minority view highlighting China as a formidable ideational foe of the US see e.g., Halper (2010).
2   For an overview of that narrative in English see e.g., Zhang (2012); Jacques (2012); Bell (2015).
3   Friedberg (2000).
4   www.bbc.co.uk/news/world-asia-china-23975037
5   See e.g., McCarthy (2011).

6 Foot and Walter (2010). For a discussion of China's political economy and the extent to which it converges with the dominant neoliberal discourse in the West see e.g., Breslin (2011);Lim (2014a).
7 www.ft.com/cms/s/0/20a43d16-878d-11e5-8a12-b0ce506400af.html#axzz3xPByY9Ka; http://usa.chinadaily.com.cn/world/2015-07/15/content_21285326.htm
8 www.nytimes.com/2015/11/27/world/asia/china-military-presence-djibouti-africa.html?_r=0; http://nationalinterest.org/blog/the-buzz/why-does-china-want-aircraft-carriers-14686
9 See e.g., Pillsbury (2015); see also http://foreignpolicy.com/2015/03/31/the-aiib-is-a-threat-to-global-economic-governance-china/
10 Liu (2009).
11 See e.g., Makeham (2008); Bell (2010); Solé-Farràs (2013).
12 www.wsj.com/articles/why-china-is-turning-back-to-confucius-1442754000; www.economist.com/news/china/21659753-communist-party-turns-ancient-philosophy-support-confucius-says-xi-does; http://time.com/3547467/china-beijing-xi-jinping-confucius-communism/; www.scmp.com/news/china/article/1603487/xi-jinping-endorses-promotion-confucius
13 See e.g., https://theconversation.com/confucius-doesnt-live-here-anymore-33006; www.theguardian.csom/commentisfree/2014/sep/29/fight-for-democracy-not-just-people-hong-kong; www.scmp.com/news/china/article/1603487/xi-jinping-endorses-promotion-confucius
14 Brzezinski (2007).
15 Luttwak (2011).
16 On the Middle East see e.g., Murphy (2009).
17 www.telegraph.co.uk/news/worldnews/asia/japan/11216844/Japan-and-China-agree-to-reduce-tensions-over-Senkaku-islands.html
18 For an overview of the debate in Chinese academe see e.g., Leonard (2012).
19 www.aisixiang.com/data/related-96215.html
20 See e.g., Fewsmith's excellent report (2005); He Bingmeng (2015).
21 www.scmp.com/news/china/policies-politics/article/1943469/xi-jinpings-stance-chinas-economy-laid-bare-he
22 Scobell and Harold (2013).
23 See e.g., Chen Weiss (2014).
24 See e.g., Shirk (2010), Introduction; Kurlatznick (2008); Brady (2009).
25 See discussion in Haar (2000). For an assessment of the Ming era in that context see e.g., Johnston (1998).
26 See e.g., van Ness (1970).
27 http://yaleglobal.yale.edu/content/modi%E2%80%99s-visit-china-marks-new-tone-no-concrete-progress
28 In reality, slavery did abound in the Tang era, and steppe-land slaves far outnumbered ethnic Han ones. Yet, in the words of Marc C. Abramson (2008, p. 137), the Tang state also ". . . directly or through the initiatives of local officials restricted the slave trade and prohibited the enslavement of other non-Han people, particularly Koreans and autochthonous inhabitants of southern China and Southeast Asia." Arguably, by the eighteenth century, racially grounded slavery (not to be confused with slavery purely deriving from indebtedness, concubinage or *devşirme*-style war captivity) greatly diminished in China compared with Christendom or Islamdom. Zanzibar-style plantation slavery never reached Mainland China, certainly not on a large scale. No minority ethnicity in China was consonant with slavery to the degree Slavs, and later Africans, were in both Christendom and Islamdom. See e.g., Clarence-Smith (2006); Eaton (2006); Klein (2014).
29 See e.g., www.nytimes.com/2011/11/21/opinion/how-china-can-defeat-america.html; http://blogs.nottingham.ac.uk/chinapolicyinstitute/2015/06/29/war-monger-or-judicious-realist-liu-mingfu-as-historically-minded-america-watcher/

30 Zhao (2015).
31 See e.g., Zhang and Hu (2010); for cogent, comprehensive and policy-relevant dis-
    cussions of China's pre-modern tributary relations in English, see e.g., Kang (2012);
    Wang and Zheng Yongnian (2008), Introduction.
32 Johnston (1998), pp. 116–117.
33 www.nytimes.com/2014/05/20/opinion/brooks-the-big-debate.html; for a similar streak
    of wonderment at East Asian achievements and anxiety about America's future, see also
    Roger Cohen's recent *New York Times* columns, e.g., www.nytimes.com/2014/12/04/
    opinion/roger-cohen-feeling-uneasy-about-the-future.html?_r=0
34 Shen (2011). Chinese liberal Li Datong was one of very few who enthused about
    Obama's election observing, by comparison, that it would be unthinkable for the
    CPC to appoint an ethnic-minority member as General Secretary. See Leibold (2013),
    pp. 30–31.
35 See, for example, Pan Wei's, *The Chinese Model of Development*, Working Paper,
    11 October 2007, posted by the London-based think-tank, the Foreign Policy Centre,
    http://fpc.org.uk/fsblob/888.pdf
36 See e.g., Yu Maochun (1996), pp. 65, 269–270, 157–158); Steve Tsang (1988).
37 www.nytimes.com/2009/06/04/us/politics/04obama.text.html
38 Kaufmann (2004), especially pp. 214–215.
39 Nathan (2015), pp. 156–170.
40 Wested (2005), pp. 9–12.
41 Chua (2007), Introduction.
42 Abramson (2008).
43 Han (2013), pp. 32–34.
44 Callahan (2013), pp. 98–123; Dikötter (1992).
45 Pines (2005a); Wyatt (2012).
46 Pan Wei (2007).
47 Yu (2000).
48 For a historically-contexualised discussion of contemporary notions of *minben* in
    China see e.g., Shi and Jie (2010).
49 See Pines (2005b); Holloway (2013), pp. 58–62.
50 See *Lunyu*, 'Wei Ling Gong' verse 22.
51 Levine (2008), pp. 26–49.
52 Pines (2012), p. 40.
53 Quoted in Nivison (1959), pp. 209–243.
54 See Cameron (2013); Puett (2015), pp. 230–259.
55 Zhao (2005), pp. 14–15, 154–160.
56 Zürcher (1972), p. 106; pp. 231–239.
57 Bol (2008). Note in that context that Manichaesim was persecuted both in Christen-
    dom and in Tang China. However, whilst it disappeared in Western Eurasia by the
    sixth century, small communities of Mani followers survived in South China right up
    to the fourteenth century. See e.g., Lieu (1985).
58 Von Glahn (2004), pp. 130–179. See also Hansen (1990). On labour and asceticism in
    Chinese Buddhism see Yü (1994), pp. 158–171.
59 See e.g., Hsiao (1960), pp. 184–158.
60 Goossaert and Palmer (2011), pp. 20–22, 28; cf. Feuchtwang (1992).
61 On the enduring "this-worldly" quality of Chinese thought, see e.g., Yü (2010), p. 62.
62 www.bbc.co.uk/news/business-22160989
63 See Leyser (1994).
64 Holt (2005), p. 156.
65 Taylor (1990), pp. 126–157, p. 131.
66 Elman (2013), pp. 68–70, 170–179.
67 Israel (2001), pp. 588–589.
68 Pak (1974), pp. 55–57.

69 Elvin (1973), pp. 69–70.
70 See Lach (1965), vol. I, p. 787. European visitors to China before the Jesuit advent, like the Dominican friar Gaspar da Cruz or the Portuguese soldier-of-fortune Galeote Pereira, broadly agreed Chinese cities to be (ibid., pp. 764) plush and technology to be fairly advanced. But they also marvelled at the intensity of farming, the great density of the rural population and the existence of poverty, albeit without mendicants.
71 www.ft.com/intl/cms/s/0/3c521faa-baa6-11e5-a7cc-280dfe875e28.html#axzz3x Fnm5EI8
72 Pines (2012), Ch. 5, *passim*.
73 Fan (2009).
74 For a classic work problematizing the notion of inherently hereditary nobility in European Middle Ages, see Bloch (1961).
75 Dirlik (1978).
76 Lin (2014), p. 16.
77 Lin (2012), pp. 22–54.
78 See e.g., Smith (2003), Introduction.
79 Elvin (1973), pp. 59–63, 73–77.
80 Somers (1986), vol. 45, no. 5, pp. 971–994. See Wechsler (1993).
81 See e.g., Rowe (2010), pp. 60–62; see also Thornton (2007), Chs. 2–3.
82 The word *fengjian* had originally referred to a system of dividing the country into appanages of the ruler's relatives and allies. By the 3rtd century BCE, it was contrasted with uniform centralized control, the *junxian* 郡縣 system. There was a major reversal to decentralized and personalized (*fengjian*) mode of rule in the early Han; renewed centralization under Han Wudi (BCE 159–87); and then lengthy coexistence of symbolic *fengjian* (i.e., granting aristocratic titles such as *wang* 王 or *gong* 公 to the emperor's kin but without real power) with de-facto centralized control. However, substantive *fengjian* re-appeared later periodically, e.g., under Western Jin, early Yuan and early Ming. Even as late as the Qing dynasty (CE 1644–1911), *fan* 番 territories were ruled as "feudal" principalities. So substantive *fengjian* never disappeared entirely. Yet it was not much welcomed, hence Tang Taizong's failure to restore a real *fengjian* during his rule.
83 See e.g., Song (2011), vol. 97, pp. 301–343.
84 Flüchter and Schöttli (2014), pp. 108–109; Schrecker (2004), pp. 264–270.
85 Twitchett (1995), pp. 49–65.
86 Will and Wong (1991).
87 See e.g., Puk (2016), pp. 163–166.
88 Sara Hsu, *China's Debt Problem*, University of Nottingham, China Policy Institute, Policy Paper Series 6, 2014, www.nottingham.ac.uk/cpi/documents/policy-papers/ cpi-policy-paper-2014-no-6-hsu.pdf; see also Beardson (2014), p. 120.
89 See e.g., Liu (2015), pp. 48–78; Goldstone and Haldon (2008), pp. 3–29.
90 See e.g., Twichett (1959), pp. 97–133.
91 See e.g., Terrill (2009), p. 56.
92 See e.g., Palmer (1987), pp. 1–119.
93 www.bbc.co.uk/news/blogs-china-blog-24865658
94 http://thediplomat.com/2012/11/is-singapore-worth-emulating/
95 See e.g., Wang Hui (2011), p. 135; Victoria Tin-Bor Hui (2005), p. 148.
96 Shih *et al* (2012).
97 Zeng (2013).
98 Ho (1964); Woodside (2006). See also Kracke Jr. (1947).
99 Herbert (1988). On the seminal pre-imperial discourse meritocracy, see Pines (2013).
100 Pan Wei (2009), pp. 3–85.
101 Elman (2000), especially Table 10 on p. 114. See also Hymes (1987) cf. Rowe (1990), pp. 51–81.
102 Yu Ying-shih (2010), pp. 16–42.

103 Chang (2005), pp. 76–80.
104 Colley (2005).
105 www.nytimes.com/2015/03/03/world/asia/in-chinas-legislature-the-rich-are-more-than-represented.html?_r=0
106 Wu Junqing, *State and Heretics: The Construction of 'Heresy' in Chinese State Discourse*, Unpublished PhD Dissertation, University of Nottingham, 2014.
107 www.rand.org/content/dam/rand/pubs/research_reports/RR100/RR118/RAND_RR118.pdf

3   CPC elite perception of the US since the early 1990s

Zheng Bijian, Wang Huning and Liu Mingfu as test cases

Introduction

Policymakers are not purely rational actors. Instead, they view other countries through tainted lenses shaped by their own belief systems, ideology and domestic shade of governance. Policymakers' perception of a foreign country often frames their long-term, if not day-to-day, approach to that country. Behaviour is to a large extent a function of perception.[1] Thus, it is expedient to try decoding the perceptions of the US of the top echelon of the CPC to better understand both Chinese policymaking regarding the US and infer how China's "alternative futures" might be seen through the eyes of its own leaders. Chinese policymakers' deeply embedded strategic distrust of the US can be, in part, attributed to their negative perception or misperception of the US and the degree to which they see China as charting an alternative aspirational narrative of global leadership.[2] Given a paucity of information and immense difficulty to get in touch with Chinese policymakers, however, it is impossible to directly draw on Chinese policymakers as test cases in gauging their perceptions of the US. Scholars have to employ other methods to indirectly gauge Chinese policymakers' perceptions of the US.

Scholars of Sino-American relations basically employ two methods to indirectly reveal Chinese policymakers' perceptions of the US. First, some scholars make use of public opinion polls, which survey the general public's attitudes towards the US, with Alastair Lain Johnston and Mingming Shen's monograph titled *Perception and Misperception in American and Chinese Views of the Other* as the latest example.[3] It is noteworthy that David Lampton also uses public opinion polls to illuminate security-relevant perceptions in Sino-American relations.[4] Second, there are nowadays more Western scholars who study China's "America watchers" and their perceptions of the US by making use of interviews and/or textual analysis of their writings. The American watchers on whom they focus include academics in Chinese universities, journalists and policy analysts in government and government-affiliated research institutions.[5]

What makes this chapter distinct from previous research is that it juxtaposes two of the most influential, yet under-studied, America watchers within the top echelon of the CPC, Zheng Bijian and Wang Huning. To be sure, the two have indelibly shaped CPC attitudes, yet surprisingly enough, although Zheng has been written about extensively in the English language, Wang has hitherto largely remained out-side academics' purview. This chapter then explores linkages between Wang's and Zheng's ideas and those of other well-known America watchers like Liu Mingfu and, to a lesser extent, Yan Xuetong. It is hoped that this comparison will offer clues about the extent to which the current advisory shaping CPC thinking on the US differs from the previous generation and as to whether CPC thinking is un-American or anti-American in essence. The conclusions will tie the study together by speculating based on Wang's and Zheng's views about the degree to which New Confucianism, as opposed to neoliberalism, will shape Chinese society in the future.

Zheng Bijian: a pro-American dove?

Zheng Bijian has been an influential theorist within the CPC since the 1970s. He played an important part in drafting a number of key documents of the CPC between the late 1970s and 2002.[6] What makes him a famous pragmatic theorist within the CPC is that he was one of the key architects of "cat theory" (*mao lun*), "national conditions theory" (*guoqing lun*) and "characteristics theory" (*tese lun*), which were key components of Deng Xiaoping theory. It is worth noting, on the other hand, that Zheng had earlier been damned as one of the two designers of the notorious policy of "two whatevers" (*liangge fanshi*), which sought to enshrine Hua Guofen and Maoist zealotry.[7] Notwithstanding these, it goes almost without saying that Zheng is best known as the midwife of the theory of China's peaceful rise. This section explores Zheng's perception of the US by dissecting his writings and speeches.[8]

To counter both the "China threat" theory and "China collapse" theory, which were prevalent in the US throughout the 1990s, Zheng introduced a new concept termed "peaceful rise" in his speech at the Boao Forum in November 2003.[9] The term peaceful rise quickly became popular around the world following the-then Chinese Premier Wen Jiabao and President Hu Jintao's public support in their speeches in December 2003.[10] According to Zheng, twenty-first century China will not repeat mistakes of twentieth century rising powers, such as Japan, Germany or the Soviet Union. Instead, China will advance organically without colonising or expropriating natural resources in other parts of the world.[11]

It is a surprise that he avoids talking about the rise of the US, which can be regarded as a typical example of peaceful rise.[12] What are the similarities and differences between China's peaceful rise and the US's peaceful rise? If he had answered this question, his theory of China's peaceful rise would have been more convincing. Barry Buzan and Michael Cox compare China's peaceful rise with the US's peaceful rise in terms of similarities and differences and then draw six lessons for China's peaceful rise in the future. According to Buzan and Cox:[13]

> Peaceful rise is possible for China, and in the very narrow sense of it not triggering great power war, very probable. The choice is between what kind of peaceful rise – warm or cold. There is still time and possibility to choose

about this, but on the present trajectory China is heading for a cold peace, both in its neighbourhood and in the world.

Zheng talks about China's peaceful rise mainly in economic terms. From his perspective, China's peaceful rise not only refers to China development path, but also refers to China's development goals. China's development path is that China "is to build up socialism with Chinese characteristics independently in the process of participating in economic globalization instead of isolating from it and in the process of achieving mutual benefits and win-win results with the international community".[14] China's development goals are "to accomplish modernization basically, to enable China to shake off its undeveloped status and achieve the level of medium-developed countries by the mid-twenty first century".[15]

The term peaceful rise is a highly controversial concept, provoking a heated debate amongst Chinese and Western scholars.[16] In light of its controversy, the term was soon replaced by the anodyne and diplomatic term "peaceful development",[17] which has become China's official rhetoric since then, on grounds that the term "rise" sounds too provocative in the West.[18] Nevertheless, the terms "peaceful rise" and "peaceful development have no real difference in substance. According to Zheng, "China's 'peaceful development' and 'peaceful rise' mean the same thing with exactly the same essence and connotations, though in different terms".[19] To be sure, the major targeting audience for Zheng's theory of peaceful rise/development is the US. By upholding China's peaceful development, the Chinese government intends to send reassuring messages to the US, which worries about negative impacts of a rising China on its preponderance in the world order.

The formulation of his theory of peaceful rise marks a watershed in Zheng's perception of the US. Before 2003, he largely took a negative view of the US's role in world politics, although he would later reminisce that even back then he had much greater disdain for the Russian "polar bear".[20] According to Zheng's prognosis in the 1990s, the world would inevitably become multipolar following the end of the Cold War, and the US's hegemony would therefore embark on downward trend.[21] Building a multipolar world "implies to 'multipolarize' the American unipolarity and counterbalance the U.S. hegemony".[22] He was enthusiastically in support of the establishment of a new international order on the basis of the five Principles of Peaceful Coexistence, a counterweight to the unipolar international order dominated by the US.[23] In Zheng's words, "[T]he huge contradictions between America's meddling in other's business and its own strength limit, and between seeking a hegemonist status and the historical tide of world multipolarisation, are historical contradictions impossible to resolve".[24] Zheng's advocacy of anti-hegemony and a multipolar world implies that he agrees with the argument that "China would be pleased by a weaker United States".[25]

Since 2003, Zheng has purposefully played down Sino-American divergences and instead talked more about opportunities of cooperation between China and the US. Such a transition of his attitude towards the US is not a surprise, given that to develop a good relationship with the US is significant to the success of China's peaceful rise. Sticking to anti-American hegemonism would complicate China's efforts to develop a positive relationship with the US. Instead of upholding a banner of anti-American hegemonism, China should seek to expand cooperation with the US. According to Zheng, there exists a high degree of convergence of national interests and mutual needs between China and the US in areas like trade and non-traditional security cooperation and "if China and the United States can work in closer cooperation, the twenty first century will be a wonderful century".[26]

Moreover, since 2011, Zheng has been advocating a "convergence of interests" and "communities of interests" between China and the US in economy, security and global governance.[27] Many Chinese readers tend to find Zheng's views to be overwhelmingly pro-US. A few neo-Maoist intellectuals even accused Zheng of betraying China's interests and regard him as a betrayal of the Han race.[28]

Zheng is a representative of doves with regard to Sino-American relations. By contrast, Colonel (Ret.) Liu Mingfu is a well-known representative of Chinese hawks. Wang Huning can arguably be situated on that scale in the middle, taking a more realist view towards the US than Zheng, but also more pragmatic one than Liu.

Notably, unlike Wang and Liu, Zheng's writings and speeches rarely spotlight the domestic affairs of the US. Yet, in one talk, he expressed a historical view of American slavery as constituting the country's 'original sin'.[29] His views on that matter are quite similar with Liu's. When discussing the Taiwan question, Zheng argues that President Lincoln's overarching purpose in abolishing slavery was to keep the unity of the US.[30]

Unlike Wang, who criticises American individualism and favours China's Confucian culture, Zheng has not so far expressed his attitude towards American individualism. But his speeches regarding China's peaceful rise implicitly demonstrate his confidence in China's Confucian culture in helping China to rise peacefully. As Zheng argues in one speech, "Two Chinese sayings may help illustrate the logic. One is 'Do not do unto others what you would not have them do unto you' and the other is 'He who helps others helps himself.' This is how peaceful rise comes about".[31]

For him, China's self-perceived peace-loving would continue to distinguish its rise from the rise of other great powers in history. In other words, he believes China's exceptionalism, underpinned by Confucian culture, makes China's peaceful rise possible.[32] Can such a version of China's exceptionalism stand examination? Wang Yuan-kang challenges China's exceptionalism and Confucian pacifism in his book titled *Harmony and War: Confucian Culture and Chinese Power Politics*. By analysing China's behaviour in the Song Dynasty (960–1279) and the Ming Dynasty (1368–1644), he argues that the historical facts fail to support the rhetoric that Confucian pacifism makes China peace-oriented, and instead, China expanded when strong and retracted when weak. According to Wang, "Confucian culture did not constrain Chinese use of force: China has been a practitioner of realpolitik for centuries, behaving much like other great powers throughout world history".[33] From the perspective of some Western realists, the Chinese government's claims of peaceful development is a mere strategy of deception when it is still weak, and it will revert to power maximising behaviour when it becomes a risen power.[34]

Zheng's theory of peaceful rise/development was the hallmark of President Hu Jintao's foreign policy idea, as evidenced by two foreign policy white papers published by the Chinese government in 2005 and 2011.[35] Since he came to power in late 2012, President Xi Jinping has adopted the "Chinese dream" as his signature foreign policy idea. As a matter of fact, Zheng put forward the term "Chinese dream" as early as November 2005. In his words, "So far as China's peaceful rise is concerned, it is only a cherished 'Chinese dream' based on China's national condition and it aims at solving China's own problems, but certainly not any other dream".[36] Like Xi, Zheng argues that the purpose of "Chinese dream" is to achieve China's national rejuvenation. According to Zheng, "The 'Chinese dream' of 1.3 to 1.5 billion Chinese people, in the final analysis, is to put an end once and for all to the miseries and humiliations the Chinese nation suffered in the past century and more".[37]

The idea of the Chinese dream is a continuation of China's peaceful development strategy.[38] The Chinese dream and China's peaceful development are consistent, in the sense that Chinese dream can only be achieved by continuing to walk on peaceful development road.[39] As Chinese State Councilor Yang Jiechi argues, "The 'Chinese dream' requires a peaceful and stable international and neighbouring environment and China is committed to realising the dream through peaceful development".[40]

Compared with his immediate predecessor, President Xi is more assertive in pursuing China's peaceful development. Scholar Zhang Jian regards China's new foreign policy under Xi as "Peaceful Rise 2.0".[41] In essence, China's foreign policy is moving from *taoguang yanghui* ("hiding one's capabilities and biding one's time") to *fenfa youwei* ("striving for achievement").[42] Under President Xi, China has taken a bolder and more assertive approach in safeguarding its so-called core interests, as demonstrated by its dredging activities in the South China Sea and its November 2015 announcement of intention to build its first overseas military base in far-flung Djibouti.[43]

Twelve years have passed since Zheng first proposed the theory of China's peaceful rise in November 2003. Sino-American relations, however, have not improved much over the past decade. Zheng's ideas of "convergence of interests" and "communities of interests" between China and the US seem naïve, given that the competitive nature of these two countries' relations becomes increasingly evident. Tensions between China and the US, though manageable, have increased during the Obama era. Sceptical voices about the peaceful nature of China's rise have become stronger in Washington. The Chinese government's advocacy of China's peaceful development sounds less convincing for the US and the Obama administration saw China as a more serious challenger to American dominance, as evidenced by its opposition to the China-initiated Asian Infrastructure Investment Bank (AIIB),[44] as well as its more vocal voice against China's assertiveness in South China Sea.[45] With the conclusion of Trans-Pacific Partnership (TPP), the US solidifies its pivot to the Asia Pacific, sending a message to Beijing that the US will not withdraw its influence in the face of China's growing influence in this region.[46]

It will be more challenging for China to rise peacefully, given that there is very likely to be backlash from the US against China's assertiveness in the South China Sea. Strategic distrust runs deep in Sino-American relations. Zheng's speeches about Sino-American relations demonstrate that he lacks a comprehensive understanding of the complicated relationship between China and the US. He is right to point out that China and the US have a lot of common interests in areas of trade and non-traditional security. But strategic distrust prevents these two countries from engaging in deep cooperation in these areas. As long as the US sees China as an untrustworthy peer competitor, and as long as American-led global leadership is quietly resented by China, Zheng's vision of sanguine Sino-American relations will be only a pipe dream.

Wang Huning: a US sceptic?

In 1991, David Shambaugh famously damned China's American studies establishment as advancing a "shallow and seriously distorted" understanding of US culture, history, society and politics.[47] Nevertheless, in the intervening two and a half decades, a new generation of experts has come to inform CPC thinking on the US. Shambaugh's 1991 study focused on prominent figures like Zhang Wenjin[48] (d. 1991), Han Xu[49] (d. 1994) and their lesser-known policy-wonk contemporaries. It is noteworthy that neither Zhang nor Han had had hands-on, in-country US experience before rising to the top echelons of CPC US policymaking.

Born well after the establishment of the PRC, China's senior America watchers at present are nevertheless much better informed about the US, albeit not necessarily more pro-US. The best examples are perhaps Yan Xuetong (b. 1952) of Tsinghua University, who actually studied for years in the US before earning a PhD from Berkeley in 1992, or Wang Huning (b. 1955), who held visiting fellowships at Berkeley as well as at the University of Iowa (1988–1989).

Surprisingly, whilst Yan Xuetong's thoughts on the US are, like Zheng Biji-an's, not entirely unfamiliar to Western readers,[50] Wang Huning's remain largely unknown. Yet, it is Wang who commands far more influence within the CPC, as reflected in his 2012 promotion to the rank of politburo member. The purpose of this section is to better familiarise Western readers with Wang Huning's formative experiences in, and impressions of, the US, as captured in a travelogue he published after returning from his visiting fellowship.

A Fudan University graduate fluent in both French and English, Wang Huning has had a remarkable career, not least because his close relationship with Jiang Zemin did not result in side-lining by Hu Jintao or Xi Jinping, but quite the contrary. Wang is thought, in fact, to have intellectually shaped Jiang Zemin's "Three Represents" reform. Though often dubbed "hawkish" and anti-Western, and despite rumours of his advocacy of the 1989 Tiananmen crackdown, Wang is also on record as supporting the rule of law.[51] Leaving academia for officialdom in 1995, Wang has ever since remained in the inner circle of the CPC foreign policy advisory, and he is reported to have established a rapport with Xi Jinping too. One report even suggested that he played a role in shaping Xi's new "Chinese Dream" discourse.[52]

So is Wang a genuine rule-of-law enthusiast, and to what extent is his worldview shaped by his experiences living in the US? In 1992, well before Wang made the transition from academia to government, he published a memoir-cum-travelogue that sheds light on these questions. Entitled *America versus America (Meiguo fandui Meiguo)*, it is a book of recollections and formative thoughts penned against the background of the Bush–Dukakis presidential run-off.[53] Despite Wang's prominence in the CPC later on, *America versus America* never received the attention it deserved in the West, and it is therefore discussed here.

Right from the introduction, Wang is scathing in his portrayal of how vested-interest lobby groups and big business work to impede the American democratic process. Wang also denounces time and again what he sees as the litigious excesses of the American lifestyle. He alleges, for example, that reliance on expensive lawyers in all walks of life systematically erodes the presumption of individual freedom and equal opportunity.[54]

Here, we shall try to foreground what redeeming characteristics of American society he points to, alongside other revealing anecdotes he shares with his readers. Upon arrival in San Francisco airport for example, Wang is surprised at the hordes of "pushy" Japanese tourists he sees around him. To be sure, Wang was writing at a time when far fewer PRC passengers were seen in Western airports, and just before Japan's "Lost Decade" had dampened the number of Japanese tourists worldwide. Presumably coming with very high expectations about American efficiency and technological advancement, Wang, who by then had become a seasoned domestic passenger, also reveals his disappointment at how long it took passengers to reclaim luggage from the carousel.[55]

He would consistently, from then on, express wonderment in the book at how tech savvy Americans were, whilst at the same time finding moral flaws with that very same feature. Thus, for example, he marvels at the facility of magnetic card use in lieu of cash in everything from public phone booths to supermarket credit cards, but observes somewhat sanctimoniously that this facility leads to spend-thriftiness on the part of ordinary Americans.[56]

The impression Wang might leave on Western readers is that he often over-simplifies the complexity of multi-ethnic and multicultural American society. Whilst acknowledging the generally higher standard of living in the US and whilst on occasion giving away his admiration for the American "can-do" attitude, scientific progress and lack of hereditary nobility, Wang Huning is also at pains to point to Native Americans as an especially disenfranchised minority group. To him, Native Americans merely enjoy formalistic equality but are largely absent from the political conversation. Curiously, there is no sign in the book that this critical assessment of American society is stimulating him to draw any comparisons with the plight of ethnic minorities in the PRC.[57] In that sense, the book is devoid of profound reflective qualities.

Where Wang uniquely offers a glimpse into the makeup and thinking of senior CPC officialdom is in the personal and family realms. Wang suggests time and again that it is not just geo-politics that inherently divides China and the US, but also fundamentally different day-to-day behaviour patterns that feed, in turn, into fundamentally different world views. Coming from what was still a very poor country in 1991, Wang perceives middle-American family life as insular and self-indulgent.[58] His focus on selfishness and individuals shuts out, for the most part, alternative interpretations and plays down the role of philanthropy and civic solidarity in American society. Similarly, it is an interpretation that does not invite much reflection on the real extent of civic solidarity in China behind the veneer of Marxist and, more recently, Confucian rhetoric. Nowadays, foreigners actually hear from their Chinese interlocutors just how materialistic and politically apathetic their society had become during the 1990s.[59]

Wang divulges perhaps moral outrage, perhaps amusement when portraying inter-generational relations in American society. For him, the US is a veritable paradise for children and a battleground for adolescents. For the elderly, the US, in Wang's view, is hell on earth when compared with their exalted status in East Asia.[60] In much the same vein, Wang ridicules the American notion of marriage as something that would be an anathema to most Chinese and Japanese. In his view, most American couples treat each other to an excessive show of public endearment, yet are cold to one another in the privacy of their own homes.[61]

It is therefore no wonder, Wang infers, that the divorce rate in America is sky-rocketing and family morality is in decline. With so many households broken, drug abuse and weapon possession atomise American society. Crime and homelessness further marginalise minority groups, leading, amongst other ailments, to wholesale African American immiseration. Wang decries African American poverty, and at the same time condemns the poor's reliance on government benefits.[62] Of course, this litany comes across as incorrigibly naïve in hindsight. For today, income inequalities have split PRC society asunder. The divorce rate in the PRC is also on the rise, and single-parent families are not unheard of. President Xi Jinping himself had divorced his first wife because she allegedly wanted to live abroad, and many other CPC officials are re-married, including the now disgraced Bo Xilai.[63] Wang himself got divorced after he came back from his study leave in the USA.

Then, Wang goes on to valorise the Singaporean experience as demonstrating how a society can industrialise whilst maintaining its Confucian mores and respect for the elderly.[64] His thinking here speaks to an enduring fascination the CPC has had since 1978 with the Singaporean Model of economic development as being better suited to China than the Western one. Indeed, far from neoliberal, China's reforms have been described by Leong Liew as "a loose hug rather than a warm embrace" of economic liberalism.[65] As late as 2011, prominent political scientist and PRC government advisor Zheng Yongnian also observed that China's economic and social experimentation in the reform era owes much to the Chinese cultural concept of *zhongyong* ("the art of the mean"), and therefore, China has by and large rejected the excesses of Western neoliberalism and market fundamentalism.[66] Zheng suggests that China's ultimate aim should not be a Western-style system, because not even Western-style individual freedoms and democracy can prevent wholesale corruption and abuse of power, as Berlusconi's Italy shows.[67] This streak of critique of the Western discourse on democracy does not only apply to the West: prominent Taiwan scholar Chu Yun-han has, for example, pointed to the Philippines and Thailand as examples of lower-income countries that are hypocritically glorified and supported by the West as "democratic", where the votes of the poor are routinely bought off by ruling elites and the military is used to intimidate real opposition.[68]

Yet not all of Wang's impressions of the US seem immutably pre-conceived. Thus, Wang apparently arrived in America believing he would encounter a very progressive society. He thus found himself surprised: despite the stories he had heard of San Francisco hippies, the mischievous rock-and-roll scene and gay-community outspokenness – he finds most of those he engages with to in fact be exceedingly conservative. Wang notes, for example, how rare interracial marriage is (in that sense, he might find a different San Francisco nowadays).[69]

Later on, Wang seems to admit that Chinese and other Confucian societies are actually encumbered by *guanxi* and rigid hierarchies when compared with American social dynamism and mobility. But, quite perceptively here, he notes in the same breath that despite the absence of hereditary nobility – family connections still matter in the upper rungs of US society. The power structure, he observes, is not always purely meritocratic when it comes to elite university admissions or presidential nominations.[70]

For Wang, the American preoccupation with privacy, in all walks of life, engenders superficiality. Americans, he avers, look much warmer, open and friendlier than the Chinese when first encountered. They willingly strike up conversations with strangers but would rarely let a friend into their inner sanctum. During his stay, Wang concludes that it proved very difficult to form all-weather, true friendships (*moni zhi jiao*) with Americans. Most Chinese, he reflects by way of comparison, look aloof on first encounter. But once reciprocity is discreetly established through deeds – Chinese are more easily able to form meaningful friendships (*shenjiao*).[71]

Wang sounds particularly wrathful when lunging at the notion that corruption is less rampant in the US than in East Asia due to more transparent governance norms in all walks of life. Firstly, he notes, even at the university where he was hosted, personal connections were all-important in, for example, mobilising funding for sabbaticals. He recounts, for example, how a certain head of department had approved an extended fieldtrip to Africa by another professorial staff member, only to be "invited" in return for a tour of that African country later on.[72] When it comes to national politics, Wang is even more damning to the point of misrepresentation: for him, the two main parties in America are completely devoid of ideology or coherent platforms; rather they constitute an agglomeration of vested interests and lobby groups with a loose common denominator.[73]

Equally problematic is Wang's portrayal of the American electoral system. He likens that system to pyramidal corporate shareholding where each share-holder has one vote on the board in theory, but in reality, minority-shareholders can amass a controlling stake, to the detriment of diffuse shareholders, because the former are better organized and better funded.[74] For Wang, this amounts to broad-daylight gerrymandering, which in turn leads to voter apathy and low participation. The system is further encumbered by what Wang sees as costly, protracted presidential campaigns and complex voter registration systems.[75]

Then, like many others in China, Wang alludes to the fact that the notion of professional civil service in the West may actually have borrowed much, or historically derived from, the Chinese imperial bureaucracy. But the US variant thereof seems to him flawed in that an incoming administration can re-appoint, at will, the entire upper echelons of the advisory.[76]

Finally, Wang comes closest to discussing the realities of reform in China when decrying US managerial style as too rigid and intellectually restrictive (*siban, yan'ge*). He contrasts that style with what he sees as Chinese managers' penchant for flexibility and dynamism (*linghuo, jidong*).[77] To be sure, there is a touch of Occidentalism (read: Asian supremacism) in Wang's portrayal of the American economy in the early 1990s. Whilst openly spiteful towards the Japanese he came across in America, Wang recounts with glee how Japan's economic success had bewildered Americans to the point that Japanese collectivist managerial approaches are accepted as superior to American individualistic ones. Chillingly, he concludes the book with a prophesy: in the twenty-first century, another mighty Asian nation (*minzu*) would come to vigorously challenge American primacy; the American system would eventually implode, Wang avers, because the kinds of individualism, equality and freedom it champions are, at their heart, inherently contradictory.[78]

Interestingly, scholars like Yan Xuetong, who had spent a longer period of time in the US than Wang, are not necessarily more complimentary in their assessments of US society. Chinese understanding of the US has, to be sure, improved a great deal since Zhang Wenjin. What has changed is that that understanding is, at present, less anchored in a Marxian frame of reference than it is coloured by a New Confucian nomenclature that draws on the Singaporean experience.[79] Yet the tiny city-state of Singapore always sought strategic closeness with America; it never aimed to offer an alternative to US hegemony, whilst the PRC always has, either explicitly or surreptitiously.

In Wang's 1992 book, what we can arguably trace out are the origins and formative intellectual underpinnings of what would later become – cloaked in a New Confucian mantle – the PRC's aspirational narrative of global leadership.[80] Whether that narrative foreshadows a genuine alternative to the current American-led neoliberal world system, let alone an attractive one, is in the eye of the beholder. The narrative, at any rate, is hardly pro-American.

Liu Mingfu: war-monger or judicious realist?

The publication of Liu Mingfu's *China Dream* in English in 2015 makes for an opportune occasion to critically take stock of his ideas.[81] In 2010, the original book the retired colonel (b. 1951) published in Chinese caused quite a sensation with his sub-title reading: "soldiers must speak out". Though it is said to have foreshadowed, even informed, President Xi Jinping's first use of the term *China Dream* in November 2012,[82] the original book never received the kind of page-by-page detailed critical and semantic analysis it deserved. Instead, Liu was mostly dismissed in the Western media as a typically loose-lipped People's Liberation Army (PLA) commissar: triumphalist, anti-American, hawkish and conspiracy-obsessed.[83] Aside from Chris Hughes and Philip Saunders' online overviews – no serious attempt, to our knowledge, has been made to engage with Liu's rationale in detail, particularly as regards his insistence that China is inherently "war averse" or as regards his historical heurism.[84]

The following passages try to cast a deliberative sidelight on the book by engaging with the Chinese original version, rather than the recently published English version, which is now being promoted in the US.[85] Far from re-dismissing Liu offhand as a sensationalist, the aim here is to show the extent to which Liu dwells on other Chinese and Western thinkers in reading international relations and the extent to which his ideas are shared by others. It is hoped that Liu's narrative can thereby be more lucidly interpreted and its policy relevance better construed. In the main, the review will be taking issue with the paradox of Liu's calling for greater military budgets, whilst clinging to a self-perceived Chinese tradition of "war aversion" (*bu duwu* 不黷武) as the most desirable strategy for the country.[86]

In the West, Liu's positions were perhaps understandably cast as militaristic without due reference to their underlying historical mainspring. In fact, that streak of militarism is for Liu a counterweight to what he sees as a "scholarly-civilian" (*yanwu xiuwen* 偃武修文) ethos that came to over-script Chinese society since the fall of the Northern Song Dynasty (1127) and the subsequent entrenchment of what Liu sees as pernicious, superstitious and effete neo-Confucian tendency through much of the late-imperial era.[87] The historical generalisation offered here is hardly unique. It is reminiscent, to one degree or another, of ideas pronounced in two other highly popular books that have been published in China over the last decade and have gained some notoriety in the West: *Wolf Totem* and *China Can Say No*. The former, whilst written by Tiananmen democracy movement veteran Jiang Rong (pseud.), is a novel that nevertheless idealises throughout the martial spirit of the nomadic steppe people living on the fringes of the Chinese sedentary heartland.[88]

Described at once as a novel of nomads and settlers and their relations with wolves, a guide to doing business in New China and an ecological handbook, as well as a piece of military strategy, *Wolf Totem* is partly based on the author's own experiences as a Red Guard who left Beijing during the Cultural Revolution to work with Mongolian shepherds. Indeed, Jiang Rong repeatedly condemns his own Han ethnic in-group for their placid "sheep-like" Confucian obedience to authority and ignorant destruction of nature. Ironically, Jiang Rong may have been imprisoned a number of times by the Chinese authorities for his non-conventional views, yet his idealisation of the martial spirit has brought Wolfgang Kubin, a world-leading expert on Chinese literature, to label *Wolf Totem*, as no less than "fascist".[89]

China Can Say No is a collection of sensationalist anti-American political essays rather than a novel. Yet it, too, was authored by individuals who are thought to have at least in part been sympathetic of the Tiananmen democracy movement back in 1989, only to turn to the nationalistic tide less than a decade later.[90] The essays are by and large devoid of overt pokes at Confucianism or prevailing Chinese societal norms. In fact, they can be read as scathing critiques of American individualism rather than a rallying cry for more thereof in China. But they do share a platform with Jiang Rong and Liu Mingfu in calling for more assertive Chinese foreign policy, particularly vis-à-vis the USA and Japan.[91]

Where Liu arguably innovates beyond the two aforementioned books is in the analogies he draws from Western history. The case is not made for more military power alone but for the right balance between military and scholarly (read: economic) power. Liu's example is the Dutch Republic, which had been a great rival to England in the seventeenth century but – in his somewhat idiosyncratic account – then invested too heavily in peace-time mercantile prowess to the neglect of its fighting navy until it was finally subdued in 1713. The Dutch parable is told, it seems, specifically to warn Chinese leaders of focusing on GDP growth alone and letting their people become too livelihood-oriented (经济民族).[92]

The Anglo-Dutch preoccupation speaks to a broader research agenda amongst Chinese scholars of international relations. At Tsinghua University, Sun Xuefeng has argued, for example, that the common Western perception of democratic countries as less likely to go to war with one another ('democratic lineage theory') was irredeemably naïve. Notably, Sun pointed to the three Anglo-Dutch wars, fought over hegemony of global maritime trade during the latter part of the seventeenth century, as a classic counter-example. England had been at the time a nascent parliamentary democracy and the Netherlands was a progressive republic, but neither showed 'liberal trust' in its neighbour and mutual demonisation was rampant. As its power declined in the early twentieth century, the British Empire did not go to war with an ascendant US: this was *not* because the two countries shared cultural baggage, but because containing the Kaiser was considered a more achievable goal by Britain. By 1900, America's GDP was nearly double than that of Britain, but Germany's GDP had just edged above Britain's and so the temptation to check the advancement of that middle-European power was more compelling.[93]

***

Underlying Liu's narrative is a frustration often expressed in private by many Chinese: China is big and populous, has illustrious imperial history and has posted stellar reform achievements over the past three decades. Yet, it is still punching well below its weight on the world stage from sports through to science, popular cultural or military might. In order to bear out the illustriousness of premodern China, and in construing the Sino-American relationship in the modern era, Liu draws heavily *not* on Chinese authors but in fact on English-language literature from Paul Kennedy, through Warren I. Cohen to Angus Maddison. The latter's quantitative work is popular in China but controversial in the West in that it suggests China remained the biggest economy in the world as late as 1830s.

Neither is Liu's book simplistic to the extent he tars all facets of American life with the same brush in the manner of *China Can Say No*. He heaps superlatives on the Clinton Presidency, for example, for unleashing America's creative spirit and community mobilisation. He also favourably compares the stability of post-bellum America with the incessant revolutions in nineteenth and twentieth century Europe. For Liu, America – in contrast to the older European powers (*lieqiang*) – is a relatively *benign* imperialistic power that aims at cowing strategic competitors rather than occupying them outright.[94] Nevertheless, China, in Liu's view, would make an even more benign world power because it has a track record of "internalising" conflict: whilst European over-population, religious dissent, social inequalities and scarce resources led in the sixteenth century to outward expansion – demographic stress and scarce resources were resolved in China through peasant rebellions.[95]

More specifically, Liu praises Abraham Lincoln for his abolition of slavery, interpreting it above all as a pragmatic exercise in nation-building rather than an expression of morality. He uses the American Civil War as a rallying cry with which to denounce the rationale of Taiwanese independence and US arms sale to Taiwan. China, he avers, would never contemplate selling arms to Hawaii separatists.[96]

In a departure from mainstream prominent Chinese foreign policy commentators like Wang Jisi or Shi Yinhong, Liu seems to be expressly arguing that a Sino-American showdown is inevitable in the long run, despite economic and other geo-strategic complementarities.[97] Nevertheless, in his view, that either side has recourse to nuclear weapons means the showdown would be determined in points rather than knock-out; indeed, precisely like his personal friend but ideological arch-enemy, Pentagon insider Michael Pillsbury, Liu likens Sino-American rivalry to a "marathon". In the face of popular Chinese adulation of Putin as "macho", Liu seems to discount Russia as a global contender, when averring that the choice for the world is between America and China. He predicts China would eventually win the hearts and minds of people elsewhere because China does not seek to shape the world in its own image, hence it is more difficult for Americans to demonise China than it was for them to demonise the now-defunct USSR.[98]

What is then China's aspirational narrative of global leadership? China, in Liu's view, would create a fairer world for the great bulk of humanity because it is not hobbled by an "original sin" – colonialism in the European case, and slavery as well as Native-American annihilation in the US's case. Liu then reverts to classic Maoist clichés in suggesting China would not seek hegemony but would instead rid the world of any kind of hegemony; he uncharacteristically signs off with overt chauvinism when stating that China possesses "superior cultural genes" (中国具有最优秀的文化基因) that would help it stake a claim for global leadership.[99]

Hardly trigger-happy, Liu counsels China, above all, patience in dealing with the US. Its ultimate decline may be inevitable, but it would be a long process and obituaries this decade are premature. History teaches Liu that the USA had in fact been written off many times in the past – most recently in the waning days of the Carter presidency – only to come back on the world stage with a vengeance.[100]

The secret of that vitality, in Liu's historical judgement, is the fact the USA had a much longer "hide and bide" incubation than Deng Xiaoping's China. It announced the Monroe Doctrine after half a century of unique isolationism (美国特色的韬光养晦), during which successive presidents strove to disentangle themselves from European strife. In that sense, the USA nurtured hegemonic aspirations in a low-cost, surreptitious manner.[101] Moreover, Liu tells his readers China must emulate the American historical trajectory when it comes to isolationism. Like Sun Xuefeng, Liu suggests American economic might, for example, had long overtaken Britain's by 1900; yet the US did not out itself as the global power *par excellence* until 50 years later.[102]

Contrary to how Liu is sometimes depicted in the West, he is in fact extremely wary of overt Chinese triumphalism. The best way forward for China, in his view, would be to fight complacency. Chinese leaders should continue to be, Liu hints, haunted by paranoia and embrace a crisis mentality as drivers of self-improvement. In that sense, US "China imminent collapse" seers are rendering an important service to the cause of China's rise as they help obfuscate the true dimensions thereof. Furthermore, for Liu, a continual, haunting sense of crisis would ensure China's leadership would not degenerate into Brezhnev-like mediocracy and conservatism.[103]

Granted, Liu does repeatedly call for China to increase its military budget. But he emphasises throughout the book that this should be used as a deterrent only. The point is that for China to deter the US from all-out war it would need a stronger army.[104] Perhaps unsurprisingly, all the paragons of military vitality (蓋世武功) in his narrative are from pre-Song era: the First Emperor of Qin, the Wudi Emperor of the Han, and Emperor Li Shimin of the Tang.[105]

Yet, what China desperately needs in equal measure in his narrative is a vigorous set of values with which to re-vitalise society as a whole. Liu observes that in the US organized faith tempers heady capitalism and individualism. Although neoliberalism as such is not discussed here, he does seem to be hinting at his displeasure at the growing inequalities and materialism within Chinese society. To him, that most Chinese are mildly secular leaves a vacuum that needs to be filled, yet he stops short of suggesting more nationalism is the answer. What he does explicitly decry, however, is the paucity of new Chinese works of literature that are translated into other languages, as opposed the plethora of translated material at any Chinese bookshop.[106]

In trying to come up with new sources of societal inspirations, Liu even comes close to hinting that the CPC needs to share more power with other parties by way of curbing abuses of power. Yet, more discerning readers aware of the "China Model" discourse can easily tell this as trite, non-committal lip service to CPC "United Front" tactics.[107] For although China enshrines the single-party leadership of the Communist Party, it nominally retains a consultative system of eight democratic parties alongside. And the Chinese government insists that China is a multiparty state. Prominent Chinese international relations expert Yan Xuetong, who is also well known for his hawkish views, is on record saying much the same non-committedly:[108] ". . . China must make the moral principle of democracy one of those it promotes". Oblivious to the Judeo-Christian equivalent, Liu then cites the Daoist adage connoting "they shall beat their swords into plowshares" (化干戈為玉帛) and the Confucian one connoting "do not do unto others as you would not have them do unto thee" (己所不欲勿施於人) as unique Asian wisdom, which is presumably a guarantee China would not bully weaker countries when it supplants the US. If anything, it should more proactively come to the rescue of the oppressed (打抱不平). Here, Liu perceptively draws on Sun Yat-Sen's more vehement anti-colonial tracts depicting China as a follower of *wangdao* 王道 ('enlightened kingly way') as opposed to the Western penchant for *badao* 霸道('hegemonic bullying').[109] But what Liu does not tell his readers is that the preoccupation with *wangdao* as an alternative, which scholars like Yan Xuetong share, was actually stoked up in the early 1920s through Japanese notions of pan-Asianism, which Sun tried to harp on at the time. Depiction of Western nations as bullies served, in a sense, to legitimize Japan's own pre-war colonial empire as a "liberator" of not just Chinese but all Asians.[110]

Liu's postulation of the PRC as a twentieth century power that, unlike Japan or the West, never attacked first is otherwise historically problematic, and it is certainly not assisted by borrowing from the Japanese pre-war vocabulary of pan-Asianism; indeed, many in the West would contend this argument is easily belied by PRC intervention in Korea in the early 1950s, as well as its flash campaigns against India in 1962 and against Vietnam in 1979.[111]

Liu's efforts in exhorting PRC against complacency and triumphalism come across on balance as fairly genuine, even to the Western eye. By far, the least palatable aspect of his narrative to lay Western readership could turn out to be *not* his military bent – after all he is a retired PLA officer – but rather his penchant for conspiracy theories, one he seems to share with many other best-selling PRC-born authors.[112] Citing the influential strategist Nicholas J. Spykman (1893–1943), Liu contends for example that America had set its sights on pre-emptive containment of China as a future competitor long before the CPC came to power.[113]

Indeed, the conspiracies Liu marshals can be seen as the real culmination of the book rather than its putative chauvinism. Perhaps most thought-provoking of these is the contention that the USA had cunningly foiled Japan's rise in the 1980s as a warm-up for its China showdown this century. By way of warning China of succumbing to US pressure for devaluing the RMB, Liu controversially argues that Japan's "Lost Decade" did not arise in fact from internal weaknesses of the Japanese economy. Rather, it was supposedly a result of the Americans dropping a "financial atomic bomb" (投放金融原子弹) on Japan in the image of the 1985 Plaza Accord. In Liu's view, the Accord forced Japan to revalue the yen, absorb subsequent damage to its exports, pay more in return for US military deployment and enhance its Overseas Development Aid (ODA) to Western-favoured destinations.[114]

Nevertheless, despite his many incendiary claims, Liu chooses to strike a somewhat more judicious tone at the conclusion of his book. That perorational quality of his work went perhaps unnoticed in the West and is therefore worth highlighting in the teeth of sensationalism.

Towards the end, Liu actually confides in his readers: the US is *neither* devil *nor* angel. After all, for all its faults, it did fight the Japanese enemy in World War II alongside China. Rather, for Liu the problem is the US itself is prone to Manichean rhetoric, *not* China; the US needs a fearsome, imaginary ideological enemy with which to galvanise its populace and to oil the wheels of its military-industrial complex. Liu therefore predicts that China, before long, would be demonised in the US with racial overtones, and that it would one day in the near future find itself in the dock, accused of being a leading member of the 'Axis of Evil'.[115]

Conclusion

Elite members of the CPC have never had a unitary perception of the US. Rather, a variety of voices compete for influence within the CPC, as shown by divergent perceptions of the US by Wang Huning, Liu Mingfu and Zheng Bijian. By and large, Zheng Bijian is a foreign policy-oriented dove who embraces the Americanised economic globalisation and advocates a closer Sino-American partnership in global affairs. Zheng has not, so far, shown his attitudes towards American society. From his writings and speeches, however, we can infer that at least he does not dislike American society, values and lifestyle.

Rather, when speaking of China, he harks back to socialism and Confucian culture in a low-key manner. In contrast, Liu Mingfu is a hawk critical of not only America's role in world affairs, but also American society, and he argues that a China with superior cultural "genes" can offer a better future for the world than the US does.

Compared with Liu, Wang Huning is a milder critic of American foreign policy and American society. Nonetheless, Wang shows more unfavourable feelings towards the US than Zheng does. Given that Wang's and Liu's critical observations of the US touch on both foreign policy and society, their writings are more useful than Zheng's to help understand China's trajectory under President Xi.

With socialism losing traction in Chinese society, the CPC has increasingly adopted a Confucianised political discourse to maintain the legitimacy of one-party rule in China. President Xi "has become obsessed with citing Confucian classics and using Chinese history to present China's domestic and external policies".[116] The ideal society Xi dreams of is far removed from a democratic and liberal American-style society with individualism and freedom at its heart.

Instead, the CPC under Xi is at pains to consolidate what Christopher A. Ford has termed "meritoligarchy" by advocating an idealised society with Confucian values emphasising hierarchy, communitarianism and paternalism.[117] It is therefore unsurprising that Wang's and Liu's critical observations of the American society strike a chord with many other elites within the CPC. Wang, in particular, is not a big fan of US social inequality. From his writings, we can infer that he thinks Singapore can be a much better welfare model for China to follow. It is almost certain that the CPC will continue to make efforts to engineer Chinese society in an opposite direction to Western liberal values. Neither is China under the rule of the CPC likely to continue acquiescing in American-led neoliberal globalisation.

However, it is useful to recall that, despite its well-known public housing system, Singaporean society today suffers from one of the highest degrees of income inequality in the industrialised world, well ahead of South Korea and slightly ahead of even the USA.[118] And if that is the model Xi's China is to follow, then increasing anti-American posture in foreign policy and New Confucian rhetoric may not necessarily augur a complete relinquishment of neoliberalism at home. That, in turn, might impede any Chinese claims to forging a genuine alternative to American-led neoliberal globalisation. We shall further explore Singapore as a very complex and at times problematic source of inspiration for China in the next chapter.

Notes

1 Shambaugh (1991), p. 3.
2 Kenneth Lieberthal and Wang Jisi, *Addressing U.S.-China Strategic Distrust*, The Brookings Institution, March 2012, www.brookings.edu/~/media/research/files/papers/2012/3/30-us-china-lieberthal/0330_china_lieberthal.pdf, pp. 7–19.
3 Alastair Lain and Mingming Shen, eds, *Perception and Misperception in American and Chinese Views of the Other* (New York: Carnegie Endowment for International Peace, 2015). It is available at: http://carnegieendowment.org/2015/09/22/perception-and-misperception-in-american-and-chinese-views-of-other/iics.
4 David Lampton, Security-relevant perceptions in U.S.-China relations: Elites and society, 11 November 2013, http://china.usc.edu/david-m-lampton-security-relevant-perceptions-us-china-relations-elites-and-society.
5 Shambaugh (1991), pp. 10–16; Saunders (2000), p. 43; Wang (2000), pp. 27–52; Yufan Hao and Lin Su (2005), pp. 19–40; Zhang (2012), pp. 22–23; Huiyuan Feng and Kai He (2015), p. 84.
6 Glaser and Medeiros (2007), p. 296.
7 "Two whatevers" refers to "We will resolutely uphold whatever policy decisions Chairman Mao made, and unswervingly follow whatever instructions Chairman Mao gave". See John Gittings, Hua Guofeng, *The Guardian*, 21 August 2008, www.theguardian.com/world/2008/aug/21/china.
8 We rely here in the main on the English translation of Zheng's collected work, entitled *China's Road to Peaceful Rise: Observations on Its Cause, Basis, Connotation and Prospect* (Peter Nolan ed., Routledge, 2013).
9 Zheng (2011), pp. 168–172.
10 Suettinger (2004), pp. 3–5.
11 Zheng (2011), pp. 229–230.
12 Wang (2011), p. 150.
13 Buzan and Cox (2013), p. 132.
14 Zheng (2011), pp. 264–265.
15 Zheng (2011), p. 265.
16 Dominik Mierzejewski categorizes Chinese scholars in terms of their viewpoints on "peaceful rise" into three schools, namely, optimists (yes group), dubious optimists (yes but group) and sceptics (no group). See Dominik Mierzejewski, *Public Discourse on the 'Peaceful Rise' Concept in Mainland China*, Discussion Paper 42, China Policy Institute, University of Nottingham, 2009, www.nottingham.ac.uk/cpi/documents/discussion-papers/discussion-paper-42-mierzejewski-power-rise-discourse.pdf.
17 Buzan and Cox (2013), p. 3. Yan Xuetong (2004, p. 52) argues the term "peaceful rise" can better guide China's foreign policy and safeguard China's overall interests than

the term "peaceful development". "Development" refers to self-improvement while "rise" refers to narrowing the gap with other countries. He thinks that it is dangerous for a country to only satisfy its own improvement without caring about to what extent it narrows the gap with others.

18 Glaser and Medeiros (2007), p. 304; Buzan (2014), p. 4.
19 Zheng (2011), p. xxix.
20 Zheng (2011), pp. 245–247.
21 Zheng (2011), p. 3, 14, 91, 137.
22 Guo (2006), p. 2.
23 Zheng (2011), p. 24, 49.
24 Zheng (2011), pp. 69–70.
25 Buzan (2010), p. 20.
26 Zheng (2011), pp. 246–247.
27 Zheng (2011), pp. 296–302; Zheng Bijian, Sino-American cooperation is the core, common development in the Asian Pacific Region, *China Institute for Innovation & Development Strategy*, 20 June 2014, www.ciids.cn/content/2015-10/14/content_11707792.htm.
28 Callahan (2015), p. 990. Han Xiya (韩西雅) and Ma Bin (马宾), Strange and doubtful: The relationship between Zoellick and Zheng Bijian, *Utopia*, 3 March 2012, www.wyzxwk.com/Article/shidai/2012/03/289000.html.
29 George M. Fredrickson, America's original sin, *The New York Review of Books*, 25 March 2004, www.nybooks.com/articles/archives/2004/mar/25/americas-original-sin/; Clarence B. Jones, Talking about America's original sin, *Huff Post*, 27 July 2014, www.huffingtonpost.com/clarence-b-jones/americas-original-sin_b_5396544.html.
30 Zheng (2011), p. 219.
31 Zheng (2011), p. 185.
32 Zhang Feng (2013, pp. 310–314) argues that China's exceptionalism consists of three components, namely, great power reformism, benevolent pacifism and harmonious inclusionism. It is apparent that Zhang attributes much of China's exceptionalism to Confucian culture.
33 Wang (2010), p. 181.
34 Buzan and Cox (2013), p. 7; John J. Mearsheimer, Can China rise peacefully, *The National Interest*, 25 October 2014, http://nationalinterest.org/commentary/can-china-rise-peacefully-10204.
35 Information Office of the State Council, China's peaceful development road, *China Daily*, 22 December 2005, www.chinadaily.com.cn/english/doc/2005-12/22/content_505678.htm; Information Office of the State Council, China's peaceful development, *Xinhua News*, 6 September 2011, http://news.xinhuanet.com/english2010/china/2011-09/06/c_131102329_2.htm.
36 Zheng (2011), p. 266.
37 Zheng (2011), p. 292.
38 Sørensen (2015), p. 53.
39 Wang Yi, Peaceful development and the Chinese dream of national rejuvenation, *China Institute of International Studies*, 11 March 2014, www.ciis.org.cn/english/2014-03/11/content_6733151.htm.
40 Yang Jiechi, Implementing the Chinese dream, *The National Interest*, 10 September 2013, http://nationalinterest.org/commentary/implementing-the-chinese-dream-9026.
41 There are three key attributes in China's "peaceful rise 2.0". First, Chinese government has greater determination to forcefully protect China's national interests. Second, China's commitment to the "peaceful development" policy has become conditional and is premised on reciprocity from other countries. Third, China has a more proactive and coordinated approach to create and shape a stable external environment serving China's domestic development. See Zhang (2015), pp. 9–11.
42 Sørensen (2015), p. 53; Zhang (2015), p. 6; Yan (2014), p. 153.

43 Johnston (2013), p. 7; Kathy Gilsinan, Cliché of the moment: 'China's increasing assertiveness', *The Atlantic*, 25 September 2015, www.theatlantic.com/international/archive/2015/09/south-china-sea-assertiveness/407203/. See also Jane Perletz and Chris Buckley, China retools its military with a first overseas outpost in Djibouti, *New York Times*, 26 November 2015, www.nytimes.com/2015/11/27/world/asia/china-military-presence-djibouti-africa.html?_r=0

44 Shannon Tiezzi, America's AIIB disaster: Are there lessons to be learned, *The Diplomat*, 18 March 2015, http://thediplomat.com/2015/03/americas-aiib-disaster-are-there-lessons-to-be-learned/.

45 *BBC News*, Obama: China 'Using Muscle' to Dominate in South China Sea, 10 April 2015, www.bbc.co.uk/news/world-asia-china-32234448.

46 The Straits Times, With TPP free trade deal, Obama solidifies US pivot to Asia, 6 October 2015, www.straitstimes.com/business/economy/with-free-trade-deal-obama-solidifies-us-pivot-to-asia.

47 Shambaugh (1991), p. 41.

48 Zhang Wenjin's expertise was undoubtedly critical to Sino-American normalisation, but he had not had much hands-on experience of the US. In fact, he studied in Germany before WWII, at much the same time that Deng Xiaoping had been studying in France. Zhang would nevertheless end up playing an important role in facilitating the Mao-Nixon rapprochement and would later also advise Deng Xiaoping and serve as PRC Ambassador to Washington.

49 Han Xu studied English in the early 1940s at the American-run Yanjing University in Beijing (known as Peiping then).

50 Yan (2011).

51 Li (2005).

52 Jeremy Page, The Wonk with the Ear of Chinese President Xi Jinping, *The Wall Street Journal*, 4 June 2013, www.wsj.com/articles/SB10001424127887323728204578513422637924256.

53 Wang Huning, *Meiguo fandui Meiguo* (Shanghai: Shanghai wenyi chubanshe, 1991).

54 Wang (1991), pp. 45–46.

55 Wang (1991), p. 1.

56 Wang (1991), p. 9, pp. 126–130.

57 Wang (1991), pp. 48–49, p. 249, p. 293.

58 Wang (1991), pp. 68–69.

59 For a study of consumerism in contemporary China, see Chen and Goodman (2013).

60 Wang (1991), p. 284.

61 Wang (1991), p. 344.

62 Wang (1991), p. 353, pp. 356–360.

63 Callahan (2013), p. 20.

64 Wang (1991), pp. 347–348.

65 Liew (2005), pp. 331–352.

66 Zheng (2011), pp. 133–152.

67 Zheng (2011), pp. 287–308.

68 Chu (2009), pp. 604–620.

69 Wang (1991), p. 73, p. 91, p. 99.

70 Wang (1991), pp. 114–116 (Dan Quayle's nomination is for Wang a case in point).

71 Wang (1991), pp. 114–116.

72 Wang (1991), pp. 116–117.

73 Wang (1991), pp. 155–158, p. 165, pp. 169–173.

74 Wang (1991), pp. 182–185.

75 Wang (1991), pp. 210–211.

76 Wang (1991), p. 248. This notion is not limited to Chinese intellectuals but had in fact been famously evoked by Creel (1970).

77 Wang (1991), p. 269.

78 Wang (1991), pp. 384–390.
79 Bell (2015).
80 For a favourable Western appraisal of that narrative, see e.g. Jacques (Penguin, 2012).
81 Mingfu Liu, *The China Dream: Great Power Thinking and Strategic Posture in the Post-American Era* (New York: CN Times, 2015).
82 For an authoritative study of the term, see e.g. Callahan (2013).
83 Se e.g., http://foreignpolicy.com/2015/06/04/col-liu-and-dr-pillsbury-have-a-dream-the-inevitable-clash-between-china-and-america/
84 Chris Hughes www.thechinabeat.org/?p=1814; Philip C. Saunders www.jamestown.org/single/?no_cache=1&tx_ttnews%5Btt_news%5D=36217#.VXbTKc9Vikp
85 www.theatlantic.com/international/archive/2015/06/china-dream-liu-mingfu-power/394748/
86 Liu (2010), p. 99. The term as used by Liu is a negative derivation of the ancient idiom 穷兵黩武 (*qionbing duwu*), which describes trigger-happy, war-mongering generals. In a modern sense, the term *bu duwu* can also connote avoidance of militarism or peace-loving.
87 Liu (2010), pp. 235–238. N.B: The idiom itself, *yanwu xiuwen*, emerged almost a millennium before the Song.
88 On Jiang Rong, see www.theguardian.com/world/2007/nov/22/china.features11;
89 www.independent.co.uk/arts-entertainment/books/features/jiang-rongs-wolf-totem-the-year-of-the-wolf-768583.html
90 http://thediplomat.com/2014/08/the-china-can-say-no-effect/
91 *China Can Say No.* by Song Qiang, Zhang Zangzang, Qiao Ben, Gu Qingsheng, Tang Zhengyu; *Studying in the USA.* by Qian Ning; *China Can Still Say No.* by Song Qiang, Zhang Zangzang, Qiao Ben, Gu Qingsheng, Tang Zhengyu, Reviewed by Peter Gries in the *China Journal* No. 37 (Jan., 1997), pp. 180–185.
92 Liu (2010), pp. 246–249. N.B.: Most standard accounts of Dutch decline in 1713 tend to ascribe it to over-investment in land forces to curb French encroachment.
93 For a discussion, see Niv Horesh, In search of the China Model, *China Report*, 49 (2013): 337–355.
94 LMF, pp. 39, 47.
95 Liu (2010), p. 118.
96 Liu (2010), p. 35.
97 Liu (2010), pp. 170–173.
98 Liu (2010), pp. 56–58.
99 Liu (2010), pp. 73–76.
100 Liu (2010), pp. 134, 144–147, 192.
101 Liu (2010), pp. 151–158. N.B.: elsewhere, Liu credits Deng with lifting up China's fortunes on the world stage dramatically. Nevertheless, he is trenchantly avers it had been Mao who more significantly helped China rid itself of servile mentality, e.g. pp. 174–175.
102 Liu (2010), pp. 81–82.
103 Liu (2010), pp. 268–282.
104 Liu (2010), pp. 250–260.
105 Liu (2010), pp. 233–234.
106 Liu (2010), pp. 88–89.
107 Liu (2010), pp. 286–287.
108 Yan (2011), pp. 212–221.
109 Liu (2010), p. 98, 121, 129. N.B.: elsewhere, Liu is critical of Sun Yat-Sen for naively believing the USSR or Japan would help China rid itself of Western imperialism, e.g., pp. 166–167.
110 Saaler and Szpilman (2011), Introduction.
111 Liu (2010), p. 102.

112 See e.g., Jin Shengrong's 金圣荣 *Kill Toyota !* (English title on Chinese cover in the original; Beijing: Xin shijie chubanshe, 2010). Chinese title: <谁想干掉丰田? 美国式阴谋伏击的真相>.
113 Liu (2010), p. 169.
114 Liu (2010), pp. 183–185. N.B. Similar claims are made in Song Hongbing's 2007 best-seller *Currency Wars* (货币战争), see e.g., www.theaustralian.com.au/archive/business-old/chinese-buy-into-currency-war-plot/story-e6frg90x-1111114509943
115 Liu (2010), pp. 210–224.
116 Zhao (2015), p. 962.
117 Ford (2015), p. 1042.
118 Mukhopadhaya (2014).

4   The 'Singapore fever' in China

Policy mobility and mutation

Introduction

Much has been made of the significance of the 1992 'southern tour' of the-then 'Paramount Leader' of the CPC, Deng Xiaoping, in instituting a new round of socioeconomic reforms in China. Relatively underplayed but not lacking in historical significance was his southern tour of Bangkok, Kuala Lumpur and Singapore in November 1978. Recounting this visit, former Singapore Prime Minister Lee Kuan Yew described how Deng's tour "shocked him [Deng] because he expected three backward cities. Instead he saw three modern cities and he knew that communism – the politics of the iron rice bowl – did not work".[1] This "shock" jumpstarted a deepening engagement with the regulatory regime in Singapore, previously labelled the "running dog of imperialism" (*diguozhuyi zougou* 帝国主义走狗) by the CPC propagandistic machine. Delegations began to visit Singapore informally in the 1980s, including Jiang Zemin, who succeeded Deng as China's next leader, and a 'Singapore fever' (*xinjiapo re* 新加坡热) quickly developed across Chinese policymaking circles after Deng's imploration to CPC cadres in 1992: "Learn from the world, especially from Singapore. There is good social order there. They govern with discipline. We should draw from their experience – and we will do even better than they."[2]

More delegations were deployed to Singapore in the 1990s. The current Chinese president, Xi Jinping, went on one of these visits as a city-level official. A bilateral agreement was signed in February 1994 in Beijing to facilitate expertise transfer in the realm of urban and industrial management – portrayed by Singaporean policymakers as a government-to-government (G-to-G) 'software transfer' – to the ancient city of Suzhou. Subsequent G-to-G collaborations were launched in Tianjin (2008) and Chongqing (2015). The regulatory engagement became further institutionalised with the signing of two agreements in 1997 and 2001 to facilitate short attachments to key regulatory agencies in Singapore and longer-term enrolment in master's degree programs offered by the Nanyang Technological University (NTU) and the National University of Singapore (NUS). More recently, the CPC's enchantment with Singaporean neo-authoritarianism appears to have transcended the domains of urban public administration and industrial policy. This is interesting – if not also surprising – as it comes after reported concerns about the "cracks in the Singapore Model" following the ruling People's Action Party's (PAP) weakest ever electoral performance in 2011.[3] With the PAP's landslide electoral victory of September 2015 suggesting that it managed to reduce the socioeconomic problems that triggered a loss of confidence in its governance, it appears there are new lessons to be drawn on addressing social discontent.

This chapter evaluates the emergence and effects of lesson drawing and policy transfers from Singapore to China in the post-Mao era. It has two objectives. First, it re-examines how this Sino-Singaporean regulatory engagement – only the second overt attempt to learn from a particular country after Mao Zedong pledged during the 1950s to contour China's tomorrow on the Soviet Union prototype – came to be. Second, the chapter provides a two-fold evaluation of the concrete policies and ideas drawn from Singapore. It begins by assessing the CPC's annual cadre training and exchange programs through critical observations from Chinese scholars and policymakers. The constraints of implementing G-to-G policy transfers are then illustrated through a critical review of policymakers' comments and existing research on the Suzhou and Tianjin G-to-G software transfers.

Placed within a broad historical framework, this spectrum of evidence shows how Singaporean-derived lessons and policies mutated when rolled out across Chinese shores. Indeed, inflows of ideas and policies continue to be refracted – if at times actively resisted – by all levels of the party-state apparatus. At one level, this reinforces W. G. Huff's contention that the Singaporean experience "is unlikely to be replicated elsewhere, not only because the Republic is a city-state, but also because few others can develop services exports reliant on location, because of the unacceptability in many other polities of a heavy foreign economic presence, and because of difficulties in effecting the same degree of government control as in Singapore."[4] At another level, the mutation and, in the case of the G-to-G projects, territorial containment of policies, ideas and philosophies from Singapore reinforces David Shambaugh's observation that foreign ideas/practices have been proactively re-adapted to local contexts in China.[5] Viewed as an aggregated process over time, however, existing research remains unclear whether the overt 'learning' engagements with Singapore-based institutions and firms are of more political rather than practical value for current and future rounds of institutional reforms across China. This chapter will address this lacuna.

There are three parts to the chapter. The geographical-historical conditions that made the China–Singapore strategic engagement possible are presented in section 2. Section 3 lists different dimensions of lesson drawing and policy transfers between China and Singapore, and evaluates the challenges associated with transposing the Singaporean regulatory experience in China are then presented. The primary theoretical question – why, *in spite of* practical constraints associated with cross-border flows of regulatory logics, Chinese policymakers persist in learning from the Singaporean experience – will be addressed in the conclusion.

The geopolitical backdrop to policy mobility

The picture often portrayed of 'feverish' China–Singapore lesson drawing and policy transfers in the 1980s starkly contrasts bilateral relations of the 1960s. Just as Singapore attained independence in 1965 after leaving the Malaysian federation, Mao Zedong was about to launch the 'Great Cultural Revolution of the Proletariat' across China. At the time, the CPC still officially subscribed to the Leninist internationalist logic that a complete transition to a Communistic end-state was premised on 'liberating' the entire international community from capitalistic-imperialistic exploitation. To attain this objective, the CPC launched its own version of policy transfer by supporting insurgent movements across Southeast Asia. In the Malay peninsula, this process was to be facilitated by the Communist Party of Malaya (CPM), termed by a recently declassified US government document as "the agent of the Communist Party of China".[6]

The CPM first embarked on campaigns to overthrow the British colonial government between 1948 and 1960, a period also known as the Malayan Emergency.[7] When this failed, its leader, Chin Peng, fled to China in 1960 and began directing operations from Beijing. The CPM operated a radio station in Hunan province known as the *Suara Revolusi Malaya* (Voice of Malayan Revolution). Broadcasts aimed at Malaya complemented clandestine local cells that worked to expand loyalty to communist China through guerrilla and psychological warfare.[8] A particular target audience was a group of ethno-nationalistic Chinese in Malaya who, in Gungwu Wang's observation, refused assimilation and "wanted all Chinese to be completely and passionately dedicated to the welfare of China and China alone".[9]

Opposing this warfare was Lee Kuan Yew, the first prime minister of Singapore. After witnessing the destruction caused by Japanese colonialism and then communistic radicalism in the 1940s and 1950s, Lee became a staunch nationalist and strongly opposed communism. His primary political goal was to create a meritocratic 'Malaysian Malaysia' when Singapore was a part of Malaysia from 1963 to 1965 and, following enforced separation, for an independent Singaporean identity.[10] To ensure that newly independent Singapore could survive without an economic hinterland, the Lee administration worked at attracting and embedding transnational capital. This stance was summarised in no uncertain terms: "Singapore will survive, will trade with the whole world and will remain non Communist".[11] Lee's proclamation effectively integrated the city-state within the very expansionary system of capitalism that the CPC, then at the apex of ultra-leftist fervor, sought to negate. In addition, this integration process would have nothing to do with "communism", which meant the exclusion of political economies like China and the Soviet bloc. Unsurprisingly, Radio Beijing and the CPM broadcasts began to label Lee and his "clique" as imperialist "running dogs".[12] Sino-Singaporean relations were tense, to say the least, and Singaporean policymakers viewed Chinese foreign policy with immense suspicion.

This frosty standoff thawed gradually after the US President Richard Nixon visited Beijing in 1972 and met with the-then CPC Chairman, Mao Zedong. Prior to that, as a recently declassified "Outline Plan of Operations" from Washington reveals, the US government implored its representatives to impress on "local Chinese" in Malaya and Singapore that "help from 'Mother China' would be inviting a fate such as Hungary, North Korea and Viet Minh; that Russia and China impose special harsh treatment upon their colonies, and upon home grown communist leaders after the takeover; and that being drawn into a communist system will lower present living standards and enslave the people".[13] With the US taking the lead in engaging this "communist system", the Lee administration began to respond to these foreign policy shifts. "We thought it would be foolish", recounts former Home Affairs Minister Wong Kan Seng, "not to go and see what China had to offer. So we sent our people there . . . to understand what was going on".[14]

Despite this newfound enthusiasm, Lee was keen from the outset to emphasise Singapore was neither an ethnic nor a geopolitical outpost of China. Underpinning this emphasis was sensitivity to Southeast Asian geo-politics: the CPM remained an active – albeit fragmented – secessionist force in the Malay peninsula, whilst the Indonesian Communist Party (PKI) had just been brutally purged (which led in turn to the collapse of the Sukarno administration). And as Lee observed at a 1973 Commonwealth Heads of Government Meeting in Ottawa, Singaporean policymakers had to overtly allay international concerns that the city-state was not a territorial extension of China:

> When the Prime Minister of Australia [Gough Whitlam] said that because Singapore has a large ethnic Chinese population, therefore the Soviet ships could not come to Singapore, the Soviet Union immediately diverted four Soviet tenders, feeder ships, to Singapore for repairs, to see whether we were Chinese or Singaporeans. We repaired them.[15]

Lee further affirmed the distinction between 'Chinese' and 'Singaporeans' in his historic meeting with Mao Zedong in May 1976. Former politician Lee Khoon Choy, one of several Chinese-educated personnel to be co-opted as Lee Kuan Yew's 'lieutenants', puts the latter's position in clear perspective:

> In 1976, when I arranged for Lee to visit China . . . we saw Mao Zedong, who was already mentally and physically frail. Lee's delegation consisted of 17 members. Other than Rajaratnam [then Foreign Minister] and me, the group included Malay Parliamentary Secretary Ahmad Mattar. It was to show that the visit was not meant to be a "kinsmen Chinese" visit of Singapore ministers. The mixed group served to allay fears or suspicion by Singapore's neighbours.[16]

Although no significant foreign policy breakthrough emerged from the Mao–Lee meeting, it softened the Sino-Singaporean standoff and generated gradual modifications in Singapore's foreign policy towards the so-called 'Communist spectre' in Southeast Asia. A new position was subsequently presented by the-then

Singaporean Foreign Minister S. Rajaratnam in an address to the Association of Southeast Asian Nations (ASEAN) in July 1977:

> Within our own countries we must continue to fight our communists because in every one of the ASEAN countries the people have made it abundantly clear that Communism is not for them. But outside of ASEAN the question of whether a government is or is not Communist is irrelevant. The only test is whether it is friendly or unfriendly; whether it is under a compulsion to liberate us from ourselves or leave it to each of us to seek the better life our own way . . . I think today and in the future great powers will seek friends and allies not on the basis of increasingly irrelevant ideological affinities but on the basis of national interests.[17]

This shift from ideological internationalism to political realism established the platform for a "friendly" Deng Xiaoping to launch the previously mentioned visit to Southeast Asia in 1978. The Singapore media was keen, as was Lee Kuan Yew in several subsequent interviews, to portray Deng's visit as an eye-opening experience. Judging from Deng's October 1979 address to domestic policymakers, this portrayal might be largely correct: whilst plans to launch the Special Economic Zones (SEZs) were proposed by key cadres such as Xi Zhongxun and Yang Shangkun as early as 1977, the Singapore visit arguably catalysed the involvement of foreign capital in new rounds of socioeconomic reforms:

> I went to Singapore to understand aspects of how they utilized foreign capital. Foreigners established factories in Singapore and Singaporeans reaped several benefits . . . We must develop this resolve, weigh and be clear about the pros and cons, and do it even if it means suffering some minor losses.[18]

The commitment to learn from Singapore entailed a policy turnabout that illustrated Deng's chameleon-like approach to governance. As the memoirs of Chin Peng, then leader of the CPM, reveal, it was Deng who, in 1961, instructed Chin to not only maintain but intensify military struggle in the Malay peninsula when the CPM was planning to wind up its operations.[19] The goal was two-fold. Apart from spreading communistic revolution to other parts of Asia, the CPC also tried to drive and draw on ethno-nationalism; following Lee Kuan Yew's request, however, it was the same Deng who mandated Chin to cease the CPM radio broadcasts immediately. This sharp reversal underscored the classic 'black cat, yellow cat' instrumentalism Deng first promulgated in the 1960s – any cat that is capable of catching mice is a good cat. And the 'mice' Deng really wanted since the early 1960s was economic rejuvenation. After phasing out communistic internationalisation, the Deng administration intensified a process that was unthinkable just a decade earlier – global economic integration.[20]

Most prominent of the Sino-Singaporean exchanges in the 1980s was the 1985 appointment of Goh Keng Swee, the former deputy prime minister of Singapore, as the advisor on coastal development and tourism to the State Council of China.[21] Despite this engagement, lesson drawing from Singapore remained largely based on inspiration throughout the 1980s. Concrete policy transfers to particular cities, if and when they occurred, were neither tailored by Singapore-based agencies nor intended for nationwide adaptation. This was due primarily to the legacy of the urban-rural dual structure: 80% of the population was catego-rised as 'rural' at the onset of the 1978 'reform and liberalization', and Deng's domestic emphasis was to increase both productivity and enthusiasm through reforming rural production.[22] If anything, Sino-Singaporean relations were char-acterised by the rollback of Mao-era geopolitical animosity in order to facilitate deeper cross-border socioeconomic engagement. For the Singapore government, what specifically needed addressing was the aforementioned Chinese support for communist guerrillas operating across Southeast Asia. Lee Kuan Yew empha-sised this point to Deng in 1978:

> During his visit Deng warned us of the Russian bear using Vietnam as its cat's paw to control Southeast Asia. I told him that the Soviet Union was far away but reminded him that all the exhortations for the overthrow of local governments in Southeast Asia were coming from broadcasting stations in China and that the arms finding their way to the insurgents were being pro-vided by China. I expected an angry and vehement denial, but he unexpect-edly asked, "What do you want me to do?" I replied, "Stop it!" He responded, "Give me time." A year later the broadcasts stopped.[23]

The year 1989 proved to be the crucial watershed of transformative change in Sino-Singaporean relations. For the leaders of Singapore and other ASEAN political economies, lingering suspicions of China eased following the surren-der of the CPM in southern Thailand and the collapse of the Soviet Union and Eastern Europe. In view of this underlying concern with the 'communist spec-tre' in Southeast Asia, Singaporean foreign policymakers opted not to establish formal diplomatic relations with China until October 1990, two months after the Suharto government of Indonesia did likewise.[24] Within China, the massive social instability leading up to and after the military crackdown on civilian protesters in Tiananmen Square on 4 June triggered strong reflections on the effects and future trajectories of post-1978 socioeconomic reforms. The conjuncture was thus characterised by a strange mix of improved foreign relations with domestic socioeconomic chaos: as foreign fears of the 'China threat' were allayed and new foundations for cross-border collaborations were laid, a growing range of social problems in both rural and urban areas demanded resolution. Specifically, Deng Xiaoping and his successor, Jiang Zemin, urgently needed new approaches to manage the intensifying urbanisation that accompanied market-oriented reforms and, consequently, assuage concerns by the strong conservative faction that deep-ening reforms would exacerbate political dissent.

Against this backdrop, Deng reaffirmed the regulatory experiences of Singa-pore as a potential developmental prototype during his 1992 southern tour. What he sought was a *pragmatic resolution* to the domestic crisis, and as Huff argues,

Singapore offered a "reliable" model for emulation: "Perhaps the most important reason why interventionism succeeded in Singapore was because of a pragmatism – the test of what works – rather than rigid ideological commitment to a free market or to state direction".[25] Contrary to the more informal learning of the 1980s, what followed since the 1990s were successive waves of lesson drawing campaigns and policy transfers that collectively constituted the Singapore fever. These were accompanied by a consistent rhetorical commitment from the Chinese party-state to learn from Singapore, even as both the PRC and Singapore's strategic and economic circumstances evolved and changed at the global scale.[26] The Chinese party-state, it appeared at the time, was very serious in formulating a Singapore-styled reform blueprint.

The realities of lesson drawing and policy transfers

Institutionalised learning in Singapore: effectiveness & constraints

The first concrete expression of lesson drawing from Singapore arguably began in 1992 with the introduction of bespoke programmes for Chinese public servants in the Nanyang Technological University (NTU). The choice of NTU as the first institution of teaching-cum-learning for visiting CPC cadres is interesting: it occupies the site of what had been formerly known as Nanyang University, the first university outside China (including Taiwan) that offered Chinese-language tertiary education for ethnic Chinese from Southeast Asia. First driven by Tan Lark Sye and launched in 1955 with the assistance of private donors, Nanyang University had in fact become a hotbed of pro-communist activism in the mid-1960s.[27] Concerns over communist-ideology slippage into mainstream society prompted the Singapore government to ultimately terminate the exclusively Chinese-based educational system in Nanyang University in 1980.[28]

Yet, one might speculate that the subsequent Singaporean choice to pitch NTU as an attractive training ground for Communist Party cadres from China was connected precisely to that vexed heritage from the 1960s. Indeed, the-then NTU president, Su Guaning, even proposed renaming NTU as Nanyang University in the mid-2000s. The CPC, for its part, did not specifically indicate they wanted to engage NTU until an official agreement on lesson drawing was drawn up in April 2001. Whilst the renaming bid proved unsuccessful, the symbolism of NTU's collaboration with the CPC should not be lost on observers of Sino-Singaporean relations: it revived and fulfilled one core objective of the original Nanyang University – the use of Chinese-language syllabi for advanced studies outside China – almost four decades after its establishment.

As enrolment in these courses expanded, NTU developed the first overseas master's programme for higher-ranked Chinese officials in 1998. Whilst the medium of instruction for most courses at NTU is English, the two masters programs for Chinese officials – namely the master of science in managerial economics (MME) and master of public administration (MPA) – are both taught predominantly in Mandarin. Both programmes are dubbed the 'Mayor's Class' (*shizhang ban* 市长班)

in China today. As these programs became popular, NTU set up the Nanyang Centre for Public Administration (NCPA) in December 2009 to offer executive training for senior Chinese civil servants. Between 1992 and 2012, more than 12000 mid- and senior-level government officials from China have been trained, with many receiving promotions upon their return to China.[29]

This longstanding relationship took on more concrete institutional expressions after the Chinese Central Organisation Department and various municipal party committees named NTU the best overseas institution for the training of Chinese government officials. In 2011, NTU was certified by The People's Republic of China's State Administration of Foreign Experts Affairs as an overseas expert organization and training institution. With this certification, NTU was authorised to conduct personnel exchange programmes for Chinese officials. In 2010, NUS joined NTU in receiving Chinese officials into its professional program at the Lee Kuan Yew School of Public Policy. Only senior CPC cadres that are section chiefs with at least 10 years of working experience can be accepted. These strengthening linkages between the Chinese party-state and Singapore-based academic institutions collectively exemplify a sustained preference on the part of the CPC for emulating and drawing inspirations from Singaporean regulatory policies.

The intensification of knowledge exchange and formalised learning positively impacted CPC cadres across the party-state structure. For instance, cadres of the municipality of Shanghai and the city of Qinhuangdao published a two-volume book reflecting on their experience in Singapore and how they could adapt best practices.[30] This corresponded with discussions on the connections between the Singapore experience and the importance of the rule of law[31]; the lessons to be drawn from the Singaporean Central Provident Fund[32]; and the factors of benevolent governance.[33] In 2007, the-then party secretary of Guangdong, Wang Yang, called on Shenzhen municipal officials to "be daring in matching up to the model of Singapore" (*jiaoban xinjiapo* 叫板新加坡). A large number of delegates were subsequently mobilised on learning visits to the city-state, and in November 2008, Shenzhen University launched a new centre on Singapore studies.[34] When Lee Hsien Loong visited Shenzhen in 2014, the Shenzhen mayor, Wang Rong, proudly proclaimed the results of this 'matching up': "amongst the cities across China trying to learn from Singapore, Shenzhen is one of the closest and the best".[35]

At the national level, the current Xi Jinping administration has established a consensus to emulate and hybridise Singaporean policies. Citing an unnamed political theorist who consulted with the CPC on new ways to emulate Singaporean policies, the *New York Times* reported that Xi had a low profile meeting with Lee Kuan Yew at the beach resort of Beidaihe in October 2010 after learning he was to assume the next Chinese presidency.[36] Lee, then minister mentor in the Singapore parliament, had met earlier with Jiang Zemin, the CPC leader who oversaw the first wave of software transfers in the 1990s. According to the report, Xi and Jiang agreed after meeting Lee "to try to adopt the Singapore model down the road".[37] Xi visited Singapore a month later, and in 2011, General Liu Yazhou, an advocate of party reform, dispatched a team of military officers to live in Singapore and prepare a study.

Following these initial visits, a policy agenda developed by the Development Research Centre of the Chinese State Council (DRC) for the first Third Plenum to be chaired by Xi (in November 2013) explicitly recommended state asset management reforms (*guozi gaige* 国资改革) to be modelled on Temasek Holdings, one of the two holding-cum-investment vehicles financed directly by the Singapore government. It was soon announced that this recommendation will be adopted.[38] A cryptically named "Small Learning Group" (*xuexi xiaozu* 学习小组) affirmed the potential of the Singapore Model through an editorial in the party mouthpiece, *People's Daily*:

> The leadership team of Xi Jinping is currently searching for an effective developmental model. To China, the Singapore model allows for more liberal economic policies to coexist with one-party governance, this point is very attractive. In addition, Singapore has shaken off the "middle income trap" successfully, this is another area especially worthy of learning.[39]

In spite of these concrete engagements and rhetorical commitments, analysts have documented strong obstacles to actualising lessons drawn from Singapore. According to Fan Lei, a researcher at the Charhar Institute in Inner Mongolia, CPC cadres found it difficult to accommodate the Singaporean experience in China:

> Context is an important factor to consider when learning from Singapore. More than 50,000 government officials have been trained in Singapore over the past 20 years. This is a considerable figure; on average every township would have an official who has been to Singapore. Yet it has been more than 20 years since the first batch of officials returned from Singapore, and the impact of "learning" is not at all clear. Why is it that so many officials were sent in search of "holy scriptures" (*qujing* 取经) for dissemination at home, only to have them return and revert to their old ways?[40]

Zheng Yongnian, a Singapore-based political analyst of China–Singapore relations, offers a similar observation:

> Take the social housing construction in China for instance, it is an example of failed learning from Singapore. Although housing reforms in China are always portrayed as learning from Singapore's housing institution, that is to allow the majority of the people to buy their own housing, what goes on in practice is land-financed development, it is to rule through real estate development. The same situation [of failed learning] can be said of the provident fund institution.[41]

Underpinning "failed learning" was arguably the short-termist developmental outlook known colloquially as 'GDP-ism'. Within the administrative structure, the promotional prospects of these cadres are contingent on their ability to generate

GDP growth in their respective territories (Chien, 2008; Xu, 2011). Following the gradual implementation of market-like rule, local CPC cadres were impelled to increase extra-budgetary fiscal revenue to finance developmental projects after the 1994 national fiscal reforms granted a larger apportionment of locally collected taxes to the central government. To augment this extra-budgetary revenue stream, cadres and bureaucrats expanded land leasing to private developers, or what is commonly termed "land financing" (*tudi caizheng* 土地财政). The developers then construct residential units and sell them at prices that are out of reach of many Chinese citizens. The consequent prioritisation of such capital-friendly initiatives over social service provision (especially for migrant workers) became a *structural barrier* for the successful implementation of Singapore-styled development. It is in relation to this economistic institutional context, Fan Lei adds, that CPC trainees found it difficult to manoeuvre if they transplant policies from Singapore:

> One of the trainees [from the government who went to Singapore] told me: "who doesn't want the blue skies and green shades of Singapore, but is it realistic to have these in China? Whoever implements development in this way is only making things difficult for him or herself." Learning from Singapore inspired these trainees a lot, they gained a lot, but the appraisal-cum-promotion institution in China restricted what they could do. Be it at the level of political ecology, economic or cultural environment, and other domains, there were many restrictions. While the officials were excited to have returned from their learning journey, they discovered many good experiences [from abroad] do not have suitable environments to survive.

Obstacles to direct borrowing are also shaped by the politics of scale within the administrative structure. This is made clear in a candid reflection by the Singapore prime minister, Lee Hsien Loong, on attempts in Shanghai to adopt Singapore's compensation strategy to deter corruption:

> I think China's circumstances are very different from ours. Your scale is much different from ours. I mean, we are the equivalent of one small city. Even Shanghai has 20 million people, four, five times the size of Singapore. So what we do in Singapore is not so easy to do all over China. I once had a discussion with a vice mayor in Shanghai, and he said to me, "You pay your ministers well, and your civil servants well, properly. And if we were Shanghai, all by ourselves, we could do that also. But if I did that, people to the west of me would have a view, people to the north of me would have a view, the people to the south of me would have a view, the people in the center would have a view. So it is not so easy for me to move, and it's a real problem, it's a different situation." But in Singapore, what we have tried to do is have strict rules, to have transparent systems, so if there is an exercise of discretion, it cannot be completed without checks and balances.[42]

Yu Ying-Shih, a former advisor on Confucian ethics to Lee Kuan Yew in the early to mid-1980s, affirmed the difficulty, if not impossibility, of extending this compensation strategy across China:

> Lee was of the opinion that Asian values differed from western democracy and western notions of freedom; that it was possible to build up a country through political unity and control. He allowed economic freedom but not freedom from the opposition parties. Because of his high credibility, the high efficiency of the People's Action Party, and the high salaries to officials that precluded corruption, hence the special characteristic of a one-party rule without corruption is unique to Singapore, it is a special characteristic others cannot produce. The CPC wants to emulate him, yet the most senior cadres developed by its one-party dictatorship have all morphed into a kind of special authority. Under this situation of special authority, it is impossible not to have corruption; corruption has become its integral component. Hence to speak of the "Singapore Model" [in China] is effectively empty talk, because such a model can only exist in a place like Singapore, and it can only exist during the Lee Kuan Yew era.
>
> (Commentary for *Radio Free Asia*, 8 April 2015)

These accounts by Fan, Zheng, Lee and Yu highlight a distinct trait within the party-state apparatus in China, namely the need for *reciprocal accountability* between different administrative jurisdictions within a unitary structure.[43] As such, one jurisdiction (Shanghai, in this case) could not act autonomously – which, as Lee's account implies, refers to the implementation of "strict rules" and "transparent systems" across the country – without the agreement of actors located at other administrative levels. By extension, Singapore's capacity to respond swiftly to global economic shifts (including the 2008–2009 global financial crisis) contrasts the multi-tiered, consensus-driven administrative system in China.[44] Singaporean policymakers' ability to micro-manage social and economic affairs and simultaneously 'scale up' the regulatory outcomes to the global scale (as opposed to the provincial and central governments in China) has been predicated on an 'urbanational' entity that the economic geographers Kris Olds and Henry Yeung term the 'global city-state':

> In global city-states, the (national) state has virtually direct access to the global economy. State policies can be shaped to develop the city-state into a global city-state . . . the political power and control of a developmental city-state distinguishes it from municipal governments in most global cities because it is able to bypass national-state/provincial-city politics typical in many global cities.[45]

This tangible difference underscores three contrasting aspects of Chinese politico-economic regulation, namely the demands of maintaining a unified party-state apparatus despite increasing differentiation between party and bureaucratic functions; the challenge of aligning bottom-up initiatives after greater regulatory autonomy was delegated to local governments[46]; and the increased emphasis on policy experimentation in the post-Mao era.

Beyond the tangible realm, the historian Xue Yong attributes the constraints to effective lesson drawing and policy transfers to a 'big country mentality',[47] namely the tendency to assess others from the self. Underpinning this mentality are two schools of thought. One is termed 'neo-authoritarianism' (*xin quanwei zhuyi* 新权威主义), and the other 'neo-Confucianism' (*xin rujia sixiang* 新儒家思想). The former explores possibilities for the concentration of political power to drive market-based reforms, and many Chinese intellectuals and policymakers regard Singapore as an exemplar in this aspect. 'Neo-Confucianism' was a movement predominantly driven by Tu Weiming from Harvard University. Tu's theory was straightforward: just like the Weberian attribution of the rise of capitalism to Protestant ethics, Confucianism had the same effect on the economic 'rise' of Japan and the four Asian dragons [South Korea, Taiwan, Hong Kong and Singapore]. Because of this, mainland policymaking and academic circles erroneously believed Singapore was founded on Confucian principles.[48] A commonality of these two camps, Xue argues, is the clear lack of interest *in* the Singapore experience, but rather an interest in furthering inward-looking intellectual agendas *through* this model:

> Be it the intellectual waves of "neo-authoritarianism" or "neo-Confucianism", when people speak about Singapore in China, they are not especially interested in Singapore, nor are they willing to expend energies to thoroughly understand Singapore. It is hard to find any kind of research on Singapore in China. People are still thinking about problems that pertain to China: is it possible to drive reforms through concentrating power? Are there modern elements in China's Confucian heritage?

This narrow-mindedness was in turn an outcome of a 'big-country mentality':

> The danger of a big-country mentality is a perennial assessment of others from the self (*yiji duren* 以己度人), to understand and explain things from the thinking framework of the self. In this way, what is new immediately becomes old. This is why, despite its popularity for a period of time the "Singapore model" did not drive research on Singapore nor stimulate interest in the legacy of the rule of law within the city-state. What people are interested in are still "neo-authoritarianism" and "neo-Confucianism", they are actually talking to themselves. It is no wonder why the Chinese intelligentsia does not seem to have advanced in thinking despite enjoying huge improvements in information technology since the 1980s. That they are ignorant of the outside world is not simply limited to [their knowledge of] Singapore.[49]

To Zhao Lingmin, a prominent observer of Chinese affairs, this mentality reflects a historically entrenched form of learning philosophy:

> In reality, China cannot emulate Singapore. One reason is the Chinese learning philosophy of "adapting modern Western techniques on the bases of traditional Chinese values" (*zhongxue weiti, xixue weiyong* 中学为体, 西学为用). During the Qing dynasty, Yan Fu [a major intermediary of Western ideas] and others advocated learning from Britain, yet when it came to constitution-development towards the end of the Qing era, there was a shift towards a total emulation of Japan, just because Japan also had an emperor and there was an emphasis on ensuring the eternality of the dynastic system. Going down this path, there was ultimately no attempt to construct a modern country.[50]

Entwined with this learning philosophy, Zhao adds, is the tendency to take short cuts so that any change would not significantly affect the status quo:

> There is always this attempt to cut corners, this hope to circumvent any change that would harm fundamental tenets of the incumbent institutional structure. Hence learning only occurs in technical and management aspects that are relatively easy. This kind of half-hearted learning, this search for quick fixes, naturally does not generate clear results.
>
> (Ibid.)

A corollary of this quest for "quick fixes" is the lack of policy "innovation". As Zheng Yongnian puts it, this refers to an unwillingness to hybridise the Singaporean experience with developmental needs in China (ref. also Table 4.1): "many local government officials do not know how to learn from Singapore. To them, learning means 'duplicating' (*fuzhi* 复制), it means 'tracing over existing characters' (*miaohong* 描红); to say that learning from Singapore is impossible means it is impossible to duplicate, to trace." (Zheng, 19 May 2013). For this reason, Zheng adds, "learning from Singapore must occur at the level of its philosophy, followed by integration with the specific conditions of China in a way that leads to innovation. Innovation is crucial, if learning is simply imitation, it will surely lead to failure".[51] The broader issue, Zheng and Zhao add, is not that Singapore is of a different size in demographic and geographical terms from China; it is the inability – or, perhaps, unwillingness – of senior Chinese policymakers to genuinely adopt the Singaporean developmental philosophy in the Chinese setting:

> Many mismanaged or failed states in the world are small. Small countries are not necessarily easy to manage. Similarly, big countries are not necessarily hard to manage. The USA is so big, yet is it not well managed? Big countries are able to absorb mistakes, and it may not matter if they make a few mistakes; yet if a major policy error is made in small countries, the whole country could collapse. To ascertain on the basis of size whether it is possible to learn from another country is illogical. I feel that many people's

understanding of Singapore is confined to some concrete dimensions, such as the Central Provident Fund (CPF) institution, housing institution, industrial park management, Temasek Holdings, financial management, etc. Very few people discuss the political institution of Singapore. The senior level of the Chinese leadership is most interested in the political experience of Singapore. Without understanding this political institution, it would be hard to understand how these other concrete dimensions came to be.[52]

I do not agree with what some others are saying, that it is not meaningful to draw from Singapore's success just because it is small. In reality, it is not an inevitability that small countries become successful. Many chaotic countries in the world are also small. Be it the success of Singapore, the USA or the UK, there are specific historical contexts and a process that unfolds over a long period. The problem lies not in learning from superficial institutional design (this is not hard), but grasping the myriad connections that occurred in these specific contexts, this is something that is hard for outsiders to comprehend, not to mention replicate. On the basis of this point, it can be said that any form of success is difficult to reproduce in its original form. What can be learnt is the philosophy and essential aspects of others' success.[53]

Zheng and Zhao's insights affirm why lesson drawing and policy transfers from Singapore – when they do occur – encountered resistance after reaching Chinese shores. Viewed in relation to the previously mentioned phenomenon of local state corporatism, the failure of the housing and pension reforms in many Chinese city-regions to integrate key elements of corresponding Singaporean policies further demonstrates centrally mandated fiscal reforms in China have generated indirect but constitutive effects on the predominant type of policy transfer – copying – from Singapore (see Table 4.1).

G-to-G projects: are geographically targeted policy transfers effective?

Apart from academic-based learning, specific policy transfers were and continue to be instituted through territorially contained G-to-G projects. Primarily involving the integration of industrial park development with the provision of social amenities in targeted cities, these projects emerged out of a software transfer initiative mooted by the Singapore government in the early 1990s. Fundamental to this arrangement is the deepening of economic relations by promoting policies that have proven effective in Singapore. As Lee Kuan Yew explains in 1993:

This is an asset which we have. But if we don't transfer it, this asset is valueless. It will die with us because as we progress, we will forget how we've done it in the early stages. If we transfer this asset over seven to 10 years, it will be useful to them and in the process we will get to know them well at different working levels. Then we can do business with them well at different working levels. That's the trade-off . . . It is a microcosm of what we've been doing in Singapore, which is why they've been going down and taking videos of us. They see the result without knowing the inner planning, the reasons for it. We're prepared to take them into the backroom and say, "look, this is the reason for it."[54]

And the first tour of the "backroom" took place in February 1994, when the governments of China and Singapore signed a landmark collaborative agreement that formally allowed Singaporean state-linked and private agencies to transfer their experiences in attracting foreign investors and managing industrial investments with Chinese partners. These experiences encompass land-use planning, building control, environmental regulation, planning and management of industrial estates, public utilities management and labour management. The first designated "microcosm" was the China–Singapore Suzhou Industrial Park (CS-SIP), a 70 km2 industrial park and residential community in Suzhou. Estimated to cost US$20 billion upon completion, the goal of the CS-SIP was to consolidate Chinese capacities to create investor-friendly environments for foreign capital. A consortium of Singapore government-linked companies took a 65% stake and a Chinese consortium took the remaining 35%.

According to Zhang Xinsheng, then Suzhou mayor, the city was positioned differently from all other economic regions in China because it offered: a) Singaporean expertise in estate management and other areas; b) Singapore-style long-term planning and enforcement of industrial regulations and practices; c) long-term security and safety for foreign investors in a "worry-free environment" because the project is promoted as having the support of then Chinese President Jiang Zemin and then Singaporean Prime Minister Goh Chok Tong; and d) easier approval for investments, as the Beijing central government had granted the Suzhou Industrial Park administration committee the authority to give the go-ahead for foreign investments exceeding US$30 million that do not require raw materials from China.[55]

Lee Hsien Loong, then deputy prime minister of Singapore, claimed the transfer of policies to Suzhou will "certainly open to China a new development model, which could be replicated in other cities if it proves successful".[56] During a meeting with then Jiangsu party secretary, Chen Huanyou, and his provincial colleagues, Lee Kuan Yew made it clear that true "replication" would be defined by a philosophical shift:

> The transfer of experiences that Singapore has, into the minds of Suzhou Industrial Park (SIP) officials, so that they can adapt their experiences to China, and spread the ideas, the model, across China. Even if we succeed in having a beautiful industrial park, with housing, hi-tech factories, if we have not transferred the ideas, the concepts, in the minds of officials, we would have failed. Once the Singapore element – the Singapore officials – leave, then nothing is left behind.[57]

Despite this support, the project was unable to meet original objectives. After the SIP plan was approved, the Suzhou City government re-started the development of a dormant project, the Suzhou New District Industrial Park (SND). This was clearly a competitive, if not cannibalistic, measure: the SND was geographically proximate to the SIP. With a majority stake in the SND, the Suzhou City largely ignored the SIP and concentrated on promoting the SND instead. The-then Suzhou vice mayor, Wang Jinhua, went to Germany and advised investors to invest directly in the SND rather than the SIP because it was not only more cost-effective, but also because the-then Chinese President, Jiang Zemin, did not favour the G-to-G project in the first place.[58] This aggressive approach reportedly caused the CS-SIP to lose US$77 million between 1994 and 2001.[59] After repeated requests for assurances that local Suzhou officials were not undercutting the G-to-G project, Lee Kuan Yew went on CNN in June 1999 to announce that the Singapore consortium would be pulling out:

> Well obviously, we are not happy because we are not getting the kind of attention which we were assured we would get, special attention. Indeed, what we are getting now is competition because . . . having learnt how we are doing it, they can always duplicate it and offer it at a lower rate of land. So, I think the problem has to be sorted out and what we hope to do is to complete one sector in the way we promised to do, so that it would be done as an example of what the whole sector could have been if we had completed it. But having completed this sector, we'll say, "Now, you do it. You compete with your own rather than we compete with them and we'll help you do it as best as you can. But you will do it".[60]

Shortly after this interview, Lee elaborated on the Singapore pullback:

> We would have liked to stay, but not in the way events have developed. It isn't worth our while to go on with it and have constant friction. And it's not just over costs – it's over ways of doing things . . . The problem was to change work styles, work habits and systems. So, I think it's best that they decide what to pick and choose and adapt to their systems.[61]

The friction was officially resolved in 2001. The Singapore consortium lowered its stake to 35%, raised the Chinese consortium's stake to 65%, and reduced its involvement in the construction from a planned 70 km2 to just 8 km2. Yet a part of Lee arguably felt point-to-point transfer and subsequent nationwide adaptation was possible, had the Chinese central government ensured the project received absolute "special attention".[62] This setback triggered reflections by key Singaporean policymakers involved in the project, which in turn revealed the difficulties confronting CPC attempts at emulating, hybridising or transplanting policies from Singapore. To George Yeo, the-then Singapore minister for trade and industry, the primary impediment of successful policy transfers was cultural differences:

> Fundamentally, the problem of Suzhou is a cultural problem. To a certain extent, for China to modernise, some of its cultural characteristics must

change. But will China become like Singapore? That's impossible . . . There are some things that China can benefit from studying the Singapore experiment, but there are many things which are irrelevant because conditions are different. The difficulty of the Suzhou project, I think, has proved that we are different from the Chinese. This also gives us some comfort that the success formula of Singapore is not easily copied. If we're so easily copied, then we'll be under competitive pressure very quickly. But because the Singapore model is not easily copied, what we have is an enduring advantage, not an ephemeral thing.[63]

To Lim Neo Chian, the former CSSD CEO, a key lesson was the Chinese central government does not run local-level economic projects, even if agreements were made at the G-to-G level:

> First of all, the alignment of interests is absolutely critical in doing projects in China. There is always the potential for problems, not just in China but in other places too. But in China, the key is to ensure the alignment of interests. An understanding with Beijing and Nanjing (the provincial capital of Jiangsu province which oversees Suzhou) is not sufficient. At the end of the day, problems are often resolved at the ground level. Therefore you have to have a very good alignment of interests at the local level. Or you have to go and run around solving your problems, and given the complexity of the Chinese government, it is not easy.[64]

For Lim and Chan Soo Sen, the first CEO of CS-SIP, differences in perceptions of contracts and policies – and by extension, the rule of law – were a major issue:

> The way we look at a contract or an agreement is quite different from how the Chinese look at it. Once signed, we have every intention to stick to the contract but they don't. They are quite happy to come back and see what they can do to re-negotiate some terms or to get out of some obligations. But you cannot change the Chinese mentality and Chinese system overnight.[65]
> In Singapore, policies are very explicit, down to the last detail. But China is too big. If a policy is too explicit and not open to interpretation, it becomes useless because every province will have exceptions and need to be exempted at different points. Therefore, Chinese policies are more general. Far better to state the spirit of the policy rather than to document the exact details.[66]

Of particular interest is the gradual success of the SIP after the Singapore-based firms engaged in more intense tacit knowledge transfer. As Andrew Inkpen and Pien Wang show, the Suzhou policymakers responded competitively because of perceived "asymmetric collaborative incentives".[67] It was only after the local consortium was given more control that the SIP began generating profits and became re-emphasised as a policy template for industrial park development across China. This corresponds with Lim Neo Chian's observation and underscores an important aspect of the policy transfer process: subnational policymakers are not passive agents who respond mechanically to central injunctions. Where their vested interests are not aligned, they could sidestep or undercut existing arrangements.

Empirically, the crucial question is whether the Suzhou experience – particularly the "cultural problem", to re-borrow George Yeo's term – would re-emerge in the second Sino-Singaporean G-to-G project. Named the Sino-Singapore Tianjin Eco-City (SSTEC), this 30 km2 project was launched in 2008 at the eastern border of Tianjin, a centrally governed municipality of 15 million people. Whilst the total investment remains undisclosed, project officials claim 40 billion *yuan* (~US$6.5 billion) was invested in fixed assets by 2012.[68] Launched against a backdrop of acute environmental pollution and income inequality, the Tianjin Eco-City project represents an ongoing concern with environmentally unsustainable urbanisation. Recounting the formation of this project, former Singaporean Prime Minister Goh explains:

> China at that time was emphasising the environment, green development, urbanisation without too much pollution. So, we had the expertise in Singapore, so I was able to align our expertise with China's interest of wanting to have a clean environment for its urbanisation.[69]

Despite these top-level commitments, it remains unclear whether transfers between Singapore and Tianjin could, in Goh's terms, actualise their proponents' visions of "replication" (*fuzhi* 复制) and "expansion" (*tuiguang* 推广).[70] Through a comparative study with Dongtan Eco-City in Shanghai, Miao and Lang conclude central governmental support explains why the Tianjin Eco-City kept running whilst the Dongtan project failed.[71] Even so, differences in opinions on what constitutes an "eco city" between the Chinese and Singaporean partners became apparent. As an investigative news report reveals, regulatory short-termism endures in the Tianjin Eco-City project. Whilst Singaporean planners would like to have housing board-style public housing that catered to low-income Chinese, Tianjin Eco-City officials were reportedly lukewarm to the idea of uncertainty over the costs of subsidising the apartments.[72] A Tianjin official whispered in the ear of a Singaporean colleague:

> By the time the public housing project is completed, many of us Tianjin officials would likely be promoted elsewhere. Who would still be around to ensure that it is really the poor people who are relocated to this public housing estate?[73]

As an unnamed staff member of SSTEC adds, policy transfers could succeed only if they were aligned to local officials' agendas:

> We have very strong high-level government links – but not with officials at the lower and provincial levels. It's the Tianjin officials' support we need to get things done – be it focusing only on green projects, building a light-rail transit line in the Eco-City or creating a community mix of different income groups.[74]

Table 4.1 Sino-Singaporean lesson drawing and policy transfers: an overview

Policy domain	Characteristics & objectives	Key actors & institutions	Spatial scale of transfer	Mode of transfer	Constraints to transfer
Industrial park development & management	• Integral aspect of inter-governmental agreement in 1994 to facilitate software transfer, or expertise in producing a pro-investor climate • G-to-G projects first launched in Suzhou in 1994; now extended to Tianjin (2008) & Chongqing (2015) • Singapore government-linked corporations involved in several other joint ventures (e.g., Guangzhou Knowledge City & Jilin Food Zone)	• Government of Singapore • Jurong Town Corporation • Multiple state-linked agencies in Singapore (e.g., EDB, URA, HDB, PUB) • Proactive officials from designated local governments in China like Wang Yang, Zhang Gaoli & Huang Qifan • Chinese SOEs	• Intra-urban	• Hybrid: co-driven by state-linked actors in Singapore & specific city-regional governments (except Suzhou Industrial Park)	• Parallel competition by local governments, increasing risks of duplication • Short-termist approach to planning, based on the GDP-focused institution of cadre performance appraisal
Management of state-owned enterprises (SOEs)	• Emulate strategies of Temasek Holdings, a government-linked holding company • Enforcement of "separation of politics from firms" (zhengqi fenkai), a principle first introduced in 1988	• Development Research Centre of the State Council • Temasek Holdings • Centrally & locally owned SOEs	• National & provincial	• Voluntary (initiative of Chinese state agencies)	• Place-specific path dependencies • Resistance by established interest groups within SOEs & local governments
Public administration	• Increase efficiency & integrity; expand rule of law; and reduce resource wastage & corruption	• NCPA, NTU • Lee Kuan Yew School of Public Policy, NUS • Central & provincial cadres	• National selection, Singapore-based training	• Voluntary (initiative of Chinese state agencies)	• Interlocked & entrenched party-SOE connections • Excessive emphasis on extra-budgetary financing, creating a colossal "grey zone" in fund-sourcing

Source: Authors' compilation.

New research is beginning to demonstrate policy mutation in the Tianjin Eco-City. Comparing the Tianjin project with Masdar City in Abu Dhabi, Federico Caprotti illustrated the importance of probing beneath the association of Chinese eco-cities with functionality, rationality and efficiency.[75] Whilst Goh Chok Tong correctly depicted the Chinese party-state's concern with environmental quality, Caprotti argues that the "motivation behind new [eco-city] projects seems to be green in the financial sense only".[76] This finding overlaps that of Miao and Lang: not only were the original objectives of the Tianjin Eco-City revised to more modest levels, they were more closely aligned with economic objectives.[77] Caprotti *et al* further demonstrate how this G-to-G project "is discursively constructed as ecologically beneficial for its inhabitants rather than for the broader socio-environmental landscape".[78] These studies collectively foreground a technocratic, apolitical and ultimately economistic approach to lesson drawing and policy transfers in Tianjin Eco-City. Politically sensitive issues that require urgent attention, like intra-urban social polarisation, institutionalised social segmentation and entrenched vested interests in pollutive industries, have not been explicitly encompassed by the "eco" and "sustainable" concepts.

Conclusion

Much has been made within China of the principle of "learning" from Singapore. Yet the aggregation of lesson drawing and policy transfers from Singapore by China within a *longer* historical framework, as attempted in this chapter, complicates the story of state-to-state policy mobility. Embedded herein are *simultaneous* copying, emulation, inspiration, hybridisation and synthesis. That policymakers and planners from both China and Singapore believe some policies – such as those introduced in the G-to-G projects in Suzhou and Tianjin – are replicable across China indicates a belief in the possibility of copying. CPC cadres undergoing training in Singapore are implicitly encouraged to emulate and draw inspiration from key tenets of Singaporean public administration (e.g., minimal corruption, high efficiency, forward planning, respect for contractual laws, etc.). Other projects range from emulation [e.g., attempts to introduce the Central Provident Fund (CPF) in cities like Shanghai and Shenzhen] to more hybrid forms of adaptation (e.g., the ongoing attempt to repurpose the practices of Temasek Holdings, the Singaporean sovereign wealth fund and holding company of state-linked enterprises). Within the senior CPC echelon, the overarching characteristic of 'learning' is to draw inspiration for devising new regulatory solutions on the basis of one-party authoritarianism and global economic integration (see summary in Table 4.1).

On the one hand, this multifaceted attempt at learning from the Singapore Model exemplifies the fluidity of socio-economic reforms in post-Mao China. It recalibrates notions of 'Chinese exceptionalism' by showing how the dynamic *interaction* with foreign policies and practices constituted post-Mao reforms. On the other hand, enduring institutional aspects of the Chinese experience arguably became more pronounced after overt and tacit attempts to learn from Singapore.

As Table 4.1 shows, constraints to transfer are evident in each policy domain. This underscores, in turn, how the evolution of the Chinese political economy is not predicated on a fixed playbook of policy and practice. If some commentators claim Chinese policymakers are exporting an internally coherent developmental 'model' to less developed political economies in Africa, Latin America and central Asia, the Singapore connection actually underscores how post-Mao reforms remain an *open-ended process* of policy experimentation and adaptation that is fraught with tension and resistance.[79]

Two defining aspects could be abstracted from this multifaceted process of policy mobility and mutation. First, the "authoritarianism" of the Singapore context has been qualitatively different from its Chinese variant. Socioeconomic regulation in Singapore was and remains predicated on the principle that no entity – including the ruling party – is above the law. Across China, the CPC technically controls the legislative system, which renders it at once within and outside the legal system. This positioning injected significant flexibility in the interpretation and implementation of law amongst cadres. Second, intense competition between Chinese municipal governments has undermined Singapore's foreign-investor and knowledge-purveyor primacy. Ironically, as the Suzhou and Tianjin cases reveal, local projects launched by the central government in the name of the 'national interest' mattered only if such projects could be credited to local officials. In Suzhou, the SIP could show improved results only after more benefits – albeit in the form of tacit knowledge – were offered to local stakeholders. And emerging evidence suggests local officials in Tianjin are behaving similarly.

Given the unclear effects of policy transfers to date, why do Chinese policymakers – from local officials to Xi Jinping – continue to proclaim the importance of learning from Singapore? The most plausible rationale could be political. Specifically, it is more palatable to refer to an Asian rather than Western entity as a model for development, especially when that Asian entity has a positive record of incorporating Western practices. Indeed, whilst many observers in China recognise Japan as the Asian exemplar of successful 'Westernization', its bitter historical relationship with China renders politically impossible any overt learning attempt. Next up is Singapore. The highly-publicised approach to emulate regulatory policies in Singapore is not about "blindly copying", to borrow Xi Jinping's terms; neither do these policies represent the destination of ongoing reforms. The reference to Singapore is, rather, to subtly expose the fundamental regulatory challenges confronting the Chinese government at all levels (municipal, county, provincial and national). In other words, the ongoing quest to 'learn lessons' from the Singapore Model is to foreground and fine-tune the fluid – if at times fragmented – foundations of the 'China Model (ref. Chapter 1). After all, as Zheng Yongnian puts it, the 'China Model' is in itself characterised by dynamic change: "a model is only formed through a prolonged period, only those that are unchangeable can constitute a model. Yet policies in China change every few years, hence it might be more appropriate to term this [regular change] China's policy model or reform model".[80]

The regular reference to and changing engagements with the Singapore Model is therefore more accurately an indirect 'challenge' to developmental models inherited from earlier regulatory regimes (including those from the pre-1949 'old society'). Foregrounding the relevance, if not desirability, of Singaporean policies in China constitutes an oblique acknowledgement that existing policies have generated a drag on the national regulatory system and could potentially pose an existential challenge to CPC longevity. An overt and highly publicised commitment to learn another model thereby buys Chinese senior leadership time; it enables the central government to claim characteristics across the highly variegated socioeconomic landscape are not unripe for China to become more like another model. Whether lessons are truly learned; whether policies are truly transferred; and, indeed, whether China truly possesses the geo-historical conditions that made possible the Singaporean economic success since the mid-1960s are arguably secondary considerations.[81] What matters is the *appearance* that change is on the way; that change is not directionless but 'modelled' after global best practices. During the late Qing era, the model was Japan; the Soviet Union represented China's tomorrow for the Mao administration; to Deng and his successors, the explicit modelling process now shifts to Singapore, a tiny city-state in southeast Asia no bigger than Shunyi district of Beijing.

Notes

1 *SPIEGEL* 2005. Interview with Singapore's Lee Kuan Yew: "It's stupid to be afraid". 8 August. Ref. To 1981.
2 Deng (1993), pp. 378–379.
3 *People's Daily* 2011. Cracks appear in the Singapore model. 23 May.
4 Huff (1995a), p. 753.
5 Shambaugh (2008), p. 103; cf. de Jong (2013).
6 Planning Coordination Group, USA. 1955. Overseas Chinese students and an Asian university. 18 August. Classification: Secret.
7 Stockwell (1993); Ramakrishna (2002).
8 Cheah (2009); Wang and Ong (2009); cf. Chin and Hack (2004).
9 Wang (1970), p. 11; cf. Chang (1980).
10 Singapore Ministry of Culture, 31 May 1965.
11 Press Conference, City Hall; 26 August 1965.
12 Ref. Latif (2007), p. 52; Ong (2015), pp. 87–88.
13 US Operations Coordinating Board, 1957. Outline Plan of Operations with respect to Singapore and the Federation of Malaya. Classification: Top Secret.
14 *The Straits Times* 1995. The evolution of a policy on China. 17 June.
15 Lee (1973), p. 3. National Archives of Singapore.
16 *The Straits Times* 2013. Descendents influenced by the soil. 6 July.
17 Rajaratnam (1977).
18 Deng (1994), p. 199; authors' translation; cf. Chen (2007).
19 Chin (2003).
20 Ref. Heaton (1982); Chen (2005).
21 Desker and Kwa (2011); Zheng and Wong (2013).
22 Oi (1999); Bramall (2007).
23 *Forbes*, 15 July 2013.
24 Ref. Tan (2009).

25 Huff (1995b), p. 1435.
26 cf. Huang and Lou (2014).
27 van der Kroef (1964, 1967).
28 Yao (2008); cf. Zahari (2007), chapter 14.
29 NTU (2014); for an overview of the demographic makeup of the officials, see Yu *et al* (2012).
30 Shanghai Municipal People's Procuratorate (2003); Ma (2006a, 2006b).
31 Li (2008); Yang (2009).
32 Wang and Ren (2008); Han and Li (2012).
33 Kuang (2013); Wu (2014).
34 *Xinhua* 2008. Shenzhen daguimo paituan pu Xinjiapo xuexi [Large-scale deployment of delegations on learning trips to Singapore]. 9 January; The Straits Times, 2008. First China centre for Singapore studies. 3 November.
35 *Shenzhen Tequbao* (2014). Shenzhen shiwei Wang Rong huijian Xinjiapo zhongli Li Xianlong yixing. 14 September; cf. Zhang (2012).
36 *New York Times* 2012. Many urge next leader of China to liberalize. 21 October.
37 *New York Times* 2012. Many urge next leader of China to liberalize. 21 October.
38 *China Daily*, 2014. Singapore's Temasek to be 'model' for SOE reform. 28 January.
39 *People's Daily*, 2015. Xi Jinping, Li Guangyao yu Xinjiapo moshi. [Xi Jinping, Lee Kuan Yew and the Singapore model]. 24 March. Authors' translation.
40 Op-ed for *Lianhe Zaobao*, 29 September 2014.
41 Interview with *Phoenix Weekly*, 2014. Xinjiapo: Moshi banyang weiji. [Singapore: crisis of a model] 24 May.
42 Interview with *Caixin*. 2014. Lee Hsien Loong on what Singapore can – And can't – Teach China. 17 February, http://english.caixin.com/2014-02-17/100639482.html?p0#page1.
43 Shirk (1993). See also Saich (2010).
44 cf. Huff (1995a, 1995b); Lim (2012a).
45 Olds and Yeung (2004), pp. 508, 512.
46 Shirk (1993); for a geo-historical overview of central-local relations since 1949, see Lim (2017).
47 *Lianhe Zaobao* 2013. Xue Yong: Zhongguoren de Xinjiapo qingjie [Xue Yong: The Chinese's Singapore story]. 15 March.
48 cf. *New York Times* 1982. Singapore plans to revive study of confucianism. 20 May.
49 *Lianhe Zaobao*, 15 March 2013.
50 *Lianhe Zaobao*, 20 March 2013.
51 Zheng, interview with *Phoenix Weekly*, 24 May 2014. Authors' translation.
52 Zheng, 19 May 2013.
53 Zhao, 20 March 2013.
54 The Straits Times, 13 May 1993.
55 Ref. *The Straits Times* 1996. S'pore-style management in Suzhou Park "a critical factor', 14 April.
56 *Asiaweek*, 1 June 1996.
57 Transcribed by *The Straits Times*, 'SM urges Suzhou to work harder to get investments' 10 September 1996.
58 Teng (1998), p. 1.
59 *The Straits Times* 2004. Seeing double. 29 May.
60 Unedited transcript, Singapore Ministry of Information and the Arts (MITA), 7 June 1999.
61 *The Straits Times* 1999. Carry on? Suzhou must make a case. 25 September.
62 *South China Morning Post*, Singapore drops control of Suzhou park, 29 June 1999.
63 Interview with *Lianhe Zaobao*, 9 June 1999; translated and transcribed by Singapore Ministry of Information and the Arts. Retrieved via National Archives of Singapore.

64 The Straits Times, 6 May 2001.
65 Lim, *The Straits Times* 2001. It's a chess game; move one piece at a time. 6 May.
66 Chan, *The Straits Times* 2004. 29 May.
67 Inkpen and Pien (2006), 805; cf. Pereira (2007).
68 *MIT Technology Review* 2014. China's future city. 18 November.
69 Singapore Ministry of Foreign Affairs, 17 October 2014.
70 Singapore Ministry of Foreign Affairs, 17 October 2014.
71 Miao and Lang (2015); see also Pow and Neo (2013).
72 *The Straits Times* 2009. Rumblings in Tianjin Eco-City. 27 December.
73 *The Straits Times* 2009. Rumblings in Tianjin Eco-City. 27 December.
74 *The Straits Times* 2009. Rumblings in Tianjin Eco-City. 27 December.
75 Caprotti (2014a); cf. Rapoport (2014).
76 Caprotti (2014b), p. 101.
77 Miao and Lang (2015), p. 249.
78 Caprotti *et al* (2015), p. 495; *contra*. Yang and Lye (2009); Chen and Zhao (2014).
79 cf. Shambaugh (2008).
80 Interview with *China Value*, 29 November 2010; authors' translation.
81 cf. Ortmann (2012); Ortmann and Thompson (2014).

5   The Chongqing vs. Guangdong 'Models' of economic development

Regional and historical perspectives on the dynamics of socioeconomic change in post-Mao China

Introduction

During the late 2000s, researchers and policymakers in China began to document and evaluate the implications of two emergent developmental 'models' in the Chinese provinces of Chongqing and Guangdong. Associated with the influence of the provincial Party Secretary, Wang Yang, between 2007 and 2012, the 'Guangdong Model' is portrayed as more 'liberal' and sophisticated. Three interrelated approaches constituted this prototype, namely market-oriented economic regulation, a growing emphasis on the rule *of* law and an explicit commitment to enhancing social well-being (as exemplified by the social campaign to create a 'Happy Guangdong'). Whilst references to the Guangdong Model in political-economic research preceded the comparison with Chongqing, it came into popular consciousness following explicit comparison with the 'Chongqing Model'.[1]

First mooted by a Hong Kong-based journal, *Asia Weekly*, in February 2009, the 'Chongqing Model' is associated with Bo Xilai, who became party secretary of Chongqing in late 2007. It similarly comprises three approaches, namely extensive state intervention in economic construction; an explicit commitment to socio-spatial egalitarianism through housing and migration policies; and a hard-handed campaign against organized crime.[2] Also construed as (re)instituting the rule *by* law, prominent critics such as Hu Deping (the son of Hu Yaobang, key reform-minded ally of Deng Xiaoping), Xu Youyu (senior academic) and Wen Jiabao (the-then Premier of China) have gone to the extent of labelling the socioeconomic policies in Chongqing as the "line of thought" (*siwei* 思维) and "spirit" (*yinhun* 阴魂) of a particular "historical tragedy" (*lishi beiju* 历史悲剧) – the Cultural Revolution.[3]

Further research into these seemingly incommensurable developmental approaches is generating nuanced interpretations. One body of work views these different trajectories as outcomes of elite politics and the quest for a consensus-based political structure.[4] Here, the focal point is on the *conflictual* political agendas of specific actors in the party-state apparatus. Another body views the developmental approaches in Chongqing and Guangdong as expressions of regional capitalist varieties that could coexist and possibly constitute the structural coherence of the national political economy.[5] Whilst offering fresh insights into post-Mao socioeconomic reforms, what remains unclear in existing research is the *relationship* between these models and the broader geographical-historical context of Chinese state formation after 1949. Specifically, two questions remain open:

1   Does the emergence of different developmental models over the past decade signal the debilitating effects of elite politics on central state power?
2   Or, perhaps counter-intuitively, is institutional differentiation an *intended* policy outcome to reinforce central state power within a content of deepening global economic integration?

Drawing on policy documents, academic commentaries, statistical data and interviews with planners from China,[6] it evaluates the logics of the Chongqing and Guangdong developmental experiences within a broader geographical-historical context. The empirical presentation is *not* meant to provide an exhaustive summary of policies, career politics or for that matter ideological metonym: these are already discussed at length elsewhere.[7] Rather, it makes for a singular contribution to the existing literature by synthesising key materials to demonstrate how these two supposed models are neither divergent pathways nor two sides of the same coin. Divergence is predicated on *a priori* unity; on a previously existing 'same coin' characterised by a coherent national structure and historical exceptionalism. Yet there was never such unity and uniqueness to begin with; differences between CPC cadres have always existed at both ideological and practical levels. Place-specific development, therefore, does not comprise differentiated parts of a larger and internally coherent entity known widely today as the 'China Model'. By extension, inter-regional variations do not reflect chronological differences that would naturally 'level up' as one exceptional whole. The Chongqing and Guangdong trajectories are not compared against a template of fixed factors for this reason; their respective socioeconomic policies and economic data have to be evaluated as geographically and historically grounded expressions of the *joint demands* of national regulation and transnational capital reproduction.

The chapter is organised in four parts. Section 2 delineates the geographical-historical context within which the analysis is framed. Focusing on "the whole country as a chessboard" (*quanguo yipanqi* 全国一盘棋) regulatory philosophy officially adopted by top CPC leaders since the late 1950s, the section demonstrates how the CPC's insistence on integrated national governance developed generates tension with place-specific developmental initiatives in the post-Mao era. Ironically, this tenuous relationship is an internal contradiction generated by Deng Xiaoping's spatial strategy to privilege industrialisation along the eastern seaboard. Section 3 then explain how the Guangdong and Chongqing trajectories came to be. It shows how conditions that shaped what appear today to be distinct developmental approaches in Guangdong and Chongqing are constituted by dynamic interactions between local initiatives and agents positioned at different scales (the provincial, regional, national and supranational). An evaluation of these approaches is presented in section 4. In so doing, the chapter makes the argument that the experiences in Chongqing and Guangdong are place-specific outcomes of *and* responses to successive national-level policies. The implications of these outcomes on the 'chessboard' philosophy and 'ladder step' logic will be explored in the concluding section.

The 'chessboard' regulatory philosophy: emergence and contemporary implications

The "China" that Mao Zedong's CPC sought to "liberate" in the late 1940s was constituted by a patchwork of socio-culturally disparate economies. As Fitzgerald puts it, China was (and arguably remains) a 'nationless state' constituted by "the motif of a unitary state reconstituting itself from the rubble of a disintegrating empire".[8] What this meant in economic-geographical terms was an absent national economy *of* China; there were many territorially distinct economies *in* China. When it became clear that the CPC would succeed in capturing power in Beijing, the imminent military success transposed into a political-geographic challenge – namely, the integration of these economies into a structurally coherent nation-state. This process was in and of itself a major encumbrance to the CPC's state building objectives because the geopolitical dimensions of 'new China' were slippery at the edges and unstable within. Meisner sums up the magnitude of this challenge:

> [It] had to be undertaken in conditions of extreme economic backwardness, in a country which possessed only the most primitive system of communications and transportation, in a land where the persistence of strong traditional localistic and regional loyalties had retarded the development of a modern national consciousness and where the dominance of largely precapitalist forms of economic life provided only the most fragile basis for national integration.[9]

Fundamental to the CPC's success in the 'protracted people's war' in October 1949 was its ability to share power – albeit in an *ad hoc* manner – with leaders of regional economies since the 1920s.[10] After securing political power, its first major regulatory strategy was to fortify its political control by re-designating spatial divisions of regulation. To this end, six 'big strategic regions' were created (*dazhanlüequ* 大战略区). These regions were, namely, North China (Huabei 华北), Northeast China (Dongbei 东北), East China (Huadong 华东), Central and South China (Zhongnan 中南), Northwest China (Xibei 西北) and Southwest China (Xinan 西南). Before long, however, parts of the new administration (including Mao himself) feared potential provincialism could morph into reality and undermine the fragile coherence and stability of 'new China'. For this reason, the six newly appointed regional leaders – Deng Xiaoping, Liu Shaoqi, Gao Gang, Rao Shushi, Lin Biao and Peng Dehuai – were re-deployed to Beijing in 1952 and 1953 and two of them, Gao and Rao, were purged from their positions in 1954.[11] These regions were then swiftly dissolved.

Accompanying the re-elevation of the provincial scale as the second highest level of administration was a growing emphasis on the necessity to align local interests to the national developmental pathway. Understanding this political emphasis on the 'national interest' is important for framing the Chongqing–Guangdong relationship and, more importantly, for understanding why Bo Xilai was purged in 2012 (ref. section 3). Mao offered a thorough explanation of this approach during a meeting in April 1956:

> The central government must focus on developing enthusiasm in the provinces and municipalities, and provincial and municipal governments should also focus on developing enthusiasm at the levels of the county, district and village, they must not be framed too tightly. Of course, it is also important to tell comrades at lower levels what tasks are to be handled holistically. In sum, anything that could and should be integrated should be integrated, anything that cannot or should not be integrated should not be forcefully integrated. Provinces, municipalities, counties, districts and villages should possess and contest for legitimate independence and power. The contestation of power in the name of holistic national interest rather than for localized benefits cannot be termed localism or independent-minded.[12]

As it emerged that disparate local practices were undermining the Great Leap Forward industrialisation project, the-then Shanghai mayor, Ke Qingshi, urged national socioeconomic coordination in an article in the Party's leading journal, *Red Flag* (红旗). This article has now attained touchstone status in Chinese policymaking and academic circles due to its metaphor 'the whole country as a chessboard':

> Regardless of class struggle or struggle in economic production, regardless of any form of work, planning, doing things, thinking about problems, there must be a holistic view . . . This entire agenda correctly reflects the relationship between different departments in the economy and the relationship between the whole and the partial, it makes clear they are intertwined into a national chessboard, not a board of scattered sand.[13]

The reference to "a board of scattered sand" (*yipan sansha* 一盘散沙) reveals how the CPC leadership regarded the previously mentioned disparate economies that constituted post-1949 'new China'. Integrating these economies, Ke argued, entailed an *a priori* conception of "the whole":

> It is only through holistic planning in economic work, through the concentration of labor power, materials and finance to ensure focal construction projects are completed, that the question of further leaps forward can be resolved. Whether these focal projects succeed or fail not only affect holistic victory or defeat, they also affect the fates of each partial part. If the whole cannot be managed well, the partial cannot do well; if the whole attains victory,

problems faced by partial units can be easily solved. This is especially important for a large country like ours, we have limited resources, to attain fast-paced economic growth . . . we cannot scatter our energies.[14]

Ke's article delineates two regulatory considerations of relevance for framing the Chongqing–Guangdong relationship in this chapter: centralised economic control and political balance between different administrative levels. In the context of the Great Leap Forward, the implication was to prioritise the funneling of resources for the prevailing national economic project and, in turn, preclude an "imbalanced" situation between the national goal and local agendas:

> Whatever that needs to proceed first should proceed first; whoever should and could step aside in a time of necessity should do so; anything that can be postponed should be postponed . . . If resources and energies were spread evenly . . . it would be impossible to construct socialism on the basis of speed, quantity, quality and economy. It could even lead to a loss of direction in economic construction and lead to the danger of economic imbalance. We definitely cannot allow such an imbalanced situation to occur.[15]

The chessboard regulatory metaphor would soon resonate in the speeches of the senior leadership. Four days after the publication, the-then vice premier of the state council, Deng Xiaoping, commented on the national alignment approach in Shanghai:

> The crux to actualizing the plan is a good management of "the whole country as a chessboard". We must realize our plan from this vantage point. No local area should have "backdoors" [i.e., direct local-to-local collusions]. Work should be done and enthusiasm developed within the "whole chessboard". Of course, there is some flexibility within the chessboard regardless of the size of the region or industry, but these flexible components should also be placed within the regional and national plan.[16]

In spite of these proclamations, the chessboard philosophy neither led the Great Leap Forward program to success nor enhanced economic production during the Mao era. The chaos during and unprecedented death toll that followed the Great Leap Forward impelled Mao to adopt more radical measures to consolidate political power in Beijing. This was launched through the Third Front Construction program in 1964 (*sanxian jianshe* 三线建设), on the premise of growing threats from "imperialism and their running dogs" (*diguozhuyi jiqizougou* 帝国主义及其走狗). Mao ordered means of production to be relocated from the coastal city-regions (the 'First Front') to those in the relatively sheltered interior (the 'Third Front').[17]

The intensification of the ideological-political campaign against domestic political rivals meant economic reconstruction slowed down during the first two years of the Cultural Revolution (1966–1968). To ensure absolute political control, cell-like administrative units were tied hierarchically to Beijing in tandem with geo-economic insulation (under the nationalistic slogan of 'self-sufficiency'). The central government granted significant autonomy to the provinces to self-finance developmental projects. In return, a minimal trade policy was enforced. For almost a full decade prior to the 1978 reforms, the Chinese economy resembled a customs union more than a common market; it was an entity with a common barrier against the global economy, within which free trade did not exist. What existed across the rural communes and urban *danwei* was effectively a "cellular" and "fragmented" economic structure that comprised of cell-like, self-sufficient and regionally uneven administrative units.[18]

More interestingly, the unwillingness of these units to work with one another meant the whole country as a chessboard philosophy regularly encountered resistance in Mao-era China. The former Chinese premier, Zhao Ziyang, puts the situation in perspective:

> The highly centralized planned economy looked upon the entire nation as a grand chessboard and relied on the state to invest in the development of natural resources in the western regions and transport them far away to the coastal regions for manufacturing. This path could no longer continue. Since the inland provinces had become unwilling to sell their resources cheaply to coastal provinces, the conflict between inland and coastal regions had intensified.[19]

The conflicts generated by this cellular and protectionist structure ultimately triggered experimental reforms *after* Deng Xiaoping took over the CPC leadership from Hua Guofeng in 1978. Calculations within different levels of government continued to prioritise self-interest and competitive advantage through the 1980s, which led to what Oi (1992) terms "local state corporatism". Under this mode of governance, which had deep historical antecedents, local cadres managed their jurisdictions as if they were businesses and sought to out-compete other territories to gain promotional opportunities.[20] This unsurprisingly generated tensions with the previously mentioned system of reciprocal accountability. As the next section will elaborate, fierce inter-territorial competition persists in the present and underpins the contemporary positioning of Chongqing and Guangdong within the national chessboard.

Working on the premise of pragmatism and yet cautious not to jettison the Marxist–Leninist ideological foundations of the CPC, the Deng Xiaoping government built on this legacy of inequality through a developmental approach known as the "ladder-step transition theory", or *tidu tuiyi lilun* (梯度推移理论). Enabling this competitive relationship was another Mao-era legacy: the inability to fully negate the capitalistic techniques the CPC inherited in 1949. In a meeting with the Danish Premier, Poul Hartling, in October 1974, Mao observed that approaches to socioeconomic regulation in post-1949 new China were "not much different from the old society".[21] Following this, a November 1977 *Guangming Ribao* article acknowledges, "egalitarianism is still the biggest problem in China . . . Before Liberation it was more or less like capitalism. Even now we practice an eight-grade wage system, distribution to each in accordance with work done and exchange by means of money, and all this scarcely differs from the old society". What these references to the pre-1949 period meant was that the retention of capitalistic organizational techniques inevitably generated uneven development.[22] To ameliorate the debilitating impact of persistent uneven development – income, output and consumption equalisation did not occur during the Mao era – on the ideological vision of egalitarianism, the Deng administration *inverted* this legacy in the 1980s by pledging to deliver egalitarianism across the country *on the basis* of techniques adopted in the "old society".

This inversion was guided by a macro-scale approach to economic-geographical reconfiguration, the ladder step transition theory. First espoused by the Shanghai-based academics Xia Yulong and Feng Zhijun in 1982, this prescriptive 'theory' attracted the attention of a senior CPC cadre, Bo Yibo, and subsequently permeated central policymaking circles. It was instituted as a policy blueprint during the seventh Five-Year Plan (1986–1990).[23] Specifically, the blueprint delineated the Chinese political economy into three economic-geographical belts: the eastern (coastal), central and western. The Deng administration gave one belt (the eastern seaboard) the priority in ascending the development 'ladder'. It assumed that the fruits of development in the 'first mover' belt would diffuse downwards to other rungs of the ladder. This template of instituted uneven development became the basis for market-oriented reforms: the Deng administration expanded China's re-engagement with the global economy by permitting foreign investments beyond the first four SEZs, of which Shantou, Shenzhen and Zhuhai were (and remain) in the Pearl River Delta region of Guangdong.[24] Prior to the 1994 fiscal overhaul that (re)concentrated fiscal resources at the central level, preferential fiscal policies were given to selected coastal provinces to accelerate their respective developments, whilst subsequent tax reforms continued to benefit these provinces.[25]

At the same time, however, the placement of this approach within a nationally oriented spatio-temporal framework assured party conservatives that the chessboard approach to national governance remained relevant.[26] Deng made this point clear in a 1988 publication "Two Big Pictures" (*liangge daju* 两个大局):

> The coastal areas must accelerate its opening up to enable this broad region of 200 million people to first develop, from which it will stimulate even better development in the interior. This is a matter that involves a big picture. The interior must understand this big picture.

Deng was, however, more specific in his exposition than Mao on the issue of socio-spatial egalitarianism: he identified an equally important 'big picture', which entailed residents of the coastal provinces to reciprocate the party-state's decision to first implement reforms in their provinces by *accepting* the subsequent redistribution of accumulated value accruing from economic liberalisation for the development of the interior:

> Upon attaining a certain level of development, the coastal areas are requested to give more energy to assist in the development of the interior, this is also a

'big picture' . . . It is an obligation for economically-advanced areas to help those that are more backward, and it is also a major policy.[27]

Despite prioritising the development of the eastern seaboard in the 1980s, it is important to note that the first decade of market-oriented reforms was centred on rural production led by quasi-private individual entrepreneurs called *getihu* (个体户) and Township and Village Enterprises (乡镇企业); nationwide engagement with foreign capital did not occur.[28] It was only in 1990, right after the 1989 military crackdown on civilian protests in Beijing's Tiananmen Square, that a distinct urban focus overlapped the 'ladder step' approach. Growing concern that delegating too much individual power to the masses (particularly in the rural areas) might lead to a loss of power in the centre, the Deng administration decided to concentrate market-based reforms in the cities.[29] The development of Pudong New Area in Shanghai arguably marked the beginning of a shift from rural reforms to an urban-industrial approach to economic development driven by two primary sources of capital – state capital, embodied in SOEs, and foreign capital, initially only through compulsory joint ventures with state-approved domestic firms, but now permitted to operate in wholly owned forms. Corresponding with the previously mentioned tax reforms of 1994, this shift jumpstarted the (still ongoing) attempt by the central government to reassert control of the means of production across China.

The contradiction internal to Deng's ladder step logic was the lack of a designated moment for coastal provinces to reciprocate their first-mover advantage. Until Deng's passing in 1997, it was unclear *when* wealth was to be proactively transferred from the coastal belt to the central and interior regions to attain long run spatial equilibrium. There was also no detailed plan that explains what would happen to the coastal provinces' economic development as resources are re-directed westwards. Does it mean a temporary stagnation in growth? Or, if growth is to be sustained, could this be achieved in a manner that can be constituted as a Pareto improvement (i.e., the eastern provinces do not feel that they are worse off as resources get redistributed)? With no forthcoming answers, the coastal provinces' share of the national GDP grew to approximately 62% over the period 1978 to 1997, whilst the central and western provinces accounted for 24% and 14% respectively.[30] Quite clearly, the economic geography of China became more uneven by the end of the 1990s. Deng's fear of the Chinese economy splitting into distinct classes of "haves" and "have-nots" (*liangji fenhua* 两极分化) thus seemed to be materialising; the economist Hu Angang went further by showing that uneven geographical development was so pronounced in the late 1990s, it was actually possible to identify "one China, four worlds".[31]

It was within this context of "four worlds" that Deng's successor, Jiang Zemin, proclaimed the importance of redeveloping the poorer western interior. Reiterating Deng's philosophy, Jiang issued a reminder that "reducing the developmental disparities within the entire country, developing in a coordinated manner and *ultimately* attaining Common Affluence is a basic principle of socialism" (*People's Daily*, 10 June 1999; authors' translation and emphasis). Soon after, in November

1999, the Jiang administration announced the next most significant national development program – officially termed "the Great Western Development" (*xibu dakaifa* 西部大开发) – to alleviate the widening income and output gaps between coastal and interior provinces. Ratified by the State Council in 2001, this program represented the beginning of more targeted approaches towards developing the interior. The original plan involved enhanced fiscal redistribution to the western provinces; more commitment by the central government to infrastructural development; opening up more sectors for foreign investments; and implementing preferential policies to attract foreign capital to the interior parts. Several large-scale projects were subsequently implemented – the two most significant projects were arguably the Three Gorges Dam, built along the Yangtze River, and the high-speed rail network linking Beijing to Lhasa, located at an altitude of 4500 m on the Tibetan plateau – and more foreign capital did flow into western provinces.[32]

Crucially, however, the coastal-interior income and output gap persisted during Hu Jintao's presidency through the 2000s. Firms that were more globalised were increasingly clustered in the coastal regions.[33] These trends highlight, in turn, the tensions between the chessboard philosophy of inter-regional economic integration and the fragmentary effects of post-Mao instituted uneven development.[34] Against this backdrop, pushbacks in the form of apparently competing models, all in search for a greater share of the economic pie, began to emerge. As the next section will show, the proactive role by the state to institute more egalitarian policies in Chongqing and launch investments friendly to capital accumulation were direct outcomes of Deng's ladder step approach, *as was* the ability of the Guangdong government to build on its initial economic success by calling for more political openness. Yet, *pace* Sebastian Heilmann and Elizabeth Perry, these different responses cannot be construed as distinct intra-national models competing for eventual national supremacy; their respective policies now respond, *simultaneously* and *directly*, to the two-fold demands of global circulatory capital and inherited national-level institutions.[35] How these different approaches impact the relevance of the chessboard regulatory philosophy and, by extension, notions of an internally coherent China Model, will be addressed in the remaining sections of this chapter.

The Guangdong and Chongqing developmental pathways after 2007: institutional change as continuity?

Within a decade of urban-based re-engagement with the global system of economy, new territorial reconfigurations of financial capital and labour power took shape across China. A definitive expression of this new economic geography was accelerating industrialisation in the Pearl River Delta (PRD) extended metropolitan region of Guangdong. The province ranked as China's top province by GDP annually since 1989. Placed in relation to national-level import/export figures, Guangdong on average accounts for almost 30% of the national total since China's accession to the WTO in 2001.[36] Under the stewardship of Zhang Dejiang, Guangdong province experienced accelerating inflows of foreign capital. It also received the largest number of inter-provincial migrant workers – also known widely as the "floating population" (*liudong renkou* 流动人口) – between 2000 and 2010.[37] According to the Chinese national population census of 2010, a third of this floating population of around 200 million was concentrated in Guangdong. A separate national report published in 2014 indicates that Guangdong remained the leading destination at the time of writing: it absorbed 29.4% of the floating population, which has since increased to 245 million by the end of 2013.[38] These levels of trade and employment enabled Guangdong province to reinforce the leading position it held after the ladder step approach was rolled out in the 1980s.

Geographical proximity to the post-colonial cities of Hong Kong and Macau reinforced this position. Currently designated as Special Administrative Regions (SARs) of China, these cities have functioned as financial and logistical platforms for firms looking to invest in China. Emerging from these connections was a cross-border, "front shop, back factory" spatial division of labour that Lin terms "red capitalism in south China".[39] Reflecting the effect of national-scale "retain the big and letting go of the small" (*zhuada fangxiao* 抓大放小) industrial policies, medium and small enterprises have taken the role of manufacturing subcontractors, whilst the major financiers and lead investors comprise state-owned enterprises (SOEs) and transnational corporations (TNCs). This multi-dimensional relationship with foreign capital in and through Guangdong offers an important prism through which to evaluate post-1978 socioeconomic reforms in China.

At one level, the intensifying engagement with foreign capital generated new demands of the Guangdong government over the past two decades. This was primarily attributed to transparency requirements and the growing consciousness of a new middle class. Xiao Bin, a leading China-based observer of reforms in Guangdong, explains why this led to a more advanced administrative system that underpinned the much-celebrated Guangdong Model:

> The reason why the administrative and public services are better in Guangdong relative to other places is because the degree of marketization is higher. The pressure of the market on the government is higher. So many businesspersons and excellent entrepreneurs here, like in Shenzhen, place demands on the government, if services are not good they will move their headquarters away, so will the government play the game? Pressures from the public are also a factor, this is because social organization is active and the awareness of public rights are relatively higher, citizens are more proactive in enforcing their rights, which impels the government to provide better services.[40]

It is important to note, however, that the putative provision of better services has no causal relationship with the decline of state authoritarianism. Whilst foreign capital investments allowed GDP to grow in Guangdong (and also across the other coastal provinces), there was no concomitant emergence of a large private capitalist class that was capable of undercutting CPC interests.[41] What "red capitalism" in Guangdong exemplifies, rather, is the ability of the CPC to *subsume* the enlargement of the non-state economic sector to party goals. Zhang puts this state-capital relationship in clear perspective: "the political power of capital in China remains fundamentally embedded in, and interlaced with, the sprawling institutional machinery of the Leninist party-state and the political capacities of the CPC".[42]

The Guangdong Model associated with the Wang Yang administration effectively built on and enhanced this relationship. Soon after he took office in 2007, Wang made clear his intentions to negotiate structural and technological "lock in" that resulted from the labour-intensive and export-oriented economic structure. According to data from the Guangdong Bureau of Statistics, the foreign trade to GDP proportion (also known as the trade dependency ratio[43]) for Guangdong province as a whole averaged 150% per year from 2001 to 2007; the figure for Dongguan, a major manufacturing hub within the PRD, was consistently above 250% in the same period. By comparison, the national average was (an already-high) 66.2% in 2007.[44] Research has also demonstrated foreign investments into the PRD, particularly those via Hong Kong, did not generate the spillovers that enable industrial upgrading through the 2000s.[45] What ensued, instead, were intra-provincial polarisation and a recognition that externally driven growth was unsustainable.[46] Chen sums up the constraining effect of this lock in:

> Most PRD-based firms and factories may be trapped in the assembling and manufacturing segment of the production chain and earning merely labor-processing fees rather than engaged in acquiring technology, developing their own brand-name products, and creating international markets directly.[47]

Wang's path-changing agenda was complicated as the global financial crisis became full-blown within a year of his tenure. Guangdong-based industries' heavy exposure to international trade morphed into a double-edged sword. Specifically, the crisis precipitated a sharp fall in effective global demand for manufactured goods from Guangdong-based industries. The province's total volume of imports and exports decreased for eight consecutive months from November 2008, with the largest monthly decline rate reaching 31.1%. Foreign capital investments dropped by over 50%. According to customs statistics, the total import/export value in Guangdong recorded 257.87 billion *yuan* (~US$40.1 billion) in the first half of 2009, a 20.7% decrease year-on-year.[48] Through an investigation spanning three years, the *Nanfang Dushibao* reported that two waves of factory closures followed after the crisis struck.[49] Between 2008 and 2009, the report estimated that half of the 58,500 Hong Kong-owned export-processing subsidiaries would not survive, whilst more sectors were affected following a new wave of closures in 2011. Against this bleak economic backdrop, the Wang administration decided not to back off; what ensued, instead, was a form of 'shock therapy' through an approach analogous to that adopted in Chongqing – *direct state involvement in economic practices.*

Rather than signal a move towards a smaller government and expanded market influence on social relations, a two-pronged response to reconfigure the provincial industrial structure was instituted. First introduced was an industrial policy known as "double relocation" (*shuang zhuanyi* 双转移). This involved shifting labor categorised as "low-skilled" and firms categorised as "high in pollution, high in energy use and low in efficiency" (*lianggao yidi* 两高一低) from the core PRD region to the underdeveloped regions of the province.[50] Accompanying this policy were attempts to 1) encourage inflows of higher-order industries to leverage on the PRD's growing reputation as an info-communications hub and 2) "scale up" the national significance of three "nationally strategic new areas" (*guojia zhanlüe xinqu* 国家战略新区)[51] in the PRD, namely Hengqin (横琴), Qianhai (前海) and Nansha (南沙), in 2009, 2010 and 2012, respectively. These intra-urban territories were subsequently designated sub-provincial status and currently function as sites of policy experimentation in domains deemed to be significant to both the Chinese central government and the economies of Macau and Hong Kong SARs. This two-pronged approach was officially termed "emptying the cage, changing the birds" (*tenglong huanniao* 腾笼换鸟), the "cage" referring to an economy regulated by the CPC, and the "birds" referring to firms that require some flying space to survive and thrive. Underpinning this approach was a straightforward political objective to fortify Guangdong's leading position within the national structure of socioeconomic development.

Problems emerged when provincial-level path generation undermines preexisting national-level logics of socioeconomic regulation. The implementation of the 'double relocation' policy reflects the extension of the previously mentioned "political logic" of reforms that invites developmental initiatives of national significance from local governments.[52] At the same time, however, the policy was contested because not all senior policymakers felt the double relocation policy would generate benefits at the national scale. As previously mentioned in section 2, CPC policymakers have been preoccupied with effective national governance. Whilst the regulatory context of the 1950s differed significantly from that of contemporary China, the chessboard philosophy continues to underpin central policymaking.[53] Opposition to the double relocation policy emerged against this backdrop: some senior cadres did not perceive the economic restructuring of Guangdong during and after the 2008 crisis to be a strategic 'move' vis-à-vis the national chessboard.

Tensions between two developmental pathways emerged as a consequence of these strategies. At the national level, the designation of the three "nationally strategic" territories "scaled up" the importance of Guangdong province to the central government and consolidated Deng Xiaoping's ladder step logic of economic development. Its rationale was to facilitate new capital into Guangdong just as industries deemed redundant were either relocated to the outlying parts of the province or allowed to shut down without further state support. These territories were then incorporated within the broader Guangdong Free Trade Zone, launched officially in April 2015. The zone currently offers more liberal policies on credit inflows from Hong Kong and Macau. Accompanying this series of state-driven industrial reconfiguration was strong GDP growth in the aftermath of the crisis (ref. Figure 5.1). As a Shenzhen-based planner said, "it was clear Wang had a clear idea where to go. For years talk of greater levels of integration between Guangdong and Hong Kong have only been lip service, but change took place very quickly after he arrived".[54]

Whilst it is premature to ascertain the impact of policy experimentation in these areas, the national designation engendered a fresh wave of fixed capital formation (driven primarily by provincial- and central-level SOEs), ensured GDP remained positive in spite of declining effective demand in the aftermath of the global financial crisis, and arguably reinforced Guangdong's strategic importance in the national economic-geographical structure (ref. Figure 5.1). Perhaps more importantly, the high and growing rate of fixed capital formation (of which an unknown proportion is state-driven) relative to Chongqing problematises critiques of investment-led growth in Chongqing (Figure 5.2). It is in this regard that the constitutive role of geography on the system of reciprocal accountability becomes pronounced: whilst Wang was party secretary of Chongqing, he felt "the government should eliminate institutional and operational barriers as soon as possible in order to create a fair economic platform"; these very barriers – in particular the state ability to control population flows and unilaterally institute industrial policies – became the very *premise* of 'emptying the cage, changing the birds' between 2008 and 2012.[55] What appears to be a market-friendly Guangdong Model is thereby more accurately an expression of strategic – if not also opportunistic – responses by political actors to specific geographical-historical conditions in order to gain 'political results' that would be viewed favourably by the senior CPC echelon in Beijing.

Also embedded within the chessboard and ladder step approaches is Chongqing, one of the four[56] province-level cities (*zhixiashi* 直辖市) under the direct control of the Chinese central government. It assumed an important economic-geographical position within China since modern industrialisation began towards the end of the nineteenth century. Developed into imperial China's first inland open port in 1891, connections with Britain, France, Germany and Japan were established by the turn of the twentieth century. Chongqing went on to become the primary trading centre along the upper Yangtze River. This preexisting economic position, coupled with its strategic location behind several mountain chains, far from potential naval landings by foreign armed forces, were arguably the reasons why the Nationalist party (also known as the Kuomintang or KMT) selected the city region as the temporary capital of the Republic of China[57] during World War II (1937–1945) and the Chinese civil war (1945–1949).

During this period, the KMT transferred a colossal amount of capital goods and labour power from other parts of China to Chongqing. This produced a vast military-industrial complex in the municipality and further enhanced its position as a major economic centre. Whilst the CPC removed Chongqing's province-level status and merged the city with Sichuan province after it became the official government of China in 1949, the Mao administration would, interestingly, repeat what the KMT did in Chongqing. Indeed, the CPC would go on to model its state-owned enterprise (SOE) system on the organizational structure of these inherited industries.[58] After launching the previously mentioned Third Front construction program in 1964, many industrial and military complexes were consequently relocated to or constructed in Chongqing, adding a new layer of industry and labour power to an industrial structure well-established by the KMT.

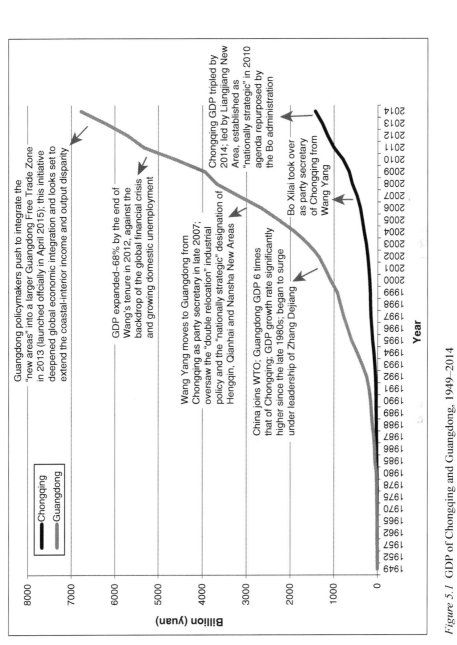

Figure 5.1 GDP of Chongqing and Guangdong, 1949–2014

Source: Guangdong Bureau of Statistics (2015); Chongqing Statistical Bureau (2015); authors' captions.

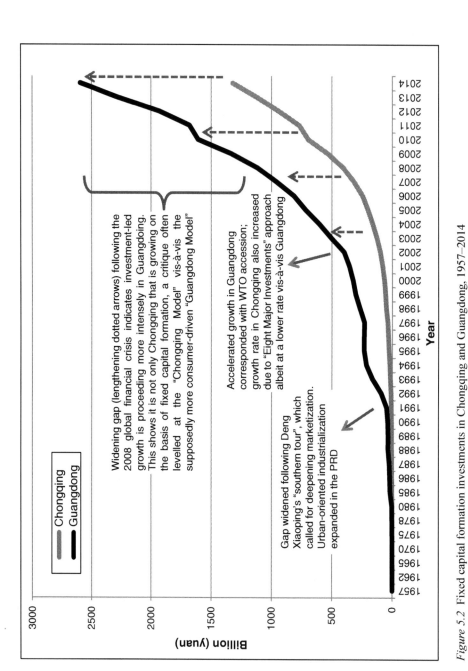

Figure 5.2 Fixed capital formation investments in Chongqing and Guangdong, 1957–2014

Source: Guangdong Bureau of Statistics (2015); Chongqing Statistical Bureau (2015); authors' captions.

Interestingly, the Third Front construction was not the first instance in which Mao-era regulatory logics re-expressed regulatory logics of the KMT era. Rather than overturn the inherited regulatory structure in the governance of the People's Communes, the CPC reproduced this structure by appointing peasants to take the place of the "tyrannical landlords and gentry" (*tuhao lieshen* 土豪劣绅). This development is of theoretical significance for conceptualising the tensions between path-generation and path-dependency: logics inherited from earlier regimes were not totally jettisoned but *repurposed* to suit new regulatory contexts. The Mao administration combined selected techniques used by the KMT with new policies, in turn generating new developmental pathways (e.g., collectivised production, rural industrialisation, the re-concentration of heavy industries in inland provinces, etc.). The selective adaptation of inherited policies would similarly characterise post-Mao development, where Deng and his successors retained specific Mao-era regulatory programs (e.g., land nationalisation and the *hukou* system of demographic control) and combined them with new experimental policies in targeted territories. It is this dynamic interaction between the past and the present that underpins Chongqing's emergence into a major frontier of reforms in contemporary China.

Before its socioeconomic resurgence, however, Chongqing's significance within the national structure of capital accumulation faded in the initial post-Mao era (i.e., between the 1980s and the late 1990s). This was because the CPC tried to drive growth through the previously mentioned ladder step logic. For more than two decades, then, Chongqing's economic growth – like many cities and provinces in China's western interior – lagged behind provinces along the coast. Relative to the leading province, Guangdong, income inequality and fixed capital formation worsened correspondingly (ref. Figures 5.1 and 5.2). It was only in the mid-1990s, after the Three Gorges Dam national energy project was launched, that Chongqing was repositioned as a strategically significant city in the national reform agenda.

Many settlements in the upstream valleys of the Yangtze River had to be flooded because of the sheer size and scale of the dam construction. An estimated two-thirds of the eight million affected residents were originally located in Sichuan province, the majority of them living in poverty. This engendered a colossal logistical and governance issue: the Sichuan provincial government, which already had to manage a huge and relatively poor population, had to take on the new challenge of resettling and then re-employing the affected residents without further straining its administrative and fiscal resources. An important alternative at the time was the proposal to create a new province known as the Three Gorges region.[59] It soon became apparent, however, that the central government was keen to avoid the costly administrative duplication and politics associated with establishing a new province. According to a 1986 diary account from the former premier, Li Peng, the primary concern for the CPC leadership was to prioritise the dam-building project over the redrawing of provincial boundaries.[60]

Chongqing was identified as a more feasible location for the population resettlement issue because Chengdu, the provincial capital of Sichuan, was not close to the flooded areas. The central government eventually agreed to administer the districts of Fuling, Wanxian and Qianjiang, then amongst the poorest areas in

Sichuan, as resettlement areas to ease the financial impact on the Sichuan government. These districts were then merged with Chongqing's core urban zone to form the sprawling Chongqing Municipality. It is intriguing to see in the Chongqing experience history coming full circle: in an almost identical repetition of what the KMT regime did in 1937, the CPC "promoted" the city region into a centrally governed municipality for the second time in 1997.

Arguably because of its relative (in)significance to the initial market-oriented reforms, Chongqing policymakers were impelled to enhance the capacities of its SOEs to drive economic growth. For this reason, the state-driven industrialisation approach was not fully dismantled in the post-Mao era. Since the late 1980s, some SOEs involved in weaponry manufacturing were relocated; some fully abandoned; whilst others like Ansteel, the Jialing Group and the Changan were restructured and are now dominant SOEs based in the municipality. In addition, the Chongqing government actively encouraged SOEs to list in foreign capital markets. Building on SOE restructuring is the "Eight Major Investments" (*badatou* 八大投) program in infrastructural construction by the Chongqing government. This program involved the establishment of eight state-financed corporations, each investing in what was considered a strategic sector (see Box 5.1). The outcome, as shown in Figure 5.2, was a surge in fixed capital formation.

Box 5.1 Eight major SOEs driving infrastructural development in Chongqing

- Chongqing Expressway Development Company (CEDC): constructs, operates and manages expressways.
- Chongqing Transportation and Tour Investment Company (CTTIC): constructs, operates and manages highways; develops and manages tourism attractions.
- Chongqing Urban Construction Investment Corporation (CUCIC): develops urban infrastructure, such as bridges, tunnels, and roads, in the main urbanised districts.
- Chongqing Energy (Construction) Investment Corporation (CEIC): invests, operates and manages energy-related (i.e., electricity, gas, and coal) power projects.
- Chongqing Real Estate Group (CREG): restores, rehabitates and develops lands.
- Chongqing Development Investment Corporation (CDIC): builds and operates rail transportation and other infrastructure projects.
- Chongqing Water Works Controlling Group (CWWCG): provides water supply and drainage integrated service to the main urban area.
- Chongqing Water Resources Investment Company (CWRIC): invests in and constructs water conservancy projects, small hydropower plants and water supply and drainage projects.

Source: Authors' compilation.

Underpinning this proactive intervention, as the Chongqing mayor, Huang Qifan, points out, was the fact that Deng's ladder step regulatory policies led to an acute lack on investor interest in developing Chongqing (and by extension the broader interior):

> To repair a freeway along the coast, the local government does not have to come up with money, there could be ten companies competing for this, some-one could even engineer a "grey transaction" to obtain this project. In the western region, however, getting one boss to construct freeway is a chal-lenge, let alone attracting ten. At the time [2002–2003] I wanted to repair 2000km of freeways, which required investments of up to 100 billion *yuan* [~US$12.1 billion, in 2002 prices]. With the then backward conditions, no private domestic or foreign firms were willing to invest in infrastructural construction. This thrusted plans for urban transformation and development into a cul-de-sac.[61]

As a result of this lack of market interest, Huang explains, state intervention became a "necessary" precondition for Chongqing to move ahead with its agenda:

> I have never had the intention to help SOEs monopolize, if there is a task that private or foreign capital could do, I would not want state capital to enjoy sole benefits. Then why must there be the "eight major investments" (*badatou*)? And furthermore, investments solely financed by the state? It is not a matter of perspective or ethics that determines whether an economic domain can be relaxed [by the state], more importantly it is determined by whether pricing and resource allocation have reached a level that can be taken over by the market.
>
> My perspective is that, for domains with weak market signals, the Chongq-ing government will use SOEs to launch and experiment with investments. It is necessary to build these eight investments, it is never about securing monopolies, never about the unwillingness to "share the cake" with the non-state economy, rather it is because market signals were not in place, the non-state economy was unwilling to do the tasks that needed to be done, hence the state can only use time to change space, it moved in through estab-lishing financing platforms and got the tasks done.[62]

Providing a crucial historical counterpoint to claims of debilitating elite politics in the Chongqing–Guangdong relationship, this state interventionism since associ-ated with the Chongqing Model was launched by Wang Yang several years before Bo Xilai took office. Statistics reveal the Chongqing government increased the value of state-owned assets (excluding those of central government-controlled SOEs) from 150 billion yuan in 2000 to 1.8 trillion yuan in 2013, a twelve-fold increase.[63] Working with the-then Mayor Wang Hongju and Vice Mayor Huang Qifan, Wang was also the key driver of experimental attempts to integrate urban and rural development – and in turn overhaul the intrinsically discriminatory urban-rural dual structure instituted in 1958 – during his tenure in Chongqing.[64]

Bo's so-called "socialistic" reforms were launched on the basis of this state-oriented developmental approach and the urban-rural integration framework launched inherited from Wang Yang (see Table 5.1). To accommodate the growing number of migrants into Chongqing's core urban areas, Bo (1) targeted building 40 million square metres of affordable housing for two million people at a cost of 140 billion *yuan* (~US$21.5 billion) from 2010 to 2012, and (2) created a "land ticket" (*dipiao* 地票) system to allow rural migrants and collectives to put their land-use rights for sale in the open market. Farmers and collectives with idle land had previously been restricted to strict and often localised land-use transfer regulations; the land ticket was a mechanism for these lands to be made available to alternative uses in a way that would enhance the financial position of rural residents migrating into the city. Interestingly, these policies are framed as socially – *and* market-friendly approaches:

> Rural residents can get urban *hukou* after years of working and living in cities. But when they are settled down, they may need to think about how to deal with their rural land. Without the land ticket system, they may have to leave the land idle or give it to relatives. The land ticket offers them a way to cash in on their land . . . The land ticket system improved farmers' incomes and offered financial support to migrant workers who left their rural homes. It also better protects farmland and eases the conflict between urban demand and rural supply of land. The system also generates capital to support rural housing renovation and other activities. For instance, land ticket sales in Chongqing have been worth more than 30 billion *yuan* [~US$4.6 billion]. Of that, more than 6 billion *yuan* [~US$920 million] was paid to migrant workers who moved into cities. B y selling their rural land, each household can earn more than 100,000 *yuan* [~US$15,300], helping them to start a new life in cities.[65]

In an indirect counterpoint to coastal provinces' unwillingness to accommodate migrant workers on a permanent basis (a direct legacy of the 1958 *hukou* institution), Huang reveals how Chongqing is increasingly benefitting from a system that keeps migrant inflows *in situ* through the provision of urban *hukou*:

> In recent years, we have noticed an interesting phenomenon in which Chongqing's foreign trade surges 70 percent to 80 percent in the first quarter every year and drops to a normal level in the following quarters. After analysis, we found it is a bonus from Chongqing's *hukou* reform for migrant workers because those in coastal provinces all return home for the Lunar New Year holiday for the first couple of months in the year, and many factory owners moved their orders to Chongqing since plants here run throughout the year.[66]

Table 5.1 presents a concise summary of how policies in Chongqing and Guangdong built on inherited institutions (at both subnational and national levels) and attempted to generate new paths. Of particular emphasis are the effects of

Table 5.1 Socioeconomic evolution in Chongqing and Guangdong, 2000–present

Comparative dimensions	Chongqing	Guangdong
Key driving actors	• Wang Yang (汪洋) • Wang Hongju (王鸿举) • Bo Xilai (薄熙来) • Huang Qifan (黄奇帆)	• Zhang Dejiang (张德江) • Huang Huahua (黄华华) • Wang Yang (汪洋) • Zhu Xiaodan (朱小丹)
Path-generating characteristics	• Aligned with "Great Western Opening Up" program to overturn the effects of the "ladder step" logic instituted in the seventh Five-Year Plan • New intra-municipality migration policies to overhaul the 1958 *hukou* institution; supported by large-scale public housing provision and "land ticket" land-use transfer scheme • New experimental policy to enable freely convertible RMB onshore • New policy to develop high-end manufacturing hub in Liangjiang New Area	• Aim to jettison labour-intensive, low value-added industries through "double relocation" industrial policy • Growing emphasis on endogenous innovation • Policy experimentation in designated territories (elevated to sub-provincial status) aims to reform national-level institutions, e.g., regulation of cross-border RMB flows and tax-free movement of goods between Macau & Hong Kong
Entwinement with inherited national-level institutions	• Emphasises absolute state provision of social benefits (as opposed to growing market-based provision) • Strong state involvement, if not monopoly, of key economic sectors construed as a throwback to Mao-era economic governance	• Reinforcement of "ladder step" logic • Reinforcement of *hukou* institution, which enabled unwanted labour power to leave without generating localised social instability, which reinforces the *hukou* institution as the underlying basis of a geographically elastic labour market

Source: Authors' formulation.

contextual conditions on the calculations of leading cadres: Wang was responding to Chongqing's slower socioeconomic development by working at bridging the gap with the coastal provinces, and yet when he assumed the leadership in Guangdong, his policies were to maintain Guangdong's leading position over other provinces (which by implication negates Mao's and Deng's vision of spatial egalitarianism) in order to assure CPC bosses of sustained social stability. Bo's key economic initiative after becoming party secretary of Chongqing in late 2007 was to fortify the foundations established by the Wang Yang government. This was exemplified through policies to augment the formal positioning of the municipality within the national economic-geographical structure. In tandem with Huang Qifan, Bo lobbied the Chinese central government to institute what was then a third "nationally strategic new area", the Liangjiang New Area (两江新区). Officially approved in 2010, the Liangjiang New Area has now become a major global manufacturing hub for automobiles and computers. The Bo administration also oversaw the launch of the Chongqing-Xinjiang-EU transcontinental railway that reduced travelling time to EU markets from 30 to 13 days. As mentioned in the previous chapter, this new zone was subsequently included as part of the third China–Singapore Government-to-Government (G-to-G) project in November 2015, a symbolic expression of its growing national importance. By extension, the economic policies reflected the relationship between uneven development in China and the system of reciprocal accountability: just like Wang, Bo was incentivised to align what appeared to be contextually defined initiatives to a centrally approved agenda. How – or, indeed, whether – it differs from the Wang administration's equally, if not more, heavy-handed approach at moulding the Guangdong Model is the focus of the next section.

Implications of the Chongqing–Guangdong relationship

Four important implications for conceptualising the post-Mao Chinese political economy – and, by extension, the 'China Model' of development discussed earlier in this book – can be derived from the historically robust framing of the Chongqing–Guangdong relationship in this chapter. First, the issue is not whether there should be less or more state intervention in China; it is about the *qualitatively different* forms of intervention. The policies instituted in Chongqing demonstrate how direct state investments in key economic sectors, widely construed to be antithetical to market-driven industrialisation, were in fact an *outcome* of national-level strategies that favoured selective marketisation along the Chinese coastal seaboard (ref. section 2). This offers, in turn, a double complication of the developmental story in post-Mao China.

On the one hand, extensive state involvement in inland economies like Chongqing is neither a simple residue nor a potential resurgence of Maoist economic governance; it is ironically a reaction – if not retaliation – to the first wave marketisation pathway that shifted means of production to coastal provinces like Guangdong. Reflecting on this issue, Liu Guoguang, the former deputy head of the Chinese Academy of Social Sciences, observes and argues that the "fundamental" issue regarding inter-regional variations rests in "ownership relations":

> The fundamental point of departure of redistribution theory in Marxian political economy [i.e., the official basis of the Chinese economy] is the determination of the redistributive institution by the ownership institution, that ownership relations decide redistributive relations. Yet people often neglect this point. When analyzing the causes of our country's widening rich-poor divide, many origins were proposed, such as the expansion of urban-rural disparity, the sharpening of uneven development between regions, monopolies of specific sectors, corruption, insufficient supply of public goods, slow responses to redistributive needs, etc. All these reasons could be valid

and need to be addressed one by one. But these are not the most important reason.[67]

Referencing the Chongqing experience, Liu adds that the precondition of effective redistribution in China is public ownership:

> To address the problem of rich-poor disparity from the realm of redistribution – and redistribution alone – is far from sufficient, it cannot fundamentally reverse the trend of worsening disparity. The problem should be tackled directly from the structure of ownership, it must be dealt with directly from the level of relations of production, from the most basic economic institution; the problem should be solved through fortifying the public ownership institution, only through this could growing rich-poor disparity be precluded and "common affluence" be attained.[68]

From a discursive angle, Liu's comment corresponds with the previously mentioned oblique critique from Huang Qifan: insofar as the CPC professes to be socialistic, it *has* to enable more equitable redistribution of profits derived from capital accumulation in the first instance. Where redistribution is ineffective, as Liu suggests has been the case in post-Mao China, the other recourse is through "fortifying the public ownership structure". This was and remains precisely the *modus operandi* of the Chongqing government across multiple domains – transport, housing, utilities etc. – since the early 2000s (ref. Box 5.1).[69]

On the other hand, state construction and management of infrastructural amenities is not inherently anti-market; on the contrary, qualitatively different forms of state intervention in Chongqing and Guangdong after 2007 have generated a new wave of market-oriented industrialisation. What differ are the *objectives* of intervention: the goal from the Chongqing vantage point was to bridge the socio-economic gap, whilst Guangdong policymakers worked at retaining the status quo. A prominent China-based scholar, Yao Zhongqiu (hereafter Qiu Feng, his pen name), offers a crisp summary of the Chongqing–Guangdong relationship:

> On the whole, these two mechanisms are positioned within a state of impasse, it can also be said to be within a state of equilibrium. The Chinese economy has attained fast growth under this mixed institutional system, but this is also accompanied by serious social and political problems . . . Both models are attempts to break out of the current impasse. What this means is both models represent feedback to the tensions of the current mixed institutional system.[70]

Second, existing research has not highlighted the fact that these "tensions" were more apparent in Guangdong than in Chongqing. Specifically, Wang had to negotiate resistance at both the national and provincial level. At the national scale, the-then premier, Wen Jiabao, openly expressed concerns, and Wang was subject to a veiled critique by senior cadres through the *People's Daily*. Within the provincial bureaucratic structure, the growing numbers of complaint letters to the central government within the first two years of Wang's appointment and Wang's rumoured disagreement with the-then Guangdong Governor, Huang Huahua, which was a plausible reason behind Huang's sudden resignation in November 2012.[71] The latter point was foregrounded openly during Wang's interaction with the press in November 2009:

> Reporter: I heard you and the Governor [Huang Huahua] had differing views on the economy. You hope firms would attain competitiveness through innovation, but the Governor was more inclined to protect labor-intensive industrial agglomerations in the Pearl River Delta. I heard Governor Huang feel you are moving a bit too fast.
>
> Wang: I can honestly tell you this is roadside news you've heard in Guangzhou.[72]

It is important to note Wang did not directly deny his rumoured disagreement with Huang; as he went on to elaborate, the point was not whether Huang had differing opinions, but what he *should* be doing as governor:

> What I can do is elaborate on the division of labor within the Party and the state in China. The primary economic work of the Provincial Party Secretary is to devise the composition and determine the direction, hence people can often hear my views on areas that are identified as requiring progress. As the Governor, Comrade Huang is more involved in the operational domain; he implements the important strategies of the Provincial Party Committee and government. In reality, all the policies that involve constructing a modern industrial system and enhancing endogenous innovation are driven and actualized by Governor Huang Huahua.[73]

Wang's emphasis on the role of the provincial party secretary as an economic *strategist* was not an issue in itself; that Wang did not have to issue a similar elaboration of his relationship with Wang Hongju, then mayor and governor-equivalent in Chongqing, and Huang Qifan, then vice mayor, was significant. As mentioned in section 3, Huang played a very proactive role in devising and driving policies, which suggest the policies in Chongqing were less contentious and more nationally aligned than those instituted during Wang's tenure in Guangdong.

The third implication pertains to the Chinese central government's willingness to institute new rounds of industrial restructuring and nationally strategic policy experimentation in both Guangdong and Chongqing. This suggests that there were (and remain) political incentives in both retaining and breaking out of the ladder step developmental pathway. This point is well illustrated in Zhang Dejiang's willingness to accommodate and further intensify Chongqing's so-called 'socialistic' reforms after he replaced Bo Xilai as Chongqing Party Secretary. As mentioned in section 3, Zhang endorsed the large-scale foreign direct investment (FDI) inflows and surge in fixed capital formation whilst he was party secretary of Guangdong. Effectively, then, Zhang was building on policies instituted under Wang and Bo, whilst Wang went on to entrench policies Zhang put in place before vacating the position of Guangdong Party Secretary (ref. Table 5.1).

The tendency of cadres to maximise contextual conditions for political capital complicate, in turn, the chronological logic of Jiang Zemin and Hu Jintao's subsequent attempts to address the uneven development associated with Deng's approach. As mentioned earlier, a growing number of migrant workers continue to move to Guangdong, whilst the faster GDP growth in Guangdong relative to that in Chongqing strongly suggests the coastal-interior economic gap is not about to be bridged in the near future (ref. Figure 5.1). Qualitatively, the decision to experiment with national-scale reforms in *both* the PRD (in tandem with Hong Kong and Macau) and Liangjiang New Area (in Chongqing) exemplify further the constitutive importance of inter-regional differentiation for effective national governance. And this foregrounds the fourth conceptually significant point: the history of the post-Mao Chinese political economy is neither linear nor exceptional to the entire national territory.

It would not suffice, indeed, to view the regulatory logic of the Chinese political economy today as an outcome of events that occurred coherently in a sequential manner. Such a linear-sequential perspective, to follow Duara, obscures and/ or overlooks many aspects of the past:

> Because our own historical conceptions have shared so much with the linear History of the nation, we have tended to regard History more as a transparent medium of understanding than as a discourse enabling historical players (including historians) to deploy its resources to occlude, repress, appropriate and, sometimes, negotiate with other modes of depicting the past and, thus, the present and future.[74]

This dynamic view of historical evolution problematises Steinbock's chronological conception of the Guangdong–Chongqing relationship (ref. section 1).[75] To Steinbock, change will evolve "from Guangdong to Chongqing". Underpinning this perspective is a logic of temporal progression premised on a revised version of 'trickle down' economics: reforms in one place would *eventually* spread to other places. The initial development in selected megacities is seen to have triggered an "economic ripple" that "has been washing into new generations of Chinese cities".[76] Whilst this "trickle across" perspective is plausible theoretically, the previously mentioned economic gap between these two provincial-level regions calls into question the 'trickle across' prediction. The differentiated positioning of Guangdong and Chongqing at the *global scale* to attract foreign investments further accentuates the constitutive effects of local developmental initiatives. It suggests, in turn, that institutional differentiation has become a precondition of sustained central governance; that the "nationally strategic" aspect of local-scale experimentation is not premised on its eventual extension to the national scale, but in its ability to enhance China's *global* economic competitiveness.

Conclusion

The Chinese political economy is a dynamic entity constituted of multiple developmental trajectories. Recent debates on two seemingly divergent models in Chongqing and Guangdong has foregrounded the potential contradictions of this dynamism. Whilst existing research has attempted to evaluate these trajectories as outcomes of elite politics or ideological incommensurability, an overlooked but no less important aspect is the connections between these trajectories, Mao-era regulatory policies and the post-1978 system of reciprocal accountability. Indeed, these variations are rolling interactions between provincial developmental initiatives, overtly encouraged by the central government to stimulate enthusiasm in the reform process and inherited regulatory institutions to coordinate state formation, some extending back into the late 1940s.

As this chapter has argued, the Chongqing and Guangdong Models exemplified the intertwined spatial logics of socioeconomic regulation instituted by the Mao and Deng regimes. Deng's approach (through the coastal-oriented ladder step theory) was similar to Mao's institution of the 'cellular' national economy (through the People's Communes) in the sense that both recognised territorially fragmented development as an *inevitability*. The key difference lies in the way the *cause* of inevitability was rationalised. Mao viewed uneven development as an "irrational" historical by-product, and his objective was to obliterate this irrationality *over time* under the whole country as a chessboard philosophy. Deng, however, recognised and accepted the inevitability as a *future* outcome of his policies to integrate China with the global economy. It was with this vision in mind that Deng planned *for* uneven development during the seventh Five-Year Plan (1986–1990), with an eye to 'resetting' it to a higher level of 'evenness' in future.

Relative to Mao's approach, which was contingent on space (geo-economic insulation), Deng's was contingent on time (ascertaining a moment for the redistribution of wealth from a more developed belt to the other two). With this temporal deferral, the platform was established for coastal provinces like Guangdong, Fujian and Zhejiang to develop at a much faster pace than Chongqing and other interior provinces like Gansu, Sichuan and Xinjiang. As it became apparent that attempts at bridging regional disparities were encountering difficulties, provincial-level governments in the western interior began taking more proactive approaches to raise their respective economic competitiveness. This was done in three ways, namely through large-scale state-directed infrastructural development, like that seen in Chongqing; the 'scaling up' of new growth poles (like Liangjiang New Area) in the "national strategy" of development; and 'scale jumping' through direct engagement with transnational circulatory capital (more than half the Fortune 500 TNCs have now established operations in Chongqing). The outcome, at one level, corresponds to what Howell terms a "fragmented" Chinese political economy.[77] At another level, this fragmentation has arguably become a *fundamental* aspect of central governance against the backdrop of deepening global economic integration.

Specifically, the persistence of different trajectories refines received knowledge of what Shirk terms the system of reciprocal accountability in post-Mao

China.[78] This system refers to the approach by Deng Xiaoping to accommodate the interests of provincial officials in order to develop potent counterweights against senior conservatives in Beijing. Wang Yang and Bo Xilai's respective approaches reflect how personal agendas to attain political results are *framed by* the specific geographical-historical conditions of the locations within which cadres are deployed. It is even possible, as Wang's strategies in both Chongqing and Guangdong demonstrate, to reform one institution (urban-rural dual structure) in one place and maximise the utility of this institution (through relocating non-local labour power) in another (ref. Table 5.1). Perhaps more importantly, the resulting inter-regional differentiations exemplify a centralising logic of the 'China Model': the reformers aimed to justify their policies in the 'national interest', which foregrounds the constitutive relationship between subnational socioeconomic conditions and the system of reciprocal accountability.

What this suggests, in turn, is the CPC's attempt at sharing greater power and benefits (*fangquan rangli* 放权让利) has generated a positive feedback loop between different regulatory levels: localised initiatives stretch centrally defined parameters, entrench inter-regional variations and consequently enhance central control. This intrinsically speculative regulatory approach has come to define what the Deng administration terms "feeling for stones while crossing the river" (摸着石头过河). For this reason, differentiated developmental trajectories do not represent different stages of growth whereby one (e.g., Guangdong) is ahead of the other (e.g., Chongqing); they are conjunctural experiences that emerged out of a rolling series of interactions between 1) policymakers positioned at different levels of the administrative hierarchy; 2) private capitalists, both domestic and foreign; and 3) the effects of policies instituted since the Mao era. These interactions underscore the importance of understanding Chinese political-economic evolution in simultaneous rather than sequential terms – in terms of geographically differentiated trajectories, each with its own history, each responding strategically to the joint demands of national governance and transnational capital accumulation.

Notes

1 See Zheng (1998); Tracy and Lever-Tracy (2004).
2 Huang (2011); Su *et al* (2011); You and Lei (2013); Lim (2014a).
3 *Apple Daily* (15 March 2012); *Ming Bao* (4 December 2012); Xu (2013).
4 Zhao (2012); Cheng (2013); Zheng (2013); Lynch (2015).
5 Huang (2012); Mulvad (2015); Zhang and Peck (2015).
6 The empirical materials presented in this chapter draw from fieldwork conducted between February 2012 and January 2013 on a broad, multi-site project on policy experimentation and the shifting logics of socioeconomic regulation across China. A new round of data collection in Guangdong was undertaken in June and July 2015. Discursive materials from key political actors were sourced and translated by the authors; supporting materials were drawn from direct interviews with CPC cadres, planners and scholars in several cities in the Pearl River Delta and in Chongqing. Often on the advice of these interviewees, further follow up work was done to derive supporting evidence. The field research was supplemented by archival work conducted in Beijing, Shenzhen and Chongqing. The materials were then triangulated to align to the analytical approach,

which is similar to what Zhang (2012) terms "a social constructivist approach" that "brings to the foreground the constitutive socio-spatial context or unique historical-geographical conjuncture of policy-making activities" (p. 5). Adopting this approach entails juxtaposing a range of information to present a multi-perspectival narrative on the connections between state rescaling and institutional path-dependency.

7 Dirlik (2012a, 2012b); Cheng (2015); Godement (2015), pp. 17–27; Li (2016).
8 Fitzgerald (1995), p. 75.
9 Meisner (1999), p. 62.
10 Gurley (1976); van de Ven (1992); Groot (2004).
11 Ref. Teiwes (1990); Shiraev and Yang (2014).
12 Mao (1999), p. 32–33; authors' translation.
13 Ke (1959); authors' translation.
14 Ke (1959); authors' translation.
15 Ke (1959); authors' translation.
16 CPC Shanghai Municipal Party Committee History Research Office (2004), pp. 70–71.
17 In that context, it is worth recalling that the Cold War climate had made Mao push for Third Front industrialisation in remote parts of China precisely because he perceived pre-existing industrial hubs like Shanghai to be vulnerable to American or Russian attacks. As relations with the US continued to thaw following Nixon's visit in 1972, pragmatism eventually led back to the grooming of the southeast as the engine of Chinese growth. The post-Mao strategy of developing the southeast coastal areas of China thus had as much to do with the easing of Cold War tensions as with geographical advantages. See e.g., Naughton (1988).
18 Donnithorne (1972); Tsui (1991); Bray (2005).
19 Zhao (2009), p. 151.
20 Chien and Gordon (2008); Xu (2011); cf. Bell (2015), pp. 182–188.
21 Party Literature Research Office (1998), p. 413.
22 Cf. Harvey (1982); Smith (1984).
23 Xia and Feng (1982).
24 The fourth SEZ was in Xiamen, Fujian province.
25 Wei (1996); Dabla-Norris (2005).
26 Cf. Wang and Hu (1999); Zhu (2003); Lin (2004).
27 Deng (1993), pp. 277–278; authors' translation.
28 Cf. Shirk (1996); Bramall (2007).
29 Ma (2005); Huang (2008).
30 China National Bureau of Statistics (2014).
31 Hu (2001).
32 China National Bureau of Statistics (2015).
33 He *et al* (2008); Ge (2009).
34 Cf. Poncet (2005); Howell (2006); Chen and Zheng (2008).
35 Heilmann and Perry (2011).
36 China National Bureau of Statistics (2014).
37 See full report by Liang *et al* (2014).
38 *21st Century Business Herald* (11 April 2015).
39 Lin (1997).
40 Xiao Bin, interview with *Time Weekly* (19 May 2015); authors' translation.
41 Cf. Dickson (2008); Walter and Howie (2011).
42 Zhang (2013), p. 1614.
43 Guangdong Bureau of Statistics (2008); ratios for both Guangdong and China determined by authors' calculation.
44 China National Bureau of Statistics (2008).
45 Huang and Sharif (2009); Meyer *et al* (2012).
46 Lu and Wei (2007); Wei and Liao (2012).
47 Chen (2007), p. 193.

48 *People's Daily* (3 August 2009).

49 *Nanfang Dushibao* (2 April 2012).

50 Officially, given the lack of inter-provincial coordination, it has to be stated that reloca-tion policies remain within the province so that the government appears to prioritize the provincial interests. This is an extension of the protectionist, inward-looking tendencies of the Mao era. In reality, however, given the huge difference in infrastructural facili-ties between the PRD and the rest of Guangdong province, the Guangdong government in fact did not mind if undesirable industries leave the province altogether rather than attempt to upgrade these industries within the province (Interview, academic and regu-lar consultant to the government, January 2013).

51 Of these "new areas", Hengqin and Qianhai are designated "sub-provincial" (*fushengji* 副省级) within the administrative hierarchy, which means that they enjoy powers lesser than a province and are now the equivalent of the cities – Zhuhai and Shenzhen, respectively – in which they are located. As both Zhuhai and Shenzhen are already national-level SEZs, Hengqin and Qianhai are popularly termed "special zones within special zones" (*tequzhong de tequ* 特区中的特区). Nansha New Area is currently gov-erned by Guangzhou, which also has sub-provincial administrative status. It is likely that more autonomy will be devolved to administrators in Nansha as it is the largest of the three.

52 Shirk (1993); see also Rawski (1995); Ma (2005); Sheng (2010); ref. section 1.

53 Webber *et al* (2002); Zhao (2009).

54 Interview, planner B, Shenzhen (January 2013).

55 *Huaxia Shibao* (17 November 2007).

56 The other three province-level cities are along the coast, namely, Beijing, Tianjin and Shanghai. These cities are centrally-governed because they are deemed highly strategic to national political-economic development.

57 As an entity, the "Republic of China" is no longer recognized by the United Nations. It continues to exist in name, however, with its base on the island of Taiwan, and contin-ues to be recognized internationally by a handful of countries. For a full geo-historical discussion, see Lim (2012b).

58 Bian (2005).

59 In March 1985, the Chinese State Council mooted a plan to rescale a "Three Gorges Province" (*sanxia sheng* 三峡省). This plan would encompass the current Chongq-ing administrative area as well as western Hubei province. However, for reasons still unknown, the plan was officially cancelled in May 1986.

60 Li (2003).

61 Huang (Interview with *Chongqing Ribao* (12 July 2010); authors' translation.

62 Huang (Interview with *ENN Weekly* (21 January 2014); authors' translation.

63 *Sina Finance* (2006), p. 20; *Caijing*, 20 January 2014.

64 See Huang (2011); Lim (2014).

65 Interview with *Caixin*, 17 September 2015.

66 Huang, Interview with *Caixin* (17 September 2015).

67 Liu, interview with *Chongqing Ribao* (5 August 2011); authors' translation.

68 As above.

69 Cf. Huang (2011).

70 Qiu (2011), n.p.

71 Interview, academic, Shenzhen (January 2013).

72 Transcribed by *Nanfang Daily* (31 July 2009); authors' translation.

73 Wang Yang, transcribed by *Nanfang Daily* (31 July 2009); authors' translation.

74 Duara (1995), p. 5.

75 Steinbock (2012).

76 Steinbock (2012), n.p.

77 Howell (2006).

78 Shirk (1993).

6 China

An East Asian alternative
to neoliberalism?

Introduction

China is the world's second largest economy today. GDP growth over the past three decades has outpaced the 'miracles' posted by other 'developmental states' in East Asia, namely Japan, South Korea, Taiwan and Singapore. Chinese per-capita income relative to US levels (in purchasing power parity terms) may be, at present, roughly equal to where South Korea was situated economically relative to the USA in the mid-1990s, namely, far behind. Two decades on South Korea's per-capita GDP is almost 2/3 of that of the USA. However, income distribution in China today is much more unequal than in 1990s South Korea.[1] This naturally begs the question of how proximate Korean and Chinese economic policies have been; more importantly, it begs the question whether South Korea's path might indicate how the much bigger Chinese economy could avoid a social backlash in the face of growing inequality, and one day perhaps catch up perhaps with American living standards?

The institutional foundations of this success have been the subject of prolific research in political economy. Japan and later South Korea and Taiwan had of course been politically allied with the West since the end of World War II, and did not openly seek to conjure up an alternative to Western neoliberalism. Moreover, the Japanese and (to a lesser extent) Taiwanese economies benefited from extensive American procurement during the Korean War and were allowed to exercise protectionism afterwards due to Washington's broader Cold War considerations.[2]

From 1979, Chinese economic reformers, too, used to go out of their way to portray China as a market-friendly country. At least until Xi Jinping's accession to power they largely eschewed any kind of Western textbook labelling, be it social democracy or laissez-faire. Indeed, as late as 2008, one of China's top economists, Justin Lin, proclaimed that his country did not follow any economic model at all.[3] This stands in contrast to observers seeking to explain how this spectacular economic expansion was constituted by (a self-perceived or substantive) *historically* exceptional 'China Model'.[4] Others have questioned whether the Chinese developmental experience was underpinned by structures similar to those of East Asian 'developmental states'.[5] There is, quite clearly, no theoretical consensus on the Chinese growth story.

At one level, the emergence of multiple explanatory tropes is unsurprising. Socioeconomic reforms in post-Mao China intersected with and subsequently became the greatest beneficiary of economic globalisation. Whilst communism is still nominally relevant, self-enrichment and business entrepreneurship have been celebrated by the party leadership since the enshrinement of the "Three Represents" ideological framework at the sixteenth Party Congress in 2002. So much so that even vociferous proponents of neoliberalism in the US, like Donald Trump or hedge fund manager Ann Lee, used to urge Washington to learn from Beijing when it came to deregulation.[6] This warm embrace of marketisation within the confines of *Zhongnanhai* strongly suggests neoliberal regulatory logics have permeated the party-state apparatus; socioeconomic regulation could be plausibly characterised as "neoliberalism with Chinese characteristics".[7]

Other facets of the "miracle" demonstrate traces of East Asian state developmentalism, however. High-speed growth was engendered under administrative authoritarianism and financial repression: the CPC wielded immense influence over the allocation of financial capital and, following the reform and corporatisation of SOEs in the 1990s, has begun to reshape industrial development through the selection of 'national champions' and deliberately 'getting prices wrong' (i.e., indirect government subsidy to sectors deemed strategic). Viewed collectively, these seemingly disparate trends raise an important question for research on Chinese political-economic evolution: is the Chinese growth 'miracle' a simple hybrid of neoliberalization and the East Asian 'developmental state'?

This chapter addresses this question from a broad historical and geographical framework. It begins from the presupposition that comparisons between different political economies would be incisive only if they are historically grounded and incorporate geographically variegated expressions of development. Whilst policies in post-Mao China might often *look much like* those of other countries, they are on occasion simply *concrete extensions* of institutions, interests and ideas inherited from the 1950s or earlier. These institutions implemented different policies and practices across China, which calls attention to the multiple scales of historical-grounding: national-level policies may complement or exist in tension with those at the supranational, provincial, municipal and collective (previously commune) levels. For this reason, it would not be helpful to assess the extent to which post-Mao China has 'deviated' from or 'converged' with ideal-typical neoliberal or developmental state prototypes. Political economies are part of fluid processes that mutate over time; neither are South Korea or Japan run economically today as they were in the 1990s.[8] States drive and adapt to these fluid processes, which calls into questions the applicability of these prototypes for comparison.[9] A more incisive form of comparison should therefore take into account the *constitutive* roles of China's multifaceted economic history and geography. This is the overarching aim of the critical review presented in this chapter.

The discussion will be organized in three incremental parts. Section 2 critically evaluates the emergence and rationale of China as a modern nation-state. Section 3 then establishes connections and tensions between developmental statism (including its putative precondition, political democratisation) and residual Soviet-style corporatism. The selective adaptation of neoliberal logics in China is addressed in section 4. The concluding section synthesises the foregoing analysis and calls for a dynamic framework that is capable of explaining Chinese political-economic evolution within a broader *historical* context of global economic integration.

China as a (capitalist) state

In spite of varying national system-specific interpretations of China's contemporary economic development, existing research has largely overlooked its intrinsic role *as* a modern nation-state. Although the capital accumulation process need not necessarily depend on national-scale unity, the production, stabilisation and/or disruption of appropriate scales of accumulation in the global political economy has been premised on national-scale regulation in the first instance. The modern state, as John Holloway sees it, should not be construed as a rigidified entity that contains a definitive 'national capitalism'; rather, through actively (re)producing the conditions and relations of production within what has become a predominantly capitalist global economy, the state exists in a co-constitutive relationship with capital accumulation:

> If capitalist social relations are inherently global, then each national state is a moment of global society, a territorial fragmentation of a society which extends throughout the world. No national state, "rich" or "poor" can be understood in abstraction from its existence as a moment of the global capital relation . . . All national states are defined, historically and repeatedly, through their relation to the totality of capitalist social relations.[10]

If all national states – regardless of governance ideologies – are defined in relation to the transnational capital accumulation dynamic, it might then be more plausible to view the national territorial scale not so much as a temporally static and geographically homogeneous whole. Indeed, the national scale of socioeconomic regulation has been dynamically constituted by – and in turn re-constructed – processes occurring at the subnational and international scales.[11] How state apparatuses "relate" to the "totality of capitalist social relations", David Harvey explains, is predicated on an active and regular reconstruction of what constitutes the national:

> Adequate territorial structures of administration and power are a necessary condition for the survival of capitalism. The difficulty is that territorial powers, once formed, become relatively fixed attributes of capitalism's geography and resist pressures for change. The tension between fixity and motion in the landscape of capitalism is re-emphasized because the state is about fixity rather than motion. But the state, as the lynch-pin of regionality, is the primary vehicle to assure the production of the collective preconditions for production, exchange and consumption. State administration is always therefore an active agent in capital circulation and accumulation.

The "interventionist" state necessarily supersedes the "facilitative" state of liberal and neoliberal theory.[12]

Jim Glassman's processual view of states adds a further dimension this notion of the "interventionist state": a state is fundamentally "a process in which the state apparatus becomes increasingly oriented towards facilitating capital accumulation for the most internationalized investors, regardless of their nationality."[13] As Glassman adds, "states should not be seen as anchored solely to those social forces designated as falling within the state's formal realm of territorial authority".[14]

In relation to these propositions that states are strategic institutional agents that facilitate the accumulation of capital at different geographical scales, this chapter calls attention to the constitution of Chinese state power by forces operating within *and* beyond the national economy. To follow Glassman, there is "no reason to assume in advance that the social forces to which state officials feel affinity or a need to respond to are only or primarily national – indeed, the social construction of nationalism in this sense is precisely the sort of project needing interrogation and explanation".[15] States, in other words, should not be viewed as inherently 'strong' or 'weak', nor do they possess distinctive and seemingly static institutional traits (e.g., a developmental state, with a specific set of institutional arrangements and regulatory ideology). In tandem with large-scale territorial decolonisation after WWII, multiple state institutions have become entwined in an inherently capricious, competitive and often tension-filled relationship with the logic of capital accumulation.[16] One of these states is CPC-governed 'new China'.

After its revolutionary success, the CPC was originally committed to a gradual transition to socialism. Underpinning this gradualism were differences in opinions amongst the top policymaking circles on how to inherit the agricultural economies run by middle and rich peasants. Such was the need for positive reciprocity from middle and rich peasants, indeed, the term "socialist construction" was not included in the Common Governance Program[17] (*gongtong gangling*) of 'new China'. Perhaps most interestingly, one of Mao's most trusted aide, Liu Shaoqi, even proclaimed in a 1948 speech in Tianjin that "exploitation has its merits" (*boduo yougong*). What ensued in the early 1950s was a willingness – even on the part of Mao – to accommodate private enterprise and land ownership:

> The present-day capitalist economy in China is a capitalist economy which for the most part is under the control of the People's Government and which is linked with the state-owned socialist economy in various forms and supervised by the workers. It is not an ordinary but a particular kind of capitalist economy, namely, a state-capitalist economy of a new type. It exists not chiefly to make profits for the capitalists but to meet the needs of the people and the state. True, a share of the profits produced by the workers goes to the capitalists, but that is only a small part, about one quarter, of the total. The remaining three quarters are produced for the workers (in the form of the welfare fund), for the state (in the form of income tax) and for expanding

productive capacity (a small part of which produces profits for the capitalists). Therefore, this state-capitalist economy of a new type takes on a socialist character to a very great extent and benefits the workers and the state.[18]

Taken together, these developments bear striking similarity to Leninist "state capitalism". First introduced by the Russian revolutionary leader, Vladimir Lenin, following the victory over tsarism in 1918, state capitalism refers to the state's *control* of key factors of production whilst leaving room for private capital accumulation. It was, *pace* Lenin, a transitional stage between capitalism and socialism in which Russia was situated but of which fast-industrialising Germany was the epitome in 1918. Lenin believed socialism was inconceivable without large-scale capitalist engineering feats drawing on cutting-edge technology borrowed from the developed world. Nonetheless, he prophetically observed that state capitalism in Germany, at the time, was at the behest of *junker bourgeoisie* and would therefore end in militarism, whereas in Russia, (self-perceived) proletariat steering could use it to yield socialist outcomes.[19] Notably, however, state capitalism behooved coordination with and concessions to capitalists in both settings, with a view towards limiting private enterprise and guiding it according to state priorities.[20]

Between 1918 and 1922, Lenin put in place the New Economic Policy (NEP or *Novaya Ekonomicheskaya Politika*). It is widely seen as the reintroduction of private initiative to the preceding system of compulsory requisition known as "War Communism", during which the Soviet economy was negatively affected. Central to this was an awareness that an instant adaptation of communism was impossible because of the large Russian peasant base. Rather, Lenin introduced a tax – the *prodnalog* – that was lower than the levels forcibly collected from peasants during the civil war. Peasants could then retain and sell the surplus, which offered an incentive to raise production. The process is summed up in Lenin's terms:

> The New Economic Policy means substituting a tax for the requisitioning of food; it means reverting to capitalism to a considerable extent – to what extent we do not know. Concessions to foreign capitalists (true, only very few have been accepted, especially when compared with the number we have offered) and leasing enterprises to private capitalists definitely mean restoring capitalism, and this is part and parcel of the New Economic Policy; for the abolition of the surplus-food appropriation system means allowing the peasants to trade freely in their surplus agricultural produce, in whatever is left over after the tax is collected – and the tax – takes only a small share of that produce. The peasants constitute a huge section of our population and of our entire economy, and that is why capitalism must grow out of this soil of free trading.[21]

As is well-documented, the NEP was unable to support the state enterprises in the cities, as grains remained in short supply. Attributing this to the profiteering tendencies of increasingly influential peasants (the *kulaks*), Joseph Stalin, Lenin's successor, abolished the NEP and re-introduced totalising state control over production in 1928. What followed was a state-led model of industrialisation that prioritised urban development and led to the detention, suppression and execution of several million *kulaks*.[22]

In an intriguing analysis, Hua-Yu Li argues that Mao strongly admired the Soviet experiences of developing socialism in the 1920s and 1930s, as described in Joseph Stalin's *History of the Communist Party of the Soviet Union (Bolshevik): Short Course*.[23] So deeply rooted was Mao's Soviet – or, more precisely, Stalin – envy, that he paradoxically chose to overlook Stalin's later advice for a gradualist transition. Instead, as Li observes, Mao "relied on this work [the *Short Course*] as a roadmap to lead China to socialism".[24] The CPC's total commitment to replicate the Soviet experience could be seen clearly in a 1953 speech by Deng Zihui, one of the 'five horses' deployed from the six administrative regions to Beijing along with Gao Gang and Rao Shushi. As Deng puts it, the CPC equated its developmental trajectory with Soviet history:

> It must first be made clear what is called a transition period. I think fellow comrades are all clear, the revolution in China is divided into two stages: the first stage is New Democratic revolution; the second stage is socialist revolution. The first stage does preparatory work for the second stage, it prepares the conditions for socialist revolution in the second stage, the first New Democratic revolutionary stage has concluded, it has finished, it has passed . . . The Soviet Union implemented the New Economic Policy from 1921 to the time the first five year plan was launched in 1929, that was a transition period. Our current transition period is basically the same as that of the Soviet Union.[25]

By Deng Zihui's account, the CPC's planning logic could be interpreted according to this periodisation: pre-1953 state building was Leninistic, whilst the post-1953 transition period, beginning with China's first Five-Year Plan in 1953, was to take the form of Stalinisation.[26] This periodic shift was reflected by drastic adjustments to developmental policies between 1953 and 1958. Under a quasi-bourgeois capitalist model (i.e., that adopted by Lenin), uneven economic-geographical development was at once contingent and necessary.[27] A Stalinistic model, however, sought "balanced, proportionate development" across the whole country; by implication, uneven development was a contingency that could and had to be eased so long as its primary cause – the bourgeoisie – was first exterminated.

The repudiation process was first enabled by the confiscation and redistribution of land, the primary means of production for the majority of Chinese citizens at the time. It was introduced in June 1950 as the Agrarian Reform Law (土地改革法) and implemented over two years. Land, farming tools and animals were confiscated from landlords – labelled by the state apparatus as "class enemies" – and reallocated to peasants and sharecroppers across the country. To Bramall, this wave of land reforms did not enhance egalitarianism and raise output; it was a *function* of intensifying CPC control of the economy.[28] Underpinning this version of state capitalism was a re-adaptation – not renouncement – of capitalistic techniques. As Howe shows, accounting rules for defining the components of enterprise wage bills remained unchanged until 1965, whilst rules for calculating minimum wages in 1957 were the same as those in 1948.[29] Family land titles in the cities were also largely unchanged at first, which meant private ownership remained a legal possibility throughout the Mao's early tenure. What ensued, then, was a removal of the private capitalists without fully uprooting the laws of capital accumulation. Mao acknowledged this point during the launch of the Great Leap Forward industrialisation program, during which he explicitly sought to build on Stalin's economic management by accentuating the importance of planning and politics:

> Capitalism leaves behind it the commodity form, which we must still retain for the time being. Commodity exchange laws governing value play no regulating role in our production. This role is played by planning, by the great leap forward under planning, by politics-in-command. Stalin speaks only of the production relations, not of the superstructure, nor of the relationship between superstructure and economic base. Chinese cadres participate in production; workers participate in management. Sending cadres down to lower levels to be tempered, discarding old rules and regulations – all these pertain to the superstructure, to ideology. Stalin mentions economics only, not politics.[30]

Employing Marx's dichotomous base-superstructure conceptualisation of politico-economic development, Mao inverted Stalin's focus on the primacy of the economic "base" by prioritising the importance of the "superstructure". Emphasising "politics" meant the integration of ideological lines and the notion of "permanent revolution" into daily economic practices across the communes and state enterprises.[31] This ideological vantage point integrated economic practices with social organization to fulfill the CPC's political objectives; the economy was not an atomistic entity distinct from the party-state, an empirical fact that has important ramifications for evaluating China as a developmental state (more in section 3). For this reason, Mao argued that commodity production was not incommensurable with his quest for socialism, *so long as* the overarching objective of "socialist commodity production" was clear:

> There are those who fear commodities. Without exception they fear capitalism, not realizing that with the elimination of capitalists it is allowable to expand commodity production vastly. We are still backward in commodity production, behind Brazil and India. Commodity production is not an isolated thing. Look at the context: capitalism or socialism. In a capitalist context it is capitalist commodity production. In a socialist context it is socialist commodity production. Commodity production has existed since ancient times . . . In capitalist society there are no socialist institutions considered as social institutions, but the working class and socialist ideology do exist in capitalist society. The thing that determines commodity production is the

surrounding economic conditions. The question is, can commodity production be regarded as a useful instrument for furthering socialist production? I think commodity production will serve socialism quite tamely.[32]

This reinterpretation of commodity production involved total state expropriation – often under forceful and non-compensatory means – of preexisting private capital. Ownership of means of production in all domains of commodity production – land, labour power and money – was transferred to the state bureaucracy, which governed urban areas directly, or its rural proxy, the "People's Communes" (now known as the collectives). An economic monopoly was thus created and controlled by the CPC. With the policy emphasis on commune-driven redistribution of resources, demand was curtailed in the large rural hinterland and the CPC wielded price-setting power over manufactured goods generated by the urban-industrial units (*gongye danwei*).

Faced with the catastrophic upshot of the Great Leap Forward, senior CPC cadres like Liu Shaoqi, Li Fuchun and Deng Xiaoping sought to re-introduce private initiatives to boost output. Schurmann likened the economic recovery of the early 1960s to be a renewed attempt to launch the 'New Economic Policy', though he also presciently noted – in view of the brutal campaigns of the Cultural Revolution during and after 1966 – signs that China "may be approaching another 1928".[33] What this reveals was a strong undercurrent within senior CPC leadership that capitalistic techniques, as recommended by the NEP, were fundamental to socialist construction. Mao did not agree and went on to label Liu Shaoqi and Deng Xiaoping as 'capitalist roaders' at the onset of the Cultural Revolution.

Any meaningful attempt at reinstating NEP-styled reforms came after Deng successfully out-maneuvered Mao's appointed successor, Hua Guofeng, in 1978. Deng would subsequently affirm the value of the NEP during a meeting with Zimbabwe's Prime Minister, Robert Mugabe, in August 1985: "What really is the appearance of socialism, even the Soviet Union could not be completely clear despite working on it for many years. Maybe Lenin's line of thought is better, he developed a NEP, although the Soviet model subsequently stiffened".[34] In fact, the two latest most comprehensive biographies of Deng – whilst at loggerheads on the overall assessment of his legacy – both concur that he remained a committed Marxist who had been inspired by Lenin's New Economic Policy throughout his life: the NEP rationale thus underlay in no small measure not just much of the land reform in the early 1950s and the move away from the Great Leap Forward in the early 1960s, but also Deng's *gaige kaifang* reforms in the 1980s. To be sure, Deng's favouring of foreign investment had also been inspired by his 1978 visit to 'capitalistic' Singapore but that aspect of his thought was more pragmatic than ideological.[35] The extent of PRC policy 'borrowing' from Singapore was already examined in detail in Chapter 4. Suffice it to mention here that Deng was in fact equally impressed by Singapore's top-down 'social engineering', e.g., its heady public housing scheme.[36]

By contrast, the CPC's biggest *faux pas* in the Mao era had arguably been its belief that national economic competitiveness could be attained within an insulated system of production. Because nation-states are defined in relation to the global system of capitalism, national insulation directly contradicted capital's inherent need for circulation. It was arguably the desire to have *absolute* state control over the production and allocation of resources that condemned China in the 1960s and 1970s to fall further behind its East Asian neighbours. In fact, Mao's belief in "ongoing struggles" reached delirious heights during the Cultural Revolution, when many parts of China plunged into social chaos. Moreover, it was obvious that economic insulation and egalitarian rhetoric did not always yield Marxian egalitarianism – uneven economic status was transposed into uneven allocation of power between the central and local governments. In fact, the divide between the welfare-privileged urban and overwhelmingly rural population widened, whilst living conditions *within* urban work units (*danwei*) and rural collectives were broadly level. Regional disparity and shifting industry meant some work units and collectives enjoyed much higher living standards than others.[37]

Is China a developmental state?

Conceptual (in)commensurabilities

The notion of the East Asian 'developmental state' has received significant research attention in political-economic research over the past three decades. This began with Johnson's seminal study of post-WWII socioeconomic policies by Japan's Ministry of International Trade and Industry (MITI).[38] Whilst there are multiple definitions of the developmental state, scholars agree that this state form is characterised by (a) a nationalistic and authoritarian state ideologically committed to augmenting the competitive advantage of domestic firms and grooming them to become leading global exporters; (b) the willingness to facilitate a favourable domestic environment through protectionist international trade policies, macroeconomic policies that ensure devalued currency and interest rate stability; and (c) the existence of relatively homogeneous and egalitarian populations that were ready to work with the state to drive growth.[39]

Observers found this variant of state-led development especially fascinating vis-à-vis other state forms – in particular the neoliberal prototype based on free market principles – because it managed to deliver high GDP growth over a relatively short period of time through state-identified 'champion' industries. Such was the success of the Japanese experience in the 1970s that Vogel famously touted that it could supersede the USA as the number one economy in the world.[40] Through the 1980s (and sporadically since), Japanese policymakers and think tanks began to promote the Japanese experience as an alternative to Western-style free market capitalism. Arguably the most memorable imagery of this claim of economic-ideological superiority was the reintroduction of the 'Flying Geese' paradigm that underpinned Japanese imperial ambitions during WWII: Japan would be the 'lead goose' that elevated other East Asian economies along the industrialisation flight trajectory, insofar as these economies are integrated within a regional division of labour driven by Japanese firms.[41]

Yet, interestingly, the larger East Asian economies – namely South Korea and Taiwan – became increasingly successful through *circumventing* the Flying Geese paradigm in the 1980s–1990s. What they selectively adopted instead were key tenets of state-capital relations and competitive export orientation first instituted in Japan. Evans describes these tenets as "embedded autonomy": an effective developmental state entails a bureaucracy that is capable of making decisions without being captured by private economic interests (autonomy), yet the state needs to be "embedded in a concrete set of social ties" and establish "institutionalised channels for the continual negotiation and renegotiation of policies" in order to avoid being disconnected from society (embeddedness).[42] The term 'selective' is deliberate and deserves emphasis: the South Korean, Taiwanese and Singaporean states were arguably less 'embedded' socially than the Japanese government in that they were less inclined to encourage private firms to provide life-long employment and broad-based social benefits. More prominent was the ability of state bureaucracies to launch industrial policies in the name of national development, although these also varied in degrees.[43]

A particular streak of research on the developmental state – now extended to the analysis of the post-Mao Chinese political economy – is the attempt at cross-country comparison on the basis of an ideal-typical template. This began in the late 1980s when Johnson developed his previously mentioned thesis of post-WWII Japanese development into a comparison of government-business relationships in Japan, South Korea and Taiwan.[44] The literature was further developed through studies evaluating the state's multi-dimensional relationships with capital, labour, political ideology (primarily liberal democracy) and the global economy.[45] With the deepening of market reforms in China after the mid-1990s, scholars began to critically interrogate whether the developmental state model is capable of explaining developments in China within a very short period of market-oriented reforms.[46]

This comparative engagement with the developmental state template can be very useful in providing a contemporary snapshot of where individual states stand in relation to one another. Table 6.1 shows how China stands at the current moment vis-à-vis Japan, South Korea, Taiwan and Singapore in terms of two well-defined concepts, namely Johnson's industrial policy and Evans' embedded autonomy.[47] What this shows is not only how the Chinese experience differs from the other East Asian developmental states, but also how the others have evolved since the 1970s. The paradox of this contribution is that it accentuates the primary *limit* to this ideal-typical template: contrary to the Flying Geese imagery of leading goose (Japan) leading a skein on an upward curve, there is no fixed historical spectrum of the developmental state along which one country can evolve insofar as specific conditions are met. This can be attributed to three reasons.

First, the developmental state is a conjuncturally and geographically differentiated *fact* rather than a static conceptual model. It is, in other words, a *dynamic* entity that responds to the changing conditions of and pressures from both its domestic environment and the demands of the global economy. To abstract and generalise from this fact is problematic, given the different contextual conditions

Table 6.1 Can China be framed conceptually as a developmental state? A comparison with Japan, South Korea, Singapore and Taiwan

Concept	Characteristics	Japan	South Korea	Taiwan	Singapore	China
Embedded autonomy	• Government agencies are embedded in socioeconomic affairs through direct information sharing & deliberation with key corporate players • At the same time, they remain autonomous from private interests, seeking to attain national-level developmental goals	• Very strong between 1960s & early 1990s • State-firm relations increasingly decoupled in the wave of intense global competition, but possibly still the highest of the five countries • Firms show signs of retreat from social welfare provision	• Very strong between 1970s & early 1990s, albeit initially under state authoritarianism • Decoupling took place in financial realm, which led to harsh outcomes during the 1997 Asian financial crisis; Korean *chaebols* have since diversified ownership; Korean state became less embedded within corporate strategies	• Not as embedded as that of Japan & South Korea during the 1950s & 1960s; KMT implemented authoritarian control over socio-economic life to ensure political survival • Room was created for large-scale growth of small & medium enterprises	• Increasingly strong since the early 1970s; labour movement integrated within political structure & led by government minister • Private interests clearly autonomous, though strategies of government-linked firms overlapped with state & industrial policies (e.g., the regionalisation drive)	• Most intense embeddedness since 1949, with the CPC directly in control of decision-making in firms & regulation of social life • Lowest autonomy of the five; despite SOE reforms in the 1980s & 1990s, both the party & the state directly impact SOE interests. Private firms are not explicitly part of industrial policies but their autonomy is constricted by the state
Prevalence of industrial policy	• Industrial policies affect industrial performances through state-driven adjustments of microeconomic variables • Involves sectoral targeting & deliberately "getting prices wrong"	• Very strong between 1960s & early 1990s; declined sharply thereafter • Bureaucratic influence over firms through microeconomic variables constrained by economic globalisation	• Very strong between 1960s & early 1990s; declined sharply thereafter • Decline in bureaucratic prowess similar to the Japanese experience	• Primarily evident through the national science policy aggressively pursued since global diplomatic recognition was significantly reduced during the 1970s • Currently evident in biotech, hi-tech electronics & nuclear power	• Remains high since the 1970s; but impact primarily government-linked firms; overall effect is not as strong as in Japan, South Korea & China • Export-oriented policy of the 1970s remain, & there is minimum influence over the strategies of foreign capital	• Very strong during the Mao era; emphasis on light industry in the three decades after 1978 as the CPC pursued export-oriented growth • Grooming state-owned "national champions" in specific sectors like tele-communications, aerospace engineering & automobiles • Enabled by "Go Abroad" strategy

Source: Authors' compilation.

of other states. For this reason, the relevance of the developmental state framework vis-à-vis intensifying neo-liberalising processes is increasingly called into question over the last decade.[48] Reflecting on state-business linkages in Korea, Yun Tae Kim argues that "the developmental state has gradually eroded" as its power and capability "was increasingly affected by economic liberalization and political democratization".[49]

A similar decline in state activism, job security and social welfare is also observed of twenty-first-century Japan. In tandem with the Japanese state's deployment of the "self-responsibility" discourse is the rise of "freeters" (freelancer) and "haken-workers" (temporarily contracted employment with minimum benefits). That decline amounts in effect to a retreat from the so-called "three treasures" of Japanese industrial relations: lifetime employment, strong unions and guaranteed seniority pay.[50] Pekkanen notes how the proliferation of civil society groups in Japan has been enabled by the decline in the bureaucracy's political insulation.[51] In its heyday, the Japanese bureaucracy was protected from disruptive influences from interest groups and civil groupings and could thus institute industrial policies unilaterally. Corresponding to emergent tendencies in South Korea and Taiwan, this changed following conscious application of neoliberal logics in Japan since the 1990s.[52] "While it is clear", writes Beeson, "that Japan's developmental state played a pivotal role in shaping its post-war recovery, it is equally apparent that it has become increasingly dysfunctional".[53]

On the other hand, there is a growing body of literature that points to the resilience of developmental state thinking amongst East Asian elites, even after the Asian Financial Crisis of 1997, and more so in the wake of the Global Financial Crisis of 2008.[54] Whereas in the US and Britain, neoliberal orthodoxy prevails for the most part on the back of the new knowledge economy, in East Asia one can more often than not find frequent recourse to the developmental catch-up toolbox even in democratic settings: the use of fiscal and monetary incentives to groom industries deemed strategic; or the deployment of price controls to drive down labour costs.[55]

Nevertheless, the *private-sector* 'champion firms' historically groomed by government in Japan, South Korea and Taiwan – major examples being Sony, Samsung and Acer – have by now become transnational corporations (TNCs) in essence. These firms concomitantly prioritised the coordination of global production networks over the attainment of domestic developmental objectives. Their primary operational strategy has shifted from expanding and enhancing domestic manufacturing (which has been predominantly outsourced to different countries) to market control (which similarly extends beyond the home base). This not only explains why industrial policies have become increasingly ineffective in these countries; the attainment of social objectives (egalitarianism and growth) through moral suasion have been concomitantly destabilised (ref. Table 6.1). Henry Yeung sums up this development incisively:

Because of the deepening strategic coupling of these national firms with lead firms in global industries, the developmental state's attempt to govern the market and to steer industrial transformation through direct policy interventions has become increasingly difficult and problematic. Through this process of strategic coupling, national firms have been gradually disembedded from state apparatuses and re-embedded in different global production networks that are governed by competitive inter-firm dynamics. While the state in these East Asian economies has actively repositioned its role in this changing governance, it can no longer be conceived as the dominant actor in steering domestic firms and industrial transformation.[56]

Second, the rollback of the state from its "dominant actor" position in Japan and South Korea arguably offers the CPC a major incentive to *avoid* wholesale imitation of their "developmentalist" policies. As discussed in section 2, the CPC has re-adopted an authoritarian, Leninist variant of "state capitalism", and research has demonstrated this approach was repurposed rather than jettisoned during the post-Mao era to facilitate the transition to a "socialist market economy".[57] Otherwise put, the Chinese variant of "state capitalism" enshrines not just state ownership of "national champions" but also CPC dominance therein.[58] At the same time, persistent and widespread state ownership arguably empowers society as a whole, insofar as it retains a generous welfare-regime for those hordes of shop-floor workers that hung on to their posts through Zhu Rongji's enforced downsizing in the 1990s.[59]

Specifically, Deng inverted Mao's developmental focus, ostensibly in an effort to defer the tensions triggered by the incommensurability between capitalistic logics and geo-economic insulation. As is well known, the rural element in Deng's 1979 reform was embodied in the in the expansion of the Xiaogang-village-style style household responsibility system (*baochan daohu*) nationwide, namely, effective de-collectivisation of land tilling along nuclear family lines. Not long after followed the setup of Town and Village Enterprises (TVEs), meant to soak in excess labour in the countryside along the Eastern seaboard – something the larger urban SOEs never achieved. TVEs spread rapidly in response the surge in consumer demand that followed the agricultural productivity spurt and higher income in the countryside in the early 1980s: they dealt in mainly labour-intensive pursuits where capital entry barriers to markets could not be effectively blocked by urban SOEs – from apparel and hosiery, renovation materials, niche food and beverage, to small-scale coal mining. They came in many institutional shades too: in Southern Jiangsu, for example, they were mostly local government run, in Wenzhou more local private ownership was allowed, and in Guangdong TVESs were commonly invested by Hong Kong business people.[60]

Contrary to the negative reception towards FDIs during the inception of the Japanese and Korean developmental states, the CPC adopted a 'dual track' developmental approach that emphasised reforms of rural production on the one hand and welcomed FDIs on the other. Concomitantly, the establishment of SEZs and subsequent 'liberalization' of city-regions nationwide for foreign capital inflows emphasised how China needed to accommodate – rather than negate – transnational capital circulation if the CPC wanted to secure perpetual rule (ref.

the state as a function of global capitalism in section 2). Relative to Yeung's postulation, Chinese SOEs have not decoupled from the party-state apparatus as they partake in and drive new forms of global production over the last two decades.[61] What ensued, rather, was a three-pronged developmental approach where (1) TNCs were allowed to subcontract work with medium and small enterprises (many of which are privately owned) across China or establish joint ventures with SOEs if the aim was to produce for domestic consumption[62]; (2) financial capital was re-concentrated in central hands through a series of repressive policies, in turn enabling the state to finance SOE and local state projects in spite of perceived inefficiencies[63]; and (3) SOEs (including state-owned banks) underwent a series of corporatisation and consolidation reforms.[64] Officially termed "catching the big and releasing the small" (*zhuada fangxiao*), the latter approach strengthened the economic capacities of Chinese SOEs vis-à-vis those of other national economies, and they are now strongly encouraged to participate in the global system of capitalism through a state-driven "Go Abroad" program.[65]

Notwithstanding the CPC's Marxist rhetoric, the persistence of corporatism might partly explain the third reason why the Chinese trajectory does not fit the flying geese paradigm of developmental statism in East Asia: state-driven surplus generation and capture have been predicated on *instituted uneven development* since the Mao era. This important and still relevant precondition is diametrically opposed to the condition that engendered state developmentalism in East Asia. As Wonik Kim shows, the developmental state in northeast Asia was an outcome of a political-ideological commitment to break away from colonial-styled governance structures and lay the groundwork for socio-spatial egalitarianism:

> I argue that the developmental state fundamentally requires relative income equality as the initial socio-economic condition. Some of the Northeast Asian countries (e.g., Japan, Taiwan and Korea) undertook radical land reforms that dramatically equalised income in society. While most Southeast Asian countries inherited "extractive colonial institutions" that perpetuated income inequality, Korea and Taiwan were able to break away from the colonial legacy, which allowed the emergence of the developmental state.[66]

What emerged since the CPC took over national regulation of China was entrenched uneven development, however. Whilst the CPC inherited a mix of extractive institutions and practices from the same colonial entity – Japan – that governed Taiwan and South Korea, its commitment to egalitarianism was only the transient redistribution of agrarian land in the early 1950s. What followed thereafter was an enforced and eventually catastrophic collectivisation of means of production to facilitate state extraction of surplus value (ref. section 2). This was facilitated by the household registration (*hukou*) system of demographic regulation instituted in 1958. Modelled after the 'internal passport' system of the Soviet Union, the *hukou* system classified each Chinese citizen as either an "agricultural" (*nongmin* 农民) or "non-agricultural" resident (*fei nongmin* 非农民). A certain set of rights (and prohibitions) was associated with this classification, the primary of which was severely restricted movement between (rural) communes and/or (urban) industrial units.[67]

So all in all, it does not appear that Mao-era egalitarianism has been wound back in the name of Deng's embrace of Leninist state capitalism. To be sure, the Gini coefficient in the Mao era was very low, and the "equalizing effects" of his Cultural Revolution have left vivid rhetorical ammunition to this day for the critics of economic reform.[68] Yet, it must be recalled that China's whopping disparities and alienation between cities and villages – as well as between regions – were persistent, if not exacerbated, later in the Mao era.[69] In that sense, one has to beware of facile dichotomy. Uneven development – as a tenet of the Chinese developmental state – cannot be reduced to Deng's legacy alone: in fact we find here some overarching resonance. On the other hand, under the careful watch of the CPC, residual widespread state ownership of key enterprises and industries has stopped China from degenerating into Latin-American-style alienation of the capitalist class from the rest of society.

Keeping labour power *in place* was the primary basis of the Soviet-inspired 'price scissors' developmental approach of the Mao era. The *hukou* institution was retained to facilitate labour-intensive industrialisation in the cities as marketising reforms were set in motion. Even as individual household farming was reinstated in the early 1980s, surplus rural labour was to be denied social welfare offered to preexisting urban residents when they move to the urban-based factories. Municipal governments could therefore divert fiscal resources to capital-friendly projects and offer the 'China price' that has proven so competitive to global investors.[70] Despite attempts at reforms and widespread speculation of its abolishment, this system remains firmly in place today.[71] Ironically, then, the sustained commitment to non-egalitarian development through the *hukou* system has become a vital enabler of what are termed local corporatist or local developmental states.[72]

Enthusiasts of the "China Model" are aware of the developmental hiatus during the Mao era, to be sure, and most of them flatly reject Mao's economic legacy. By contrast, they point out that the Chinese trajectory has one compelling feature that is superior to the other East Asian developmental states; one that might usher China into the technological frontier, help it become globally more competitive and attain high income in due course: namely, greater receptivity to foreign direct investment (FDI). Remarkably, in 2014, China has overtaken the US to become the largest destination of FDI in the world.[73]

Attitudes to FDI in post-war Japan, South Korea and even Taiwan could arguably not be more different. As Bytheway has recently shown, in fact, there has been less FDI coming into Japan in relative terms in the post-war years that during the pre-war era.[74] Notably, even between the 1860s and 1930s Japan mainly relied on loans and bond issuance in overseas securities markets to raise much needed capital rather than lure in foreign investors and foreign entrepreneurs per se. Foreign borrowing thus financed the establishment of infrastructure in Japan's largest cities, the nationalisation of railways, and the rapid electrification of Japanese industry in the 1920s. To this day, there are, in Japan, relatively few local-foreign joint ventures; foreign shareholders or directors in the Japanese corporate world are a fairly rare sight – foreign investment and ownership as a whole, one might observe, is discouraged.

From the foregoing discussion, it is apparent that the developmental experience of China was and remains distinct in some important ways from those of other East Asian developmental states. In spite of the many policy similarities, underpinning market-oriented reforms in post-Mao China is a *sustained preference* on the part of the CPC for strong control over the means and relations of production. It would be problematic, as a growing literature has done, to assume China can *already* be categorised as a developmental state.[75] Rather, as introduced in Chapter 1, the developmental process in post-Mao China has been one of selective adaptation. In order to reinstate and develop Leninistic state capitalism as discussed in section 2, one aspect borrowed from the East Asian experience was financial repression.

Concrete similarity: financial repression as/for developmentalism

Arguably the most contentious dimension of the East Asian developmental state trajectory in the twentieth century, at least in the eyes of economists of rigid neoclassical persuasion, is "financial repression". What the term broadly conveys is the notion that banks in Japan, Korea and Taiwan throughout the post-war era have, at the behest of government, cheapened credit to a select group of hand-picked industrial export-geared firms at the expense of captive 'mom-and-pop' savers. That the overall private saving rate in East Asia remained high is nevertheless usually attributed to the government depriving individuals from alternative, more remunerative "financial instruments". Moreover, in China, the banking system is still largely state-owned, thus the case for "repression" in the domestic economy is, in neoclassical parlance, even more severe. Indeed, pernicious credit discrimination between state-favoured large firms and bottom-up entrepreneurs has become the bugbear of not just foreign analysts like Lardy[76] but also China's own neoclassical minded economists.[77]

And yet recent, partly dissenting studies like that of Eun Young Oh offer a more nuanced picture. In Oh's view, South Korea's remarkable economic growth in the 1980s was in no small measure a product of ". . . government intervention such as channelling resources in selected industrial sectors which can significantly increase the efficiency of credit allocation".[78] Oh further alludes to the fact that "financial repression" East Asian style can assist other emerging economies. Huang and Wang similarly opine that in a transitional, largely rural setting, Chinese economic planners were vindicated in instituting "financial repression", at least until the 2000s. They find circumstantial evidence to support the case that "repressive" policies on balance helped Chinese economic growth overall, but concludes that the pace of financial-market reform has since fallen behind and does no longer suit the re-vamped Chines economy.[79]

A study of the factors behind Japan's economic malaise since the "Lost Decade" of the 1990s is beset by much the same contention. On the one extreme, influential accounts such as *Japan: the System that Soured* by Richard Katz posited in the late 1990s that the Japanese economy is still heavily regulated as if it was still in a catch-up mode. Keeping a developmental state mindset, the gerrymandered Japanese political establishment no longer promotes industrial export-geared "winners" and full employment. Rather, in Katz' view, it shields inefficient domestic-market-geared "losers" (particularly well-connected property developers) from competition at home and from cheaper imports, whilst letting them move jobs to invest more and more overseas. The way this is done, according to Katz, is through bank excessive cross-shareholding in these 'loser' firms (the notorious *keirestu* link); on the one hand, and by all-too-cosy relations between government bureaucrats and the banks. At heart then is "financial repression" again: banks "too big and powerful" directing cheaper capital to cronies, and paying little to no interest to small-time depositors.[80]

But Katz's conventional neoclassical storyline has since been challenged. To be sure, in China that explanation has never fully sunk in. Instead, as discussed in Chapter 3, commentators on the other extreme believe it was the US that craftily foisted the "Lost Decade" on the Japanese economy through the 1985 Plaza Accord because of geopolitical concern for American global primacy if the Japanese economy continued to grow. Much more importantly, more recent Western economic accounts, like that of Richard Grossman's, suggest that, far from a case of government over-regulation, the roots of Japan's "Lost Decade" can actually be traced back to excessive financial *de*regulation in the early 1980s, allowing *keirestu* (diversified bank-centred conglomerates) to float corporate debt through bond issuance. Since Japan's saving rate did not diminish as a result, and since export-geared *keiretsu* were less in need of bank credit, Japanese banks were left with excess capital to lend out. That "easy credit" was channelled to realty, resulting in a pernicious asset bubble not unlike the one afflicting China in the late 2000s.[81]

And if Grossman by and large de-emphasises the economic and historical significance of the Plaza Accord, political scientist Leonard Schoppa's earlier account does not.[82] Somewhat in contrast to Katz, Schoppa also notes that American trade negotiators did manage to open up the Japanese domestic market to some extent in the face of *keiretsu* resistance – the Toys 'R' Us foray into the Japanese fragmented retail sector as early as 1991 being an obvious case in point. Moreover, Schoppa recounts how the Bush Sr. administration was fervently guided by neoclassical doctrine: its economists believed for example in the saving–investment principle, which heterodox economists like Ronald McKinnon reject.[83] As a result, they pressured Japan – partly successfully from 1994 onwards – to increase government spending on infrastructure, anticipating wrongly that such increase would narrow down America's trade deficit with Japan.

Earlier, when President Regan was in office, he was disinclined to intervene in trade relations with Japan out of a similar neoclassical-cum-neoliberal penchant. However, concerns that anti-Japanese sentiments in Congress might boil over if the deficit persisted led the Reagan second-term administration to reluctantly intervene on the cross-rates. The 1985 Plaza Accord was conceived as a result. Within one year, the US$ was made to lose 1/3 of its value against the Japanese yen. Yet, astonishingly, America's trade deficit remained at record-high levels, even afterward.[84] Hence, the Bush Sr. administration resorted to Japanese public spending later, instead of just pressure on Japan to revalue the yen.

Schoppa alludes to the fact that it was, in the main, the 1985 Plaza Accord that triggered recession in Japan, and at the same time it did not solve America's deficit problem. Stronger yen brought about flagging consumption and made imported raw materials, which the Japanese industry so badly needed, much dearer. However, in Schoppa's judgement, the sequence of events between 1985–1987 was utterly unplanned. What made the recession turn into over two decades of near-zero or sub-zero growth was the Bank of Japan's (BoJ) failure to intervene immediately to curb the property and asset bubble on the one hand, and prop up private consumption on the other. The BoJ lowered interest rates to stimulate the economy only in 1987, but they left it unchanged for two years thereafter – so hot money was continuing to pour into the stock exchange. The high-yen doldrums (*endaka fukyo*) finally came unstuck when the Tokyo stock exchange collapsed in December 1989. As mentioned earlier, the Japanese government tried – in line with advice from the Bush Sr. administration – to offset the recession by massively increasing spending on new infrastructure. Yet, spending did not take off until 1994: it did not whittle down the trade deficit with the US much but, on the other hand, landed the Japanese government into the red.[85] By the 2010s, the Japanese ratio of public debt to GDP has become the highest in the developed world.[86]

Constraining – and driving? – global neoliberalization

If the experiences of the East Asian developmental states provide one key reference point for the CPC, it is the increasing difficulty of navigating contradictions between US global-leadership acceptance, authoritarianism coupled with free-wheeling entrepreneurship ethos at home and heavy public indebtedness. This has specific implications for the Leninist state capitalism the CPC is trying to cultivate in the post-Mao era (ref. section 2). Whilst other facets of the Chinese economic miracle might already bear similarity to Japan, South Korea and Taiwan in terms of technological catch up and industrial and infrastructural upgrade – the latter high-income developmental states, unlike low-income China, all eventually softened up politically by embracing social welfare to a much greater extent and permitting more democratic participation in politics.[87] Will the Chinese variant of the so-called East Asian developmental state model therefore chart a different path? And if so, what would be the balance between individual freedoms, welfare, employability and free marketising?

For now, most independent observers suggest China has not internalised neo-liberalism into economic planning, even though it has been a great beneficiary of economic globalisation. Leong Liew came to the conclusion that the institutional legacy of socialism in China was still heavily tempering infatuation with small government ideology.[88] Fulong Wu similarly concluded his state-of-the-field survey with the prognosis that it would be "controversial" to dub contemporary China "neo-liberal".[89] Instead, China "selectively adapted neoliberalism under the political-economic context of strong state control". To be sure, China's New Left critics, such as Wang Hui, indict the last three decades of reforms as a "neoliberal" dismantlement of Mao-era welfare provision.[90] The "neoliberal" label here seem misguided, however, as it was mostly urban dwellers protected by *hukou* barriers and working for SOEs that enjoyed *danwei* free education, healthcare and housing in the Mao era. Life expectancy and literacy rose nationally under Mao, but peasants largely had to fend for themselves (no state pension) and pay tax to subsidise megalomaniac industrial projects in the urban sector.[91] And notwithstanding relaxed regulations on rural-urban migration, smallholding farmers continue to make up a much larger share of the adult workforce in China than in Japan, South Korea, Taiwan, let alone the cities of Singapore or Hong Kong. Nevertheless, in the context of assessing the impact of neoliberalism strictly in the urban economy, an equally critical measure would be the ratio of state-owned assets to GDP.

Here, the preponderance of China's SOEs in the economy, even after Zhu Rongji's downsizing of the 1990s, militates towards pigeonholing the country as an antidote of neoliberalism.[92] China is clearly in the lead here, followed with large margin by India, Russia and Brazil. Nowhere to be seen in this category are the earlier, high-income East Asian developmental miracles where manufacturing, if not all utilities, are overwhelmingly in private rather than government hands. To be sure, Korea's *chaebol* conglomerates are run more along family lines than Japan's *keiretsu* or Taiwan's business groups, yet in the latter two countries, the government is mostly known to spin off successful public R&D ventures rather than keeping it to themselves.[93] The vitality of government-private partnerships, and their net positive impact on society as a whole, has been critical to understanding the East Asian developmental boilerplate, as opposed to the neoliberal template espoused by the Washington Consensus. Controversially, the East Asian formula is often reduced to holding down labour costs by oppression or co-optation of docile labour unions by way of nurturing globally competitive firms.

However, there is more to the story than meets the eye: in fact, a comparison between the Southeast Asian variant of the developmental state (particularly Malaysia, Indonesia, Philippines, and Thailand) and those in North Asia (particularly Japan, Korea, Taiwan) suggests economic growth in the long run might actually depend on redistribution of rural land early on[94]; income increases across the board as firms globalise later on, as well as merit-based recruitment into the government bureaucracy as a means of offsetting clientelism. The Taiwanese experience is particularly striking as an antidote to neoliberal textbooks, as Taiwan not only reconciled land reform-cum-equality with growth; in fact, income inequality in Taiwan diminished markedly from the 1950s to the early 1980s as the country industrialised and GDP figures rapidly shot up.[95]

At the same time, income growth and redistribution might have been prodded to a greater extent by Cold War geopolitical insecurities that were present in East Asia.[96] Yusuf Shahid has, for example, observed that the decision to diversify into heavy and chemical industries in which Korea had no comparative advantage in the early 1970s was taken by President Park Chung Hee *not necessarily* as a result of far-sighted industrial grand design; rather it was "partly out of a belief in the primacy of steel and machinery producing industries, and partly in response to the American decision to taper their defence commitments in East Asia and require their allies to shoulder more of the burden of defence".[97]

The idea that government re-distributional designs explain East Asian economic success, at least in part, is of course assailed by observers of neoliberal persuasion. Their *cause célèbre* is the former Crown Colony of Hong Kong, often portrayed historically as the epitome of ultra-urban 'lean government', low taxation and laissez-faire attitude. To be sure, taxation and welfare spending in Hong Kong are still very *low* by Western standards, and its rural population has long vanished. However, what is often airbrushed from historical surveys is the fact that a merit-based, professional civil service wielded much executive power there. Moreover, under the British, the local government, in effect, nationalised all *land*, and as of the 1950s started providing cheap public housing to its residents. By the 1970s, under Governor Murray MacLehose, the scale of public housing provision was extended on a much larger scale than the one pursued in post-war Britain itself. Yet, the late 1970s also saw Hong Kong economic growth rates soar, as the colony turned into a financial hub and started benefiting from openness on the Mainland.[98] As indicated earlier, much the same debunking of neoliberal convictions can apply to Singapore: after all, it was not purely laissez faire policies that impressed Deng Xiaoping there in 1979 but also Lee Kuan Yew's heady public housing scheme.

***

Indeed, the 'freedom' associated with neoliberal reasoning is underpinned in practice by *proactive* state intervention. Even democratisation, widely heralded as the corollary of free markets, does not guarantee social equity. Rather, democratic regimes are witnessing growing levels of inequality as a consequence of economic deregulation. As Niall Ferguson concedes, as late as the 18th century, even the minimalist British "night watchman" state had in fact to rely on government monopolies and postal services to partly defray empire-building alongside excise and customs.[99] Similarly, Paul Bairoch famously described America's economic path to economic might, before its later 20th century association with neoliberalism, as one based on state planning, mercantilism and "protectionism".[100] And Jamie Peck offers an interesting argument that is helpful for understanding the CPC's engagement with neoliberal logics:

> Neoliberalism . . . has only ever existed in "impure" form, indeed *can* only exist in messy hybrids. Its utopian vision of a free society and free economy is ultimately unattainable. Yet the pristine clarity of its ideological apparition, the *free market*, coupled with the endless frustrations borne of the inevitable failure to arrive at this elusive destination, nevertheless confer a significant degree of forward momentum on the neoliberal project. Ironically, neoliberalism possesses a progressive, forward-leaning dynamic by virtue of the very *unattainability* of its idealized destination.[101]

Whether China, being much more populous and bigger in size, faced the same early Cold War economic-reform stimulus as Japan, South Korea or Taiwan is a moot point. Whilst the latter were palpably threatened by China in the 1950s, Mao Zedong had his own insecurities arising from the Korea War and Stalin's paternalistic attitude. It is often observed in this context that Japan, South Korea and Taiwan all enacted re-distributional rural land reform under American auspices in the 1950s to mitigate peasant militancy and immiseration of the kind that Westerners attributed to the rise of the CPC. Indeed, the CPC itself staked its claim to authority on the rural land reform it carried out in North China whilst still in the underground. After it came to power in 1949, the CPC continued with a more moderate form of land reform, improving the plight of millions of smallholders and tenant tillers, but often executing wealthy land owners. In the early 1960s, however, smallholding was undone by the collectivisation of land during the Great Leap Forward, hence the break from the East Asian developmental mode until Deng Xiaoping re-took the reins in 1979 to re-enshrine "market gardening".[102]

Beyond East Asia

It is important to note that proponents of the China Model within China do not – for political reasons – emphatically celebrate previous East Asian developmental miracles. Rather, they tend to point to Latin America's protracted economic ailments as proof of the inadequacies of the "Washington Consensus". India is much poorer and harder to pigeonhole due to its socialist legacy and large state-owned sector. Thus, in the Chinese narrative, the introduction of IMF and World Bank financial deregulation prescripts into Latin America in the 1990s triggered a prolonged phase of continued economic and social crises, cannily paralleling the failures of "shock therapy" following the disintegration of communist regimes in Eastern Europe. By contrast, China is seen to have averted the worst of the 1997 Asian Financial Crisis, as well as the 2008 Global Financial Crisis, precisely due to its defying of IMF and World Bank philosophy, and protecting the cardinal role of the state in the economy: particularly tight state domination of transport, telecommunication, utilities and the banking sector. Unlike Latin America, the Chinese state is seen to promote full employment through export discipline rather than import substitution.[103]

From a broader East Asian perspective, some wry irony can be found in these observations since, as late as 1980, South Korea looked up to Brazil as a model for industrialisation promotion, even though Brazilian society was, and still is, a much less equal society: both countries were under authoritarian rule at the time. Etzkowitz and Brisolla suggest South Korean economic growth fast outpaced Brazil's precisely because it had built on the gains of re-distributional land reform, which saw a transition to garden farming, whereas in Brazil the rural sector remains dominated by inefficient *latifundia* and an impoverished landless underclass.[104] Critically, the difference between Latin America as a whole and Japan or South Korea in the 1960s–1970s was the fact that the latter countries employed tariffs to shield industries with export potential and, at the same time, precluded foreign ownership of domestically geared service and manufacturing firms. China proved more open to foreign investment in the 1990s, but there too – unlike Latin America –TNCs were largely prevented from dominating domestically geared key firms through joint ventures. In other words, TNCs in China were lured to set up exporting plants, whilst in Latin America they were producing capital-intensive, expensive goods for the urban wealthy – goods they did not allow to be sold globally.[105]

To be sure, there was much more foreign capital readily available for investment in Brazil in the 1950s, but foreign investment discouraged on balance the growth of an export industry in favour of mineral exploitation and food commodities. Rather, foreign ownership translated by the 1970s into import substitution through the erection of high tariff barriers, where TNCs in effect produced inferior good for captive local markets. In Korea, by contrast, the dearth of foreign capital honed export discipline. However, in fairness to the IMF, it has to be recalled – as Bulmer-Thomas reminds us – that IMF favoured export-led growth rather than import substitution in the 1980s by way of solving Latin American chronic balance of payment deficit and indebtedness to North American banks.[106] However, for the most part, export-led growth strategies favoured – through promotion of currency exchange deregulation – agricultural commodities in the absence of capital controls of the kind in place in East Asia at the time. In other words, financial deregulation from the 1970s onwards "condemned" much of Latin America to specialise in non-industrial goods. At much the same decade in fact, South Korea switched *en masse* from policy favouring heavy industry to policy favouring automotive and electronic consumer goods for export markets.

South Koreans looked up to Brazil earlier in the 1960s, when Korean-made cars had not yet debuted in developed-world markets. Yet, at the time, it was hard to fathom the great weakness of Brazil's famous auto industry: first, its profitability and reputation were contingent not just on the MNCs that manufactured them with heavily guarded foreign technology but perhaps more on the input price of parts manufactured by state-owned plants. The industry was otherwise totally geared inward, like the USSR car industry: Brazilian-made cars were rarely exported, and thus, they increasingly lost global competitive edge, protected by high tariffs on the part of government, on the one hand, and by MNC restrictive policy in home developed markets on the other hand. To make matters worse, increasingly unequal income distribution in Brazil from 1970s onward greatly narrowed the domestic market because relatively few could afford cars.[107]

***

In the final analysis, as alluded earlier, the post-war catch up and democratisation story in the developing world cannot be told without reference to rural immiseration as well as wealth and education inequality alongside disparate industrial export-promotion policy mixes. To be sure, Chinese average rice yield per hectare is for example doubly higher than in India not just due to the human factor or land reform: precipitation is China is more evenly spread throughout the year allowing for multiple cropping. However, China's more extensive and deeper-seated roll-out of land redistribution in the early 1950s might well explain peasants' ability to overcome the havoc of forced industrialisation and collectivisation in the late

1950s. To this day, Chinese peasants save more on average and use the proceeds towards investment in fertilisers to a greater extent than their Indian peers. In that sense, we have an apt reminder that the East Asian developmental states can be seen as even less inclined towards neoliberalism in the rural sector, the initial mainspring of growth in the 1950s. And as Pranab Bardhan cogently laments, it is a bewildering fact that in democratic India – what with its independent judiciary – effective rural tenancy and landlessness partly through dispossession and indebtedness is much higher than in China even though it is nominally outlawed.[108]

Arguably, it is relative rural equality in the 1950s that explains how China – in the words of Brandt, Ma and Rawski – "an industrial pigmy" in the early twentieth century, could become, six decades later, the unrivalled "factory of the world".[109] Much the same can be said about Japanese (and South Korean) social stability since the 1950s, based as it has been even to a greater extent on rural land reform and pork barrelling. If anything, it is likely that China's rural sector will be further protected as it diminishes in size to gradually match Japan and South Korea's level of urbanisation.

In contrast to Japan and South Korea, however, relatively few private-owned Chinese firms have entered the Fortune 500 list, whilst more and more SOEs do. For now, it is begrudgingly acknowledged that some SOEs have turned a corner becoming profitable rather than net drain on rural and urban taxpayers. However, profitability is often ascribed by neoliberal-minded scholars to monopolistic posturing rather than to an emerging export edge when it comes to Chinese SOEs, or hybrid firms such as Haier.[110] If one of these SOEs, like for example globally powerful telcon giant Huawei, could one day catch up with the technological frontier, – chipping away at Apple iPhone sales – not just consumers will be in for a surprise neoliberal theoreticians may have to re-write many of their textbooks.

Conclusion

Attributing high-speed GDP growth and overall socioeconomic development in China to developmental statism and/or neoliberalism is inherently fraught with difficulties. As discussed in section 2, the question for China is one of a dynamic experimentation in state capitalism. This chapter does not posit state capitalism as a separate mode of production from liberal or 'free market' capitalism. State capitalism in China has become a variant of capitalism not dissimilar to the one emerging when wealthier states are faced with severe crisis, whether such crisis takes a primarily economic form (such as in Western countries in the 1930s or today) or a primarily political form (such as in Russia in the 1920s following the revolution and the Bolsheviks' consolidation of all political and economic power there, or in China since the CPC's takeover of power in 1949).

State capitalism itself can oscillate between two extremes in real terms: the Western, Keynesian, 'mixed economy' form, or the Stalinist form, with almost complete state ownership of the economy. Contemporary China does not fit squarely with either of these two models, however. During the early Mao era, the CPC embraced the Stalinist model and consequently developed a larger share of economic ownership relative to the former Soviet bloc, India, Brazil, Japan, Taiwan or South Korea. The CPC was therefore in a strong position to negotiate with foreign powers and capital after Deng launched reforms in 1978. This said, the lasting legacy of the Deng administration was a commitment to *coexist* with a quasi-private market economy (an integral approach of Lenin's NEP). This not only precluded the destabilising effect of the 'second economy', or informal economy, on the planned system of the Soviet bloc after Stalin's death in 1953, it enabled the state-owned economic structure to reconfigure itself. Chinese SOEs have consequently become more attuned to international-level practices (including a commitment to profitability) and in many cases have become TNCs in their own right.[111] This does not mean, however, that China is following the trajectory of other East Asian developmental states.

Whilst there appear to be some similarities in terms of China's early rural land reform, export orientation, and its current preference for 'financial repression' – the CPC's direct economic involvement in the large state-owned sector and its spatially and socially uneven development pattern indicate it has not yet "become" a full developmental state. By the same token, export orientation may explain why some analysts have mischaracterised China as oriented towards Western-styled neoliberalism. *Contra* Knight, the term "become" presupposes an ideal-typical entity known as a developmental state and that it is possible to qualify as such insofar as specific objectives are met (ref. section 3).[112] Knight focuses specifically on post-Mao policies and developments on the premise that state-driven intervention to derive rapid economic growth qualifies China as a developmental state. Rather, China's overall trajectory is characterised by a re-adaptation of Lenin's NEP on the one hand and creative lesson drawing and policy transfers from other countries on the other hand. The overarching goal, it appears, is to secure freedom to engage the global system of capitalism whilst keeping intact its primary domestic focus of state-led development. This in itself reflects a *paradoxical* relationship with neoliberal logics.

As will be elaborated in the conclusion of this book, we believe the CPC has and will continue to differentiate itself developmentally and ideationally from neoliberalism whilst *simultaneously* championing global-level free trade. From the global vantage point, the great bulk of historical evidence suggests no predominantly rural late-comer can industrialise to reach developed-world status through neoliberal policy: shrinking government size, floating currency exchange rate, full privatisation, overweening respect for intellectual property rights, tariff elimination, etc.[113] And as Peter H. Lindert observes, it appears that the CPC is increasingly impelled to commit more to social welfare in order to smooth over social unrest à la the Japanese approach in the 1950s.[114]

Notes

1 Data adapted from IMF World Economic Outlook Database, available at www.imf.org/external/pubs/ft/weo/2016/01/weodata/index.aspx; for a broader discussion of this catch-up process, see e.g., Kroeber (2016), pp. 9–11.

2 For a cogent, up-to-date overview of the literature on the "development of developmental states" see Hua (2014), Introduction.
3 *Wall Street Journal*, 29 February 2008.
4 Arrighi (2007); Naughton (2010); Breslin (2011); Bell (2015); cf. Perkins (2013).
5 Baek (2005); Boltho and Weber (2009).
6 *Jacobin* (2015).
7 Harvey (2005a); see also, Wang (2009).
8 Hsu (2016); Wan (2014), pp. 73–84.
9 For an excellent discussion see Peck and Theodore (2007); Peck and Zhang (2013).
10 Holloway (1994), p. 32.
11 Massey (1984); Peck (2002); Brenner (2004).
12 Harvey (2005a), p. 81.
13 Glassman (1999), p. 673.
14 Glassman (2004), p. 41.
15 Glassman (2004), p. 41.
16 Ref. Desai (2013); cf. Harvey (1985); Jessop (2015).
17 The Common Program was the first guiding list of governance principles for CPC leaders in the newly-established China. It would be replaced by Mao's "General Line for Socialist Transformation" in 1953.
18 Mao (1953) 'On State Capitalism', translated by The Maoist Documentation Project. Available here: www.marxists.org/reference/archive/mao/selected-works/volume-5/mswv5_30.htm
19 Buick and Crump (1986); Desai (2004), pp. 135–136.
20 Ball (1990).
21 Lenin (1966), p. 64.
22 Kuromiya (1990); Hughes (1998); Viola (2007).
23 Li (2006).
24 Li (2006), p. 3.
25 Deng Zihui (2006), pp. 182–185; authors' translation.
26 No similar equation – at least not in the positive sense – was made in reference to the "de-Stalinization" policies implemented by Stalin's successor, Nikita Khruschev. Khruschev, as Pantsov and Levine (2012) explain with great detail, was repeatedly denigrated by Mao as an ideological revisionist. During the Cultural Revolution in the mid- to late-1960s, Mao labeled the putatively pro-market Liu Shaoqi and Deng Xiaoping respectively as "China's No. 1 and No. 2 Khruschevs". This underscores the importance of Stalinism in China's developmental trajectory, the legacy of which is still very evident today.
27 Cf. Harvey (2005b).
28 Bramall (2004).
29 Howe (1973).
30 Mao (1958); translated by The Maoist Documentation Project. Available at: www.marxists.org/reference/archive/mao/selected-works/volume-8/mswv8_65.htm
31 Schram (1971); Walder (2015); Dikötter (2016); Liu (2016).
32 Mao (1977a), pp. 144–145.
33 Schurmann (1964), p. 65.
34 Deng (1993), p. 139; authors' translation.
35 Pantsov and Levine (2015), pp. 7, 38, 211–218, 373; Vogel (2011), pp. 24–26.
36 As Vogel (2011, pp. 290–291) perceptively notes, before Deng's visit, Singapore had routinely been described as a running dog of American imperialism in the PRC press. After his visit, the press started casting Singapore as an impressive hub of economic modernisation that was well worth studying. Since he had been informed by tendentious local left-wing informers, Deng expected throngs of Singaporeans to greet him upon arrival. When that did not happen, and following meetings with the thoroughly-Anglicised Lee Kuan Yew – he realised Singaporean society had, albeit majority

ethnic Chinese, become much more self-determined and free-wheeling than he had imagined.

37 Whyte (2010).
38 Johnson (1982).
39 See, for instance, Öniş (1991); Grabowski (1994); Johnson (1995); Huff *et al* (2001); for an excellent definitional review, see Stubbs (2009).
40 Vogel (1981).
41 For an overview, see Kasahara (2013).
42 Evans (1995), p. 12.
43 Huff (1995); Amsden (1992); Wade (2003); Greene (2009).
44 Johnson (1988).
45 Douglass (1994); Aoki *et al* (1997); Doner *et al* (2005).
46 Breslin (1996); Baek (2005); Boltho and Weber (2009); Beeson (2009).
47 Johnson (1982); Evans (1995).
48 See Glassman (1999); Beeson and Islam (2005).
49 Kim (1999), p. 441; see also Minns (2001); Park (2010); Yusuf (2014).
50 Honda (2004); Hook and Hiroko (2007).
51 Pekkanen (2004).
52 Shibata (2008).
53 Beeson (2009), p. 20.
54 See e.g., Thurbon (2016).
55 Chu (2016).
56 Yeung (2014), p. 70.
57 Huang (2008); Lin (2011); Coase and Wang (2012).
58 Cf. Bremmer (2010).
59 Zweig (2001); cf. Eaton (2016); Wade (2003), for South Korean and Taiwanese society.
60 Naughton (2007), pp. 271–293.
61 Yeung (2014).
62 Yang (2014).
63 Shih (2008); Huang and Wang (2011); Johansson (2012).
64 Aivazian *et al* (2005); Chiu and Lewis (2006).
65 Ref. Lim (2010); Nolan (2012); Kowalski *et al* (2013).
66 Kim (2009), p. 383.
67 For a historical overview, see Cheng and Selden (1994); Chan (2009).
68 See e.g., Wang (2011).
69 Whyte (2012); Dikötter (2016); Lim (2017)
70 Ref. Harney (2009).
71 Chan and Buckingham (2008); Lim (2014).
72 See e.g., Oi (1992); Zhu (2004).
73 Chen (2011).
74 Bytheway (2014).
75 See, e.g., Wong (2004); Beeson (2009); Chen and Lees (2016); So (2016).
76 Lardy (2008).
77 The best-known Chinese economists who have raised criticism in that vein include Zhang Weiying, Wu Jinglian and Mao Yushi. Proponents of state-led banking include the new left, neo-Maoists and Hu Angang. See e.g., *China 3.0* edited by Mark Leonard, published online 2012 by European Council on Foreign Relations. www.ecfr.eu/page/-/ECFR66_CHINA_30_final.pdf
78 Oh (2011), p. 75.
79 Huang and Wang (2011).
80 Katz (1998), mainly Chapter 14.
81 Grossman (2010), pp. 276–281.
82 Schoppa (1997).

83 McKinnon (2013), chapters 6 to 8.
84 Schoppa (1997), pp. 66–67, 81 and 118–120.
85 Schoppa (1997).
86 CIA World Factbook (2016).
87 Kim (1997); Hu (2005); Wong (2006); Morley (2015).
88 Liew (2005).
89 Wu (2010), p. 624.
90 Wang (2011).
91 Friedman *et al* (1993).
92 Kowalski *et al* (2013).
93 Colpan *et al* (2010).
94 Studwell (2013).
95 Booth (2007).
96 Wade (1990); Doner *et al* (2005).
97 Yusuf (2014), p. 92.
98 Schenk (2002), pp. 14 & 135; Carroll (2007), pp. 145–162; Tsang (2007), pp. 199 & 205.
99 Ferguson (2001), p. 90.
100 Bairoch (1993).
101 Peck (2010), p. 7, emphases in the original text.
102 Studwell (2013).
103 *Qiushi* (2014).
104 Etzkowitz and Brisolla (1999); see also Bulmer-Thomas (2003); Studwell (2013).
105 Bulmer-Thomas (2003), pp. 268–269.
106 Bulmer-Thomas (2003), pp. 270–273.
107 Bulmer-Thomas (2003), pp. 274–275; see also Haber (2006).
108 Bardhan (2012), pp. 49–50.
109 Brandt *et al* (2016).
110 For an excellent discussion of the pertinent literature, see Lardy (2014).
111 Grossman (1977, 1998); Sampson (1987).
112 Knight (2014).
113 Chang (2002).
114 Lindert (2004), p. 221.

7 Conclusions

In as much as the 'China Model' has penetrated political, policymaking and popular lexicon, it remains vague to many others observers in theory and practice. The theoretical purview – or, by association, the limits – of this 'model' inevitably relies at times on historical abstraction. In this book, we have tried to offer a fresher understanding of the model going much further back in time than is usually the case in the pertinent literature. In Chapter 2, we explored, for example, the degree to which China's exceedingly complex premodern past may be relevant to the country's future. Equally importantly, we have subsequently construed China's post-1949 trajectory as a whole in non-dichotomous terms. That is to say, whilst acknowledging the many earth-shattering departures and life-changing innovations of the Deng era, we also sought out those facets of the earlier Mao era that have partly endured and might help explain the post-1978 trajectory, not just those which obviously set China back economically.

The framing of China as an integrated entity vis-à-vis other political economies is attractive, because it provides a simplified version of economic growth and political governance. The issue with this approach lies in essentialising China's developmental *a priori*; it risks portraying a preexisting and seemingly eternal kernel around and above which new developments occur. This book is a critical appraisal of this portrayal. In that spirit, we have sought not just Chinese distinctness but also tried hard to underscore throughout the ways and means by which China is in fact a variant of earlier East Asian developmental successes. To that end, we have critiqued scholarship published in both the West and in China itself, and we did not shy away from the realm of self-perception and wishful thinking in either setting.

On its own, we have argued, China is, at present, hardly an attractive or sufficiently differentiated alternative to the US (neo)liberal world order beyond some quarters of the developing word. Neither is it likely to try exporting its model full-throttle any time soon – both because of geo-politics and because of its narrative of non-interventionism. Consequently, a convergence of power and interests between the anti-globalisation New Left in the West and Chinese officialdom seems unlikely for now.

Rather, the question we have critically assigned ourselves is whether or not the broader post-war East Asian economic success story – currently led and to some extent redefined by China – might not be seen as a more compelling global alternative to neoliberalism.[1] After all, as we mention right at the outset of this book, Japan was beginning to see itself as such alternative as recently as the 1980s.

Against this backdrop, three aspects of the 'China Model' and its apparent challenge to global neoliberal hegemony have been presented in the foregoing chapters. The notion of "apparent" cannot be overemphasised: these three aspects demonstrate how concrete aspects of Chinese political-economic evolution coexist with, if not also constitute, global neoliberalism. The Chinese developmental experience is therefore more accurately a fluid and increasingly open process, rather than an expression of historical exceptionalism.

On the one hand, we argue that the Chinese variant of the East Asian developmental state, because it is much more geared towards state ownership at the technological frontier, is more of an antidote to neoliberal thought. On the other hand, China has in many ways been a paradise for MNCs and foreign investors until Xi Jinping's ascent. Reform of China's mammoth SOEs has, over the past two decades, drawn on neoliberal precepts, even if wholesale privatisation was and remains off the agenda. Many SOEs have been publicly listed and broken up into competing units or corporatised in other ways, and the share of the sector as a whole in urban employment has rapidly shrunk. Whilst not bank-centred like Japan's *keiretsu* or family-run like South Korea's *chaebol*, Chinese SOEs are closer to the Anglo-American ideal corporate model in one sense: they are highly specialised.

Focusing on Chinese elite perceptions of both America and their own history, the book gauged the extent to which China might opt to counteract or unseat the US-led neoliberal world order both rhetorically and concretely. Naturally, one cannot know for sure whether rhetoric – or for that matter, which strain of rhetoric – will translate into foreign policy. As the greatest beneficiary of globalisation over the past four decades, China does not seem, at present, in any rush to construct an alternative regulatory architecture. It is nevertheless possible to already observe the budding of what we have called here 'China's aspirational narrative of global leadership'. That narrative has many shades. In Chapter 3, we have explained, for example, that policies implemented at the highest levels of the CPC are at times shaped by inconsistent historical imageries, such as those setting Zheng Bijian apart from Wang Huning. Neither is this newly Confucian-hued narrative always congruent with earlier Mao-era claims to global leadership.

Lower down the regulatory structure, cadres often hold differing views of developmental approaches relative to those held by the senior echelon, as shown by the variegated and relatively unsuccessful attempts at policy transfers from Singapore (Chapter 4). China's inability or reluctance to foster an independent judiciary to the extent one exists in Singapore was shown to be a watershed division of the two societies, even if they have been ruled by the same party (PAP and the CPC) since independence. Singapore's successful mass public housing programme is, on the other hand, widely admired by CPC officialdom. To be sure, subsidised urban public housing in China had also existed on a large scale until *de facto* privatisation in 2003.[2] Even Hong Kong – otherwise known as the epitome of small government – took off as a financial hub in the 1980s only after it introduced cheap public housing on a large scale over the previous decade. Bo Xilai's policies in Chongqing, the emergence of China's New Confucian narrative stressing social justice and newly relaxed guidelines regarding population mobility (*hukou*) might signal that Beijing is headed in similar direction and further away from neoliberal thinking.

The willingness on the part of the Chinese central government to engage in lesson drawing and policy transfers from a host of other countries – explicitly Singapore, and less overtly Japan, South Korea and Taiwan – does not necessarily reflect the lack of a coherent planning agenda within the context of global economic integration. Instead, as we have shown in Chapters 5 and 6, policy experimentation, a degree of market fragmentation and even inter-provincial competition were central to Deng's reform thought. Arguably, the origins of uneven development can be traced even further back in time to Mao's 'chessboard' approach to national development, his Third Front campaign of industrial relocation, and the *hukou* walls he built between villagers and urbanites, which were partly inspired, in turn, by Soviet barriers to its own population mobility.[3] Yet, although China held the Soviet Union as a developmental blueprint until the mid-1950s, it remained a much more decentralised (and rural) economy than the former's, even at the height of Mao's power, and this is no accident of history or purely the result of natural endowment.

Of course, local policy experimentation attending national best-practice is not unique to China. Many countries launch plans on a tentative basis, with the expectation of benefiting from engaging the global economy whilst circumventing crisis scenarios.[4] What is arguably unique to the Chinese – and, on a smaller scale, Vietnamese – context is the pursuit of 'state capitalism'. The CPC, in other words, insists on retaining a unitary and hierarchical political structure, even as it opens up more economic domains for engagement with transnational capital. This means that central control over subnational activities remains a key regulatory aspect, which justifies, in turn, regular "macro-level adjustments" (*hongguan tiaokong*) to local initiatives.

The internal differences in developmental approaches underscore how the China Model is in actuality fragmented by seemingly divergent pathways. As Chapter 5 showed, policies in Chongqing and Guangdong were not just vastly different in and of themselves; they were responses to strategies and initiatives introduced much earlier at varying spatial scales. Guangdong benefited from the macro-level privileging of the coastal seaboard; it was also the site of longer-standing interactions with Hong Kong during the Mao era, which provided an important first-mover advantage. Chongqing, on the other hand, has been overlooked ever since Mao Zedong's 'Third Front' campaign came to an end.

The new policies that jumpstarted growth were in part an outcome of the shift towards an incentive-based political appraisal system, which encouraged local officials to take risks in developmental programs, and in part, because the inequality generated by coastal bias provided the requisite context for more "harmonising" (Read: "socialist") reforms. The Chongqing and Guangdong experiences therefore manifest another internal contradiction: national-level policies instituted through this incentive-based system generate different responses at the subnational levels that could lead to further tensions between both locally oriented agendas and central objectives. If there were at all a stand-alone 'China Model', it would surely be one characterised by this intense contradiction rather than overarching monikers like communism or capitalism.

Taken together, then, these aspects exemplify a dynamic, if at times incommensurable, engagement between a cautious and rigid party-state apparatus with the twin processes of economic liberalisation and market-like rule. To what extent then could this engagement constitute a challenge to the global neoliberal hegemony?

Underlying the notion of "challenge" is the presupposition of one approach taking on another with the ultimate goal of supersession. Applying this notion to China's post-Mao engagement with a global economy dominated by the Washington Consensus inevitably presupposes that the Chinese government aims to supersede neoliberal logics by imposing a new developmental paradigm across the world.

But, as we have previously argued, the emergence of what appears to be an alternative developmental approach cannot always be construed in zero-sum terms. What the materials presented in this book suggest, instead, is that the China Model was gradually reconfigured – in both geographical and institutional terms – to engage positively with neoliberal logics. This was not an exclusive outcome of Deng Xiaoping's reforms in the 1980s and Zhu Rongji's deepening marketisation of the 1990s; the process had been arguably set in motion, in part, by Mao Zedong's willingness to engage with the US in the early 1970s; in part by engagements with the global system of capitalism via Hong Kong throughout the Mao era;[5] and in part because conditions for private production were never fully extinguished in spite of the Socialist High Tide (1955–1957, preceding the Great Leap) and Cultural Revolution (1966–1976).

After market reforms were launched in 1978 and subsequently expanded in the 1980s, CPC leaders began forsaking the kind of internationalism associated with Marxist ideology. In an intriguing turn, this internationalism was dropped in favour of a Stalinistic approach – the notion that "socialism in one country" is possible without corresponding worldwide revolution. It was under this premise that Deng re-introduced private production and capital accumulation into the national economic system; the overarching goal was to make use of increased output and surplus to fulfill the vision of "socialism with Chinese characteristics". This friendly engagement with the global economy – especially pronounced in its welcoming attitude to FDI after the 2001 World Trade Organization (WTO) accession – should have alleviated fears of any concrete challenge to the global neoliberal order. This then leads to the question first raised in the Introduction: why is the Chinese developmental approach increasingly *perceived* to be a challenge?

Looking into the distant future, we have argued that hints of the impending intellectual and concrete challenge can be gleaned from the discourse now present in some quarters of Chinese academe and policy advisory. Already, these have begun tentatively cohering into a narrative shaping CPC rhetoric both domestically and on the world stage. It is a narrative that by now far outweighs the legacy of Deng's low-key foreign policy. In other words, ideology and mutual perceptions matter even if, potentially, China could be *at present* much more disruptive on the world stage than it actually is.

Perhaps the answer could *also* rest in the geographies of this perception. The emergence of China's economic capacities have largely been viewed in zero-sum terms in Western media and policymaking circles. It might be easy to understand if this portrayal is based on an anxiety over the loss of economic competitiveness; the situation becomes further complicated when it is fraught with the competition for finite resources and export-market share.

Fresh developments are emerging in tandem with global political-economic conditions, primarily the simultaneous movement towards geopolitical multi-polarity and intensifying geo-economic integration. For instance, China's much-touted "One Belt, One Road" initiative can potentially be portrayed, at present, as an all-out challenge to the US-led neoliberal world order or an insidious attack on the primacy of the US$ as global reserve currency. It is also partly grounded in Chinese concerns about the growing disparity between the eastern seaboard and the western provinces.[6] A key conceptual point to note, then, is the lack of clear-cut correlation between these developments and any institutional or cultural kernel that constitute a China Model.

Crudely put, we nevertheless believe the Chinese narrative enshrines state capitalism domestically, and we therefore find it hard to believe that the mammoth SOE sector will be downsized much further, even if Xi's anti-corruption campaign and supply-side economics might sound at the moment mellifluous in neoliberal ears.[7] There are already signs that despite the pro-market rhetoric annunciated during the third Plenum of the eighteenth Party Congress, Xi's administration will deepen the social welfare measures introduced during the Hu-Wen era as regards universal healthcare, unemployment benefits and pension coverage. Since the 1990s, China has been dogged by one the highest measures of income disparity in the world, as measured, for example, by the Gini figures. It would be difficult to reverse the trend completely, but we believe great efforts will be made to prevent a further widening of gaps between villagers, migrant workers and established urbanites, even if Scandinavian welfare levels are not really on the leadership cards.

It is important to note, in that respect, that much of the New Confucian discourse in China centres on issues of social justice. That discourse arguably confers another tier of performance legitimacy on CPC Leninist state capitalism, because in premodern China, uniquely, rulers were never beholden to financiers or high priests. Whether other perceived elements of the premodern patrimony – like for example low taxation, war aversion, bureaucratic meritocracy and *tianxia* magnanimity – will be relevant to Chinese statecraft in the future is moot. The third tier of legitimacy is conferred on the CPC, of course, by the success of the other East Asian developmental states, all of which rejected, in practice, the Washington Consensus on economic policy, whilst closely aligning themselves with Washington geo-politically.

Nationalism is perhaps the last tier of CPC legitimacy, but it is not least. Its advancement in the economic realm almost by definition means rejection of neoliberalism. We noted three key features of the Chinese variant of the developmental state: the maintenance of a large SOE sector, high inequality and sweeping receptivity to FDI. Only the last two features are congruent with neoliberalism and even so – they are likely to be assiduously kept constant if not abated over the next decade. China's current efforts to groom nominally privately owned technological "national champions" like Huawei and Lenovo for global primacy is reminiscent of policies in all other East Asian developmental states, and they may betoken less acceptance of foreign ownership in the future.

All these various tiers of legitimacy have meant the CPC could cling to power during an epoch of great social transformation and growing inequality. Its hold on power is assessed as fairly secure for now.[8] To continue holding power, we expect the CPC to continue rhetorically differentiating itself, as well as concretely, from neoliberalism, whilst simultaneously championing free global trade. Indeed, the weight of historical evidence suggests no underdeveloped predominantly rural economy could attain high living standards by either religiously buying into neoliberal prescripts or through embracing a Brazilian-style import substitution strategy.[9]

For these reasons, and assuming constant GDP growth, we expect the Chinese variant of the East Asian developmental model to attract more attention over the next decade amongst low and middle-income countries around the world. However, whether that authoritarian variant can gain any ideational traction in the West remains to be seen. Whilst redolent of historical grandeur and though it is growing in sophistication – China's new aspirational narrative is not yet seen as providing anything like an alternative to the US-led neoliberal world order. This is probably because of its enduring contradictions, as well as its rejection of parliamentary democracy and judiciary independence.

Yet, for any alternative to be workable in the age of heady globalisation, it must find an audience in richer countries too. In the absence of democracy, could such a narrative as China's ever gain traction in the developed world? Perhaps this might happen if and when China begins to demonstrate prowess in developing cutting-edge consumer technology of its own, not just manufacturing others'. That is to say, when China does not merely excel in applying the latest Western internet filtering technology to muzzle the likes of Google on its soil, but nurtures new Googles of its own, Western scepticism might begin to dissipate.

Notes

1 Cf. Nolan (2008).
2 Kroeber (2016), pp. 82–83.
3 cf. Morton (1984).
4 Brenner (2004); Jessop (2016).
5 Schenk (2000, 2007).
6 Summers (2015, 2017).
7 www.bloomberg.com/news/articles/2016-09-08/china-s-supply-side-is-a-far-cry-from-reagan-s
8 Whyte (2016).
9 Chang (2002).

Bibliography

Abramson, Marc C. (2008). *Ethnic Identity in Tang China*. Philadelphia: University of Pennsylvania Press.

Aivazian, Varouj A., Ying Ge, and Jiaping Qiu (2005). Can corporatization improve the performance of state-owned enterprises even without privatization? *Journal of Corporate Finance*, 11(5): 791–808.

Allen, Robert C. (2011). *Global Economic History*. Oxford: Oxford University Press.

Ambrosio, Thomas (2012). The rise of the 'China Model' and 'Beijing consensus': Evidence of authoritarian diffusion? *Contemporary Politics*, 18(4): 381–399.

Amsden, Alice H. (1992). Asia's Next Giant: South Korea and Late Industrialization. Oxford: Oxford University Press.

Amsden, Alice H. (2001). The Rise of 'The Rest': Challenges to the West From Late – Industrializing Economies. New York: Oxford University Press.

Aoki, Masahiko, Hyung-Ki Kim, and Masahiro Okuno-Fujiwara (eds.) (1997). *The Role of Government in East Asian Economic Development: Comparative Institutional Analysis*. Oxford: Clarendon Press.

Arrighi, Giovanni (2007). Adam Smith in Beijing: Lineages of the Twenty-First Century. London: Verso.

Baek, Seung-Wook (2005). Does China follow 'the East Asian development model'? *Journal of Contemporary Asia*, 35(4): 485–498.

Bairoch, P. (1993). *Economics and World History: Myths and Paradoxes*. Chicago: University of Chicago Press.

Ball, Alan M. (1990). *Russia's Last Capitalsits: The NEPmen, 1921–1929*. Berkeley, CA: University of California Press.

Bardhan, Pranab (2012). Awakening Giants, Feet of Clay: Assessing the Economic Rise of China and India. Princeton, NJ: Princeton University Press.

Beardson, Timothy (2014). *Stumbling Giant: The Threats to China's Future*. New Haven: Yale University Press, p. 120.

Beeson, Mark (2007). *Regionalism and Globalization in East Asia: Politics, Security and Economic Development*. New York: Palgrave Macmillan.

Beeson, Mark (2009). Developmental states in East Asia: A comparison of the Japanese and Chinese experiences. *Asian Perspective*, 33(2): 5–39.

Beeson, Mark and Iyanatul Islam (2005). Neo-liberalism and East Asia: Resisting the Washington consensus. *The Journal of Development Studies*, 41(2): 197–219.

Bell, Daniel (2010). *China's New Confucianism*. Princeton, NJ: Princeton University Press.

Bell, Daniel (2015). The China Model: Political Meritocracy and the Limits of Democracy. Princeton, NJ: Princeton University Press.

Bian, Morris (2005). The Making of the State Enterprise System in Modern China: The Dynamics of Institutional Change. Cambridge, MA: Harvard University Press.

Bloch, Marc (1961). *Feudal Society*. London: Routledge.

Block, Fred and Margaret Somers (2014). *The Power of Market Fundamentalism*. Cambridge, MA: Harvard University Press.

Bol, Peter K. (2008). *Neo-Confucianism in History*. Cambridge, MA: Harvard University Press.

Boltho, Andrea and Maria Weber (2009). Did China follow the East Asian development model? In Barry Naughton and Kellee S. Tsai (eds.), *State Capitalism, Institutional Adaptation, and the Chinese Miracle*. Cambridge: Cambridge University Press, pp. 240–264.

Bonefeld, Werner (2008). Global capital, national state, and the international. *Critique*, 36(1): 63–72.

Booth, Ann (2007). Can the 'Taiwan model' of growth with equity be replicated in the Southeast Asian context ? In Robert Ash and J. Megan Greene (eds.), *Taiwan in the 21st Century*. Abingdon: Routledge, pp. 74–99.

Brady, Anne-Marie (2009). *Marketing Dictatorship: Propaganda and Thought Work in Contemporary China*. Lanham: Rowman & Littlefield.

Bramall, Chris (2004). Chinese land reform in long-run perspective and in the wider East Asian context. *Journal of Agrarian Change*, 4: 107–141.

Bramall, Chris (2007). *The Industrialization of Rural China*. New York: Oxford University Press.

Bramall, Chris (2008). *Chinese Economic Development*. Abingdon: Routledge.

Brandt, Loren, Debin Ma and Thomas Rawski (2016). *Industrialization in China*. IZA Discussion Papers 10096, Institute for the Study of Labor (IZA).

Bray, David (2005). Social Space and Governance in Urban China: The Danwei System From Origins to Reform. Stanford: Stanford University Press.

Bremmer, Ian and Devin Stewart (2010). China's State Capitalism Poses Ethical Challenges. *Global Post*. http://www.carnegiecouncil.org/publications/articles_papers_reports/0065.html/:pf_printable?

Brenner, Neil (2004). *New State Spaces*. Oxford: Oxford University Press.

Breslin, Shaun G. (1996). China: Developmental state or dysfunctional development? *Third World Quarterly*, 17(4): 689–706.

Breslin, Shaun G. (2008). Do leaders matter? Chinese politics, leadership transition and the 17th Party Congress. *Contemporary Politics*, 14(2): 215–231.

Breslin, Shaun G. (2011). The 'China model' and the global crisis: From Friedrich List to a Chinese mode of governance? *International Affairs*, 87(6): 1323–1343.

Brzezinski, Zbigniew (2007). *The Grand Chessboard*. New York: Basic Books.

Buchanan, James and Gordon Tullock (1962). *The Calculus of Consent*. Ann Arbor: University of Michigan Press.

Buick, Adam and John Crump (1986). *State Capitalism: The Wages System Under New Management*. New York: Springer.

Bulmer-Thomas, Victor (2003). *The Economic History of Latin America Since Independence*. Cambridge: Cambridge University Press.

Burdekin, Richard C. (2008). *China's Monetary Challenges: Past Experiences and Future Prospects*. Cambridge: Cambridge University Press.

Burdekin, Richard C. and Ran Tao (Forthcoming). An empirical examination of the factors driving the offshore RMB market. Forthcoming in the *China Economic Journal*.

Butterfield, Herbert (1931). *The Whig Interpretation of History*. London: Bell.

Buzan, Barry (2010). China in international society: Is 'peaceful rise' possible. *The Chinese Journal of International Politics*, 3: 20.

Buzan, Barry (2014). The logic and contradiction of 'peaceful rise/development' as China's grand strategy. *The Chinese Journal of International Politics*, 7(4): 381-420.

Buzan, Barry and Michael Cox (2013). China and the US: Comparable cases of 'peaceful rise'. *The Chinese Journal of International Politics*, 6(2): 132.

Bytheway, Simon J. (2014). Investing Japan: Foreign Capital, Monetary Standards, and Economic Development, 1859–2011. Cambridge, MA: Harvard University Press.

Caixin (2015). Chongqing Mayor says rural land reform pilot has been just the ticket. 17 September. Accessed 23 February 2015, http://english.caixin.com/2015-09-17/100851144.html

Callahan, William A. (2012). Sino-speak: Chinese exceptionalism and the politics of history. *The Journal of Asian Studies*, 71(1): 33–55.

Callahan, William A. (2013). *China Dreams: 20 Visions of the Future*. New York: Oxford University Press.

Callahan, William A. (2015). History, tradition and the China dream: Socialist modernization in the world of great harmony. *Journal of Contemporary China*, 24(96): 990.

Cameron, Maxwell A. (2013). Strong Constitutions: Social-Cognitive Origins of the Separation of Powers. Oxford: Oxford University Press.

Caprotti, Federico (2014a). *Eco-Cities and the Transition to Low Carbon Economies*. London: Palgrave Pivot.

Caprotti, Federico (2014b). Eco-urbanism and the eco-city, or, denying the right to the city? *Antipode*, 46(5): 1285–1303.

Caprotti, Federico, Cecilia Springer and Nichola Harmer (2015). 'Eco' for whom? Envisioning eco-urbanism in the Sino-Singapore Tianjin Eco-city, China. *International Journal of Urban and Regional Research*, 39(3): 495–517.

Carroll, John M. (2007). *A Concise History of Hong Kong*. Lanham: Rowman & Littlefield.

Cartledge, Paul (2011). *Ancient Greece*. Oxford: Oxford University Press, pp. 124–133.

Chan, Kam Wing (2009). The Chinese hukou system at 50. *Eurasian Geography and Economics*, 50(2): 197–221.

Chan, Kam Wing and William Buckingham (2008). Is China abolishing the hukou system? *The China Quarterly*, 195: 582–606.

Chang, Chak Yan (1980). Overseas Chinese in China's policy. *The China Quarterly*, 82: 281–303.

Chang, Ha-Joon (2002). Kicking Away the Ladder: Development Strategy in Historical Perspective. London: Anthem Press.

Cheah, Boon Kheng (2009). The communist insurgency in Malaysia, 1948–90: Contesting the nation-state and social change. *New Zealand Journal of Asian Studies*, 11(1): 32–152.

Chen, Donglin (2001). 1964nian sanxian jianshe juecezhong de fenqi jiqi dui xibukaifa de qishi [Differences during the 1964 policymaking on the Third Front and its message for the Great Western Opening Up]. *Dangshi Yanjiu Ziliao*, 6: 1-11.

Chen, Chunlai (2011). Foreign Direct Investment in China: Location Determinants, Investor Behaviour and Economic Impact. London: Edward Elgar.

Chen, Geoffrey C. and Charles Lees (2016). Growing China's renewables sector: A developmental state approach. *New Political Economy*, 21: 574–586.

Chen, Gang and Litao Zhao (2014). Translating concept into practice: Sino-Singapore Tianjin Eco-City project. In Swee-Hock Saw and John Wong (eds.), *Advancing Singapore-China Economic Relations*. Singapore: ISEAS, pp. 94–125.

Chen, Hong (2007). Zhongguo jingjitequ jianli de qianqian houhou [The before and after of Special Economic Zone construction in China]. *Wenshibolan*, 12: 4–8.

Chen, Minglu and Goodman, David S. G. (2013). *Middle Class China: Identity and Behaviour*. Cheltenham: Edward Elgar.

Chen, Minglu and Y. Zheng (2008). China's regional disparity and its policy responses. *China & World Economy*, 16(4): 16–32.

Chen, Zhimin (2005). Nationalism, internationalism and Chinese foreign policy. *Journal of Contemporary China*, 14(42): 35–53.

Cheng, Joseph Y. (2013). The 'Chongqing Model': What it means to China today. *Journal of Comparative Asian Development*, 12(3): 411–442.

Cheng, Joseph Y. (2015). Introduction. In idem. (ed.), *The Use of Mao and the Chongqing Model*. Hong Kong: City University of Hong Kong Press, pp. 1–10.

Cheng, Tiejun and Mark Selden (1994). The origins and social consequences of China's hukou system. *The China Quarterly*, 139: 644–668.

Chien, Shiuh-Shen and Ian Gordon (2008). Territorial competition in China and the West. *Regional Studies*, 42(1): 31–49.

Chin, C. C. and Karl Hack (eds.) (2004). *Dialogues With Chin Peng: New Light on the Malayan Communist Party*. Singapore: Singapore University Press.

Chin, Peng (2003). *My Side of History*. Singapore: Media Masters.

China National Bureau of Statistics (2008), *China Statistical Yearbook 2007*. Beijing: China Statistics Press.

China National Bureau of Statistics (2015), *China Statistical Yearbook 2014*. Beijing: China Statistics Press.

Chiu, Becky and Mervyn Lewis (2006). *Reforming China's State-Owned Enterprises and Banks*. Cheltenham: Edward Elgar Publishing.

Chongqing Ribao (2010). Huang Qifan jieshou zhuanfang: Kongjiang Chongqing miandui 'pochancaizheng' santian nei chouji 10 yi yuan [Interview with Huang Qifan: Airborne Chongqing faces 'bankrupt finance', raises 1 billion in 3 days]. 12 July.

Chu, Yun-han (2009). Zhongguo moshi yu quanqiu zhixu chongzu [The China Model and the Remaking of the Global Order]. In Pan Wei (ed.), *Zhongguo Moshi* [The China Model] Beijing: Zhongyang bianyi chubanshe.

Chu, Yin-Wah (2016). Introduction, in idem (ed.) *The Asian Developmental State: Reexaminations and New Departures*, New York, NY: Springer, pp. 1–26.

Chua, Amy (2007). Day of Empire: How Hyperpowers Rise to Global Dominance – and Why they Fall. New York: Doubleday.

Clarence-Smith, William G. (2006). *Islam and the Abolition of Slavery*. Oxford: Oxford University Press.

CIA World Factbook (2016). *Country Comparison: Public Debt*. Accessed 27 July 2016, www.cia.gov/library/publications/the-world-factbook/rankorder/2186rank.html

Coase, Ronald and Ning Wang (2012). *How China Became Capitalist*. London: Palgrave Macmillan.

Colley, Linda (2005). *Britons: Forging the Nation, 1707–1837*. New Haven: Yale University Press.

Colpan, Asli M., Takashi Hikino, and James Lincoln (2010). *The Oxford Handbook of Business Groups*. Oxford: Oxford University Press.

Confucius, *Lunyu* ['Annalects'], 'Wei Ling Gong' verse 22. Available at: http://www.acmuller.net/con-dao/analects.html#div-16

CPC Shanghai Municipal Party Committee History Research Office (2004) *Deng Xiaoping zai Shanghai [Deng Xiaoping in Shanghai]*. Shanghai: Renmin Chubanshe.

Creel, Herrlee G. (1970). *The Origins of Statecraft in China*. Chicago: University of Chicago Press.

Dabla-Norris, Era (2005). Issues in intergovernmental fiscal relations in China. IMF Working Paper, Working Paper 05/30.

de Jong, Martin (2013). China's art of institutional bricolage: Selectiveness and gradualism in the policy transfer style of a nation. *Policy and Society*, 32(2): 89–101.

Deng, Xiaoping (1993). *Deng Xiaoping Wenxuan*, Vol. 3. Beijing: Renmin Chubanshe.

Deng, Xiaoping (1994). *Deng Xiaoping Wenxuan*, Vol. 2. Beijing: Renmin Chubanshe.

Deng, Zihui (2007) *Deng Zihui Zishu [Speeches of Deng Zihui]*, Beijing: Renmin Chubanshe.

Desai, Meghnad (2004) *Marx's Revenge: The Resurgence of Capitalism and the Death of Statist Socialism*. London: Pluto Press.

Desai, Radhika (2013). Geopolitical Economy: After US Hegemony, Globalization and Empire. London: Pluto Press.

Desker, Barry and Chong Guan Kwa (2011). *Goh Keng Swee: A Public Career Remembered*. Singapore: World Scientific.

Dickson, Bruce J. (2008). Wealth and Power: The Communist Party's Embrace of China's Private Sector. Cambridge: Cambridge University Press, pp. 40–41.

Dikötter, Frank (1992). *The Discourse of Race in Modern China*. Stanford: Stanford University Press.

Dikötter, Frank (2010). Mao's Great Famine: The History of China's Most Devastating Catastrophe, 1958–1962. London: Bloomsbury Publishing.

Dikötter, Frank (2013). *Tragedy of Liberation*. London: Bloomsbury.

Dikötter, Frank (2016). *The Cultural Revolution: A People's History, 1962–1976*. London: Bloomsbury Publishing.

Ding, Xueliang (2011). *Zhongguo Moshi: Zancheng yu Fandui* [The Chinese Model: For and Against]. Hong Kong: Oxford University Press.

Dirlik, Arif (1978). Revolution and History: The Origins of Marxist Historiography in China, 1919–1937. Berkeley: University of California Press.

Dirlik, Arif (1996). Reversals, ironies, hegemonies: notes on the contemporary historiography of modern China. *Modern China*, 22(3): 243–284.

Dirlik, Arif (2006). *Beijing Consensus: Beijing 'Gongshi.' Who Recognizes Whom and to What End*? Working Paper, www.globalautonomy.ca/global1/article.jsp?index=PP_Dirlik_BeijingConsensus.xml

Dirlik, Arif (2012a). The idea of a 'Chinese model': A critical discussion. *China Information*, 26(3): 277–302.

Dirlik, Arif (2012b). Mao Zedong in contemporary Chinese official discourse and history. *China Perspectives*, 2: 17–27.

Doner, Richard F., Bryan K. Ritchie and D. Slater (2005). Systemic vulnerability and the origins of developmental states: Northeast and Southeast Asia in comparative perspective. *International Organization*, 59(2): 327–361.

Donnithorne, Audrey (1972). China's cellular economy: Some economic trends since the cultural revolution. *The China Quarterly*, 52: 605–619.

Douglass, Mike (1994). The 'developmental state' and the newly industrialised economies of Asia. *Environment and Planning A*, 26(4): 543–566.

Drèze, Jean and Amartya Kumar Sen (2002). *India: Development and Participation*. New York: Oxford University Press.

Duara, Prasenjit (1995). *Rescuing History From the Nation*. Chicago: The University of Chicago Press.

Eaton, Richard M. (2006). The rise and fall of military slavery in the Deccan, 1450–1650. In Indrani Chatterji and idem. (eds.), *Slavery and South Asian History*. Bloomgton: Indiana University Press, pp. 115–135.

Eaton, Sarah (2015). *The Advance of the State in Contemporary China: State-Market Relations in the Reform Era*. Cambridge: Cambridge University Press.

The Economist (2011). The Guangdong model. November 26.

Elman, Benjamin A. (2000). *A Cultural History of Civil Examinations in Late Imperial China* Berkeley, CA: University of California Press.

Elman, Benjamin A. (2013). *Civil Examinations and Meritocracy in Late Imperial China.* Cambridge, MA: Harvard University Press.

Elvin, Mark (1973). *Pattern of the Chinese Past.* Stanford: Stanford University Press.

Etzkowitz, Henry and Sandra N. Brisolla (1999). Failure and success: The fate of industrial policy in Latin America and South East Asia. *Research Policy*, 28(4): 337–350.

Evans, Peter B. (1995). *Embedded Autonomy: States and Industrial Transformation*, Vol. 25. Princeton, NJ: Princeton University Press.

Fan, Peng (2009). Zhongguo shehui jiegou yu shehui yishi dui guojia weihu wending mosgi de yingxiang. In Pan Wei (ed.), *Zhongguo Moshi* [The China Model]. Beijing: Zhongyang bianyi chubanshe, pp. 455–495.

Feng, Huiyuan and Kai He (2015). America in the eyes of America watchers: Survey research in Beijing in 2012. *Journal of Contemporary China*, 24(91): 84.

Ferchen, M. (2013). Whose China model is it anyway? The contentious search for consensus. *Review of International Political Economy*, 20(2): 390–420.

Ferguson, Niall (2001). The Cash Nexus: Money and Power in the Modern World, 1700–2000. New York: Basic Books.

Ferguson, Niall (2008). The Ascent of Money: A Financial History of the World. London: Penguin.

Feuchtwang, Stephan (1992). *The Imperial Metaphore: Popular Religion in China.* Abingdon: Routledge.

Fewsmith, Joseph (2005). China under Hu Jintao. *China Leadership Monitor*, 14 April. Accessed 22 May 2017, http://media.hoover.org/sites/default/files/documents/clm14_jf.pdf

Fitzgerald, John (1995). The nationless state: The search for a nation in modern Chinese nationalism. *The Australian Journal of Chinese Affairs*, 33: 75–104.

Flüchter, Antje and Jivanta Schöttli (2014). The dynamics of transculturality: Concepts and institutions in motion. New York: Springer.

Foot, Rosemary and Andrew Walter (2010). *China, the United States and Global Order.* Cambridge: Cambridge University Press.

Ford, Christopher A. (2015). The party and the sage: Communist China's use of quasi-Confucian rationalizations for one-party dictatorship and imperial ambition. *Journal of Contemporary China*, 24(96): 1042.

Fredrickson, George M. (2004). America's original sin. *The New York Review of Books*, 25 March, www.nybooks.com/articles/archives/2004/mar/25/americas-original-sin/

Friedberg, Aaron (2000). Will Europe's past be Asia's future? *Survival*, 42(3): 147–159.

Friedman, Edward, Paul G. Pickowicz, and Mark Selden (1993). *Chinese Village, Socialist State.* New Haven: Yale University Press.

Friedman, Edward, Paul G. Pickowicz, and Mark Selden (2007). *Revolution, Resistance and Reform in Village China.* New Haven: Yale University Press.

Fu, Zhengyuan (1994). *Autocratic Tradition and Chinese Politics.* Cambridge: Cambridge University Press.

Fukuyama, Francis (1992). *The End of History and the Last Man.* New York: Free Press.

Gao, Mobo (2008). The Battle for China's Past: Mao and the Cultural Revolution. London: Pluto Press.

Ge, Ying (2009). Globalization and Industry Agglomeration in China. *World Development* 37(3): 550–559.

Gilsinan, Kathy (2015). Cliché of the moment: 'China's increasing assertiveness. *The Atlantic*, 25 September, www.theatlantic.com/international/archive/2015/09/south-china-sea-assertiveness/407203/

Glaser, Bonnie and Evan Medeiros (2007). The Changing Ecology of Foreign Policy-Making in China: The Ascension and Demise of the Theory of 'Peaceful Rise'. *The China Quarterly*, 190: 291–310.

Glassman, Jim (1999). State power beyond the 'territorial trap': The internationalization of the state. *Political Geography*, 18(6): 669–696.

Glassman, Jim (2004). Economic 'nationalism' in a post-nationalist era: The political economy of economic policy in post-crisis Thailand. *Critical Asian Studies*, 36(1): 37–64.

Godement, François (2015). *Contemporary China: Between Mao and Market*. Lanham: Rowman & Littlefield.

Goldstone, Jack A. and John F. Haldon (2008). Ancient states, empires and exploitation: Problems and perspectives. In Ian Morris and Walter Scheidel (eds.), *The Dynamics of Ancient Empires: State Power From Assyria to Byzantium: State Power From Assyria to Byzantium*. Oxford: Oxford University Press, pp. 3–29.

Goossaert, Vincent and David A. Palmer (2011). *The Religious Question in Modern China*. Chicago: University of Chicago Press.

Grabowski, Richard (1994). The successful developmental state: Where does it come from? *World Development*, 22(3): 413–422.

Greene, J. Megan (2009). *The origins of the developmental state in Taiwan: science policy and the quest for modernization*. Cambridge, MA: Harvard University Press.

Gries, Peter (1997). China can say no. *China Journal*, 37(January): 180–185.

Groot, Gerry (2004). Managing Transitions: The Chinese Communist Party, United Front Work, Corporatism and Hegemony. London: Routledge.

Grossman, Gregory (1977). The second economy in the USSR. *Problems of Communism*, 26(September/October): 25–40.

Grossman, Gregory (1998). *Subverted Sovereignty: Historic Role of the Soviet Underground*. Research Series-Institute of International Studies. Berkeley, CA: University of California, pp. 24–50.

Grossman, Richard S. (2010). Unsettled Account: The Evolution of Banking in the Industrialized World Since 1800. Princeton, NJ: Princeton University Press.

Guangdong Bureau of Statistics. (2008). *Guangdong Statistical Yearbook 2007*. Beijing: China Statistics Press.

Guo, Sujian (2006). Challenges and opportunities for China's 'peaceful rise', In idem. (ed.), *China's 'Peaceful Rise' in the 21st Century*. Burlington: Ashgate, p. 2.

Gurley, John G. (1976). *China's Economy and the Maoist Strategy*. New York: Monthly Review Press.

Haber, Stephen (2006). The political economy of Latin American industrialization. In Victor Bulmer-Thomas, John Coatsworth and Roberto Cortes Conde (eds.), *The Cambridge Economic History of Latin America: Volume 2, The Long Twentieth Century*. Cambridge: Cambridge University Press, pp. 537–584.

Haggard, Stephan (2004). Institutions and growth in East Asia. *Studies in Comparative International Development*, 38(4): 53–81.

Halper, Stefan (2010). *The Beijing Consensus*. New York: Basic Books.

Han, Enze (2013). Contestation and Adaptation: The Politics of National Identity in China. Oxford: Oxford University Press.

Han, Rui and Jingping Li (2012). Xinjiapo gongwuyuan zhongyang gongjijin zhidu jiqi qishi. [Lessons of Singapore's civil service central provident fund institution]. *Lilun yu Gaige*, 3: 99–102.

Han, Xiya (韩西雅) and Ma Bin (马宾) (2012). Strange and doubtful: The relationship between Zoellick and Zheng Bijian. Utopia, 3 March, www.wyzxwk.com/Article/shidai/2012/03/289000.html

Hansen, Valerie (1990). *Changing Gods in Medieval China, 1127–1276*. Princeton, NJ: Princeton University Press.

Hao, Yufan and Lin Su (2005). Contending views: Emerging Chinese elites' perception of America. In idem. (eds.), *China's Foreign Policy Making: Societal Force and Chinese American Policy*. Aldershot: Ashgate.

Harney, Alexandra (2009). The China Price: The True Cost of Chinese Competitive Advantage. London: Penguin.

Harvey, D. (1982). *The limits to capital*. Oxford: Blackwell.

Harvey, David (1985). The Geopolitics of capitalism. In D. Gregory and J. Urry (eds.), *Social Relations and Spatial Structures*. London: Macmillan, pp. 128–163.

Harvey, David (2005a). *A Brief History of Neoliberalism*. Oxford: Oxford University Press.

Harvey, David (2005b). *Spaces of Neoliberalization: Towards a Theory of Uneven Geographical Development*. Wiesbaden: Fritz Steiner Verlag.

He, Bingmeng (2015). 何秉孟,'再论新自由主义的本质'《当代经济研究》年第2期, pp. 5–11.

He, Canfei, Yehua Dennis Wei, and Xiuzhen Xie (2008). Globalization, institutional change, and industrial location: Economic transition and industrial concentration in China. *Regional Studies*, 42(7): 923–945.

Heaton, William (1982). China and Southeast Asian communist movements: The decline of dual track diplomacy. *Asian Survey*, 22(8): 779–800.

Heilmann, S., and E. Perry., eds. (2011). *Mao's Invisible Hand: The Political Foundations of Adaptive Governance in China*. Cambridge, MA: Harvard University Press.

Herbert, Penelope A. (1988). Examine the Honest, Appraise the Able: Contemporary Assessments of Civil Service Selection in Early Tang China. Canberra: Australian National University Monograph.

Ho, Ping-ti (1964). *The Ladder of Success in Imperial China: Aspects of Social Mobility*, 1368–1911. New York: Science Editions.

Holloway, John (1994). Global capital and the national state. *Capital & Class*, 18(1): 23–49.

Holloway, Kenneth W. (2013). *The Quest for Ecstatic Morality in Early China*. Oxford University Press, pp. 58–62.

Holt, Mack P. (2005). *The French Wars of Religion, 1562–1629*. Cambridge: Cambridge University Press.

Honda, Yuki (2004). The formation and transformation of the Japanese system of transition from school to work. *Social Science Japan Journal*, 7(1): 103–115.

Hook, Glenn D. and Takeda Hiroko (2007). 'Self-responsibility' and the nature of the post-war Japanese state: Risk through the looking glass. *The Journal of Japanese Studies*, 33(1): 93–123.

Horesh, Niv (2009). What time is the 'great divergence'? And why economic historians think it matters. *China Review International*, 16(1): 18–32.

Horesh, Niv (2013). In search of the China Model. *China Report*, 49: 337–355.

Horesh, Niv and Kean Fan Lim (2017a). China: An East Asian alternative to neoliberalism? *The Pacific Review*. 30(4): 425–442.

Horesh, Niv and Lim, Kean Fan (2017b). The 'China Model' as a complicated developmental trope. *China: An International Journal* 15(2): 166–176.

Horesh, Niv, Hyun Jin Kim and Peter Mauch (2013). *Superpower, China?* Chicago: World Scientific-Now Publishers Series in Business.

Howe, Christopher (1973). *Wage Patterns and Wage Policy in Modern China, 1919–1972*. Cambridge, UK: Cambridge University Press.

Howell, Jude (2006). Reflections on the Chinese State. *Development and Change,* 37(2): 273–297.

Hsiao, Kung-Chuan, (1960). *Rural China: Imperial Control in the Nineteenth Century.* Seattle: University of Washington Press.

Hsu, Sara (2014). *China's Debt Problem.* University of Nottingham, China Policy Institute, Policy Paper Series 6, www.nottingham.ac.uk/cpi/documents/policy-papers/cpi-policy-paper-2014-no-6-hsu.pdf

Hsu, Sara (2016). Economic Reform in Asia: China, India, and Japan. Cheltenham: Edward Elgar.

Hu, Angang (2001). *Diqu yu fazhan: xibukaifa xinzhanlüe* [Regions and Development: The New Strategy of Western Opening Up]. Beijing: Zhongguo Jihua Chubanshe.

Hu, Ching-Fen (2005). Taiwan's geopolitics and Chiang Ching-Kuo's decision to democratize Taiwan. *Stanford Journal of East Asian Affairs,* 5(1): 26–44.

Hua, Shiping. (2014). Introduction. In idem. and R. Hu (eds.), *East Asian Development Model: Twenty-First Century Perspectives.* London: Routledge, pp. 3–9.

Huang, Can and N. Sharif. (2009) Manufacturing Dynamics and Spillovers: The Case of Guangdong Province and Hong Kong, Macau, and Taiwan (HKMT). *Research Policy* 38(5): 813–828.

Huang, Chaohan and Baocui Lou (2014). Zhongxin guanxi qianjing: Xinjiapo mianlin de xin tiaozhan. [PRC-Singapore relations: New challenges]. *Journal of Henan Normal University,* 41(1): 66–70.

Huang, Phillip C. (2011). Chongqing equitable development driven by a 'third hand'? *Modern China,* 37(6): 569–622.

Huang, Phillip C. (2012). Profit-making state firms and China's development experience: 'State capitalism' or 'Socialist market economy'? *Modern China,* 38(6): 591–629.

Huang, Y. (2008) *Capitalism with Chinese characteristics: Entrepreneurship and the State.* Cambridge: Cambridge University Press.

Huang, Yasheng and Tarun Khanna (2003). Can India overtake China? *Foreign Policy,* 137(July–August): 74–81.

Huang, Yipin and Xun Wang (2011). Does financial repression inhibit or facilitate economic growth? A case study of Chinese reform experience. *Oxford Bulletin of Economics and Statistics,* 73(6): 833–855.

Huaxia Shibao (2007). Fang Chongqing shiwei shuji Wang Yang: dazhang qigu fazhan feigong jingji. [Interview with Chongqing Party Secretary Wang Yang: Develop the non-state economy with great fanfare]. 17 November.

Huff, Gregg (1995a). What is the Singapore model of economic development? *Cambridge Journal of Economics,* 19(6): 735–759.

Huff, Gregg (1995b). The developmental state, government, and Singapore's economic development since 1960. *World Development,* 23(8): 1421–1438.

Huff, W. G., Gerda Dewit and Christine Oughton (2001). Credibility and reputation building in the developmental state: A model with East Asian applications. *World Development,* 29(4): 711–724.

Hughes, James (1998). Re-evaluating Stalin's Peasant Policy in 1928–30. In J. Pallot (ed.), *Transforming Peasants: Society, State and the Peasantry, 1861–1930.* London: Palgrave Macmillan, pp. 238–257.

Hymes, Robert P. (1987). Statesmen and Gentlemen: The Elite of Fu-Chou Chiang-Hsi, in Northern and Southern Sung. Cambridge: Cambridge University Press.

Inkpen, Andrew and Wang Pien (2006). An examination of collaboration and knowledge transfer: China – Singapore Suzhou Industrial Park. *Journal of Management Studies,* 43(4): 779–811.

Israel, Jonathan I. (2001). Radical Enlightenment: Philosophy, and the Making of Modernity, 1650–1750. Oxford: Oxford University Press.

Jacobin (2015). China fantasies. Issue 19. Accessed 24 May 2016, www.jacobinmag. com/2015/12/china-new-global-order-imperialism-communist-party-globalization/

Jacques, Martin (2012). When China Rules the World: The End of the Western World and the Birth of a New Global Order. London: Penguin.

Jessop, Bob (2016). *The State: Past, Present, Future*. Cambridge: Polity Press.

Jin, Shengrong (2010). 金圣荣 [Kill Toyota!] (English title on Chinese cover in the original) Beijing: Xin shijie chubanshe. Chinese title: <谁想干掉丰田? 美国式阴谋伏击的真相>.

Johansson, Anders C. (2012). Financial repression and China's economic imbalances. In H. McKay and L. Song (eds.), *Rebalancing and Sustaining Growth in China*. Canberra: Australian National University E Press, pp. 45–64.

Johnson, Chalmers (1982). MITI and the Japanese Miracle: The Growth of Industrial Policy: 1925–1975. Stanford: Stanford University Press.

Johnson, Chalmers (1988). Political institutions and economic performance: The government-business relationship in Japan, South Korea, and Taiwan. In F. Deyo (ed.), *The Political Economy of the New Asian Industrialism*. Ithaca, NY: Cornell University Press, pp. 136–164.

Johnson, Chalmers (1995). Japan, Who Governs?: The Rise of the Developmental State. New York: WW Norton & Company.

Johnston, Alastair Iain (1998). *Cultural Realism: Strategic Culture and Grand Strategy in Chinese History*. Princeton, NJ: Princeton University Press.

Johnston, Alastair (2013). How new and assertive is China's new assertiveness? *International Security*, 37(4): 7–48.

Jones, Clarence B. (2014). Talking about America's original sin. *Huffington Post*, 27 July, www.huffingtonpost.com/clarence-b-jones/americas-original-sin_b_5396544.html

Kang, David C. (2012). East Asia Before the West: Five Centuries of Trade and Tribute. New York: Columbia University Press.

Kasahara, S. (2013). *The Asian Developmental State and the Flying Geese Paradigm*. UNCTAD Discussion Papers No. 213, http://unctad.org/en/PublicationsLibrary/osgdp20133_en.pdf

Katz, Richard (1998). *Japan: The System that Soured*. Armonk, N.Y: M.E. Sharpe.

Kaufmann, E. P. (2004) *The Rise and Fall of Anglo-America*. Cambridge, MA: Harvard University Press.

Ke, Qingshi (1959). Lun 'Quanguo Yipanqi' [On 'the Nation as a Chessboard']. *Hongqi* 4: 9–12.

Kennedy, Scott (2010). The myth of the Beijing consensus. *Journal of Contemporary China*, 19(65, June): 461–477.

Kim, Eun Mee (1997). Big Business, Strong State: Collusion and Conflict in South Korean Development, 1960–1990. Albany, N.Y.: SUNY Press.

Kim, Wonik (2009). Rethinking colonialism and the origins of the developmental state in East Asia. *Journal of Contemporary Asia*, 39(3): 382–399.

Kim, Yun Tae (1999). Neoliberalism and the decline of the developmental state. *Journal of Contemporary Asia*, 29(4): 441–461.

Klein, Martin A. (2014). *Historical Dictionary of Slavery and Abolition*. Lanham: Rowman & Littlefield, *passim*.

Knight, John B. (2014). China as a developmental state. *The World Economy*, 37(10): 1335–1347.

Kowalski, Przemyslaw, Max Büge and M. Sztajerowska (2013). *State-Owned Enterprises: Trade Effects and Policy Implications*. Working Paper, OECD Trade Policy Papers, No. 147, OECD Publishing, Paris.

Kracke, Edward A. Jr. (1947). Family Vs. merit in Chinese civil service examinations under the empire. *Harvard Journal of Asiatic Studies*, 10(2): 103–127.

Kroeber, Arthur (2016). *China's Economy: What Everyone Needs to Know*. Oxford: Oxford University Press.

Kuang, Daoqiu (2013). *Xingdaojueqi: Xinjiapo de liguo zhihui* [Rise of a Star Island: Nation-Building Intelligence of Singapore]. Beijing: Renmin Chubanshe.

Kueh, Y. Y. (2008). China's New Industrialization Strategy: Was Chairman Mao Really Necessary.Cheltenham: Edward Elgar.

Kung, James Kai-Sing (2008). The political economy of land reform in China's 'Newly liberated areas': Evidence from Wuxi. *China Quarterly*, 195(September): 675–690.

Kurlatznick, Joshua (2008). Charm Offensive: How China's Soft Power Is Transforming the World. New Haven: Yale University Press.

Kuromiya, Hiroaki (1990). *Stalin's Industrial Revolution: Politics and Workers, 1928–1931*, Vol. 60. Cambridge: Cambridge University Press.

Lach, Donald F. (1965). *Asia in the Making of Europe*, Vol. I. Chicago: University of Chicago Press, p. 787.

Lain, Alastair and Mingming Shen (eds.) (2015). *Perception and Misperception in American and Chinese Views of the Other*. New York: Carnegie Endowment for International Peace, http://carnegieendowment.org/2015/09/22/perception-and-misperception-in-american-and-chinese-views-of-other/iics

Lampton, David (2013). Security-relevant perceptions in U.S.-China relations: Elites and society, 11 November, http://china.usc.edu/david-m-lampton-security-relevant-perceptions-us-china-relations-elites-and-society.

Lardy, Nicholas (2008). *Financial Repression in China*. Washington, D. C.: Peterson Institute for International Economics Working Paper No. PB08–8.

Lardy, Nicholas (2014). *Markets Over Mao: The Rise of Private Business in China*. Washington, D.C.: Peterson Institute of International Economics.

Latif, Asad (2007). *Between Rising Powers: China, Singapore, and India*. Singapore: ISEAS.

Lee, Kuan Yew (1973). *On the change in great power relations at the Commonwealth Heads of*

Government Meeting, Ottawa, 3 August. Available at National Archives of Singapore, http://www.nas.gov.sg/archivesonline/data/pdfdoc/lky19730803.pdf

Leibold, James (2013). *Ethnic Policy in the PRC: Where China Is Heading*. Honolulu: East West Center.

Lenin, Vladimir I. (1966). *Collected Works*. Moscow: Foreign Languages Publishing House.

Leonard, Mark (2012). *China 3.0*. Berlin: European Council on Foreign Relations.

Levine, Ari (2008). Divided by a Common Language: Factional Conflict in Late Northern Song China. Honolulu: University of Hawaii Press.

Leyser, Karl (1994). Communications and Power in Medieval Europe: The Gregorian Revolution and Beyond. A&C Black.

Li, Cheng (2016). *Chinese Politics in the Xi Jinping Era: Reassessing Collective Leadership*. Washington, DC: Brookings Institution Press.

Li, Cheng (2005). The status and characteristics of foreign-educated returnees in the Chinese leadership. *China Leadership Monitor*, 16: 1-21

Li, Huaiyin (2006). *Village China Under Socialism and Reform*. Stanford: Stanford University Press.

Li, Luqu (2008). Xinjiapo zhengzhi fazhan moshi bijiao yanjiu [Comparative research on political development in Singapore]. *Shehuizhuyi yanjiu*, 2008(1): 127–131.

Li, P. (2003). *Zong Zhi Hui Hongtu: Li Peng San Xia Riji*. Beijing: China Three Gorges Publishing House.

Li, Xiangqian (2003). 1964: Zhongguo jingji zhengzhi biandong de lishi qiyin [1964: The historical origin of changes in the Chinese political economy]. *21 shiji*, 59: 47–56.

Liang, Zai, Z. Li, and Z. Ma. (2014). Changing Patterns of the Floating Population in China, 2000–2010. *Population and Development Review* 40(4): 695–716.

Lieberthal, Kenneth and Wang Jisi (2012). *Addressing U.S.-China Strategic Distrust*. The Brookings Institution, March 2012, www.brookings.edu/~/media/research/files/papers/2012/3/30-us-china-lieberthal/0330_china_lieberthal.pdf, pp. 7–19.

Lieu, Samuel N. C. (1985). *Manichaeism*. Manchester: Manchester University Press.

Liew, Leong H. (2005). China's engagement with neo-liberalism: Path dependency, geography, and party self-reinvention. *The Journal of Development Studies*, 41(2): 331–352.

Lim, Kean Fan (2010). On China's growing geo-economic influence and the evolution of variegated capitalism. *Geoforum*, 41: 677–688.

Lim, Kean Fan (2012a). The point is to keep going: The global sub-prime mortgage crisis, local labour market repositioning, and the capital accumulation dynamic in Singapore. *Journal of Economic Geography*, 12(3): 693–716.

Lim, Kean Fan (2012b). What you see is (not) what you get? The Taiwan question, geo-economic realities, and the 'China threat' imaginary. *Antipode*, 44(4): 1348–1373.

Lim, Kean Fan (2014a). 'Socialism with Chinese characteristics': Uneven development, variegated neoliberalization and the dialectical differentiation of state spatiality. *Progress in Human Geography*, 38(2): 221–247.

Lim, Kean Fan (2014b). Spatial egalitarianism as a social 'counter-movement': On socio-economic reforms in Chongqing. *Economy and Society*, 43(3): 455–493.

Lim, Kean Fan (2017). On the shifting spatial logics of socioeconomic regulation in post-1949 China. *Territory, Politics, Governance*. 5(1), 65-91.

Lim, Kean Fan and Niv Horesh (2016a). The Chongqing vs. Guangdong developmental 'models' in post-Mao China: Regional and historical perspectives on the dynamics of socioeconomic change. *Journal of the Asia Pacific Economy*. Online version: http://www.tandfonline.com/doi/full/10.1080/13547860.2016.1263044

Lim, Kean Fan and Niv Horesh (2016b). The 'Singapore fever' in China: Policy mobility and mutation. *The China Quarterly*, 228: 992–1017.

Lim, Kean Fan and Niv Horesh (Forthcoming). The 'China Model' as a complicated developmental trope. *China: An International Journal*.

Lin, G. C. S. (1997). *Red Capitalism in South China: Growth and Development of the Pearl River Delta*. Vancouver: UBC Press.

Lin, Justin Yifu (2012). *Demystifying the Chinese Economy*. Cambridge: Cambridge University Press.

Lin, Justin Yifu (2014). *The Quest for Prosperity: How Developing Economies Can Take Off*. Princeton, NJ: Princeton University Press.

Lin, Nan (2011). Capitalism in China: A centrally managed capitalism (CMC) and its future. *Management and Organization Review*, 7(1): 63–96.

Lin, Shanwei (2003). *Dalu Jingji Jiegou Tiaozheng Zhanlüe [Economic restructuring strategy of mainland China]*. Beijing: Zhongguo Shehui Kexue Chubanshe.

Lind, Michael (2013). *Land of Promise*. New York: HarperCollins.

Lindert, Peter H. (2004). Growing Public: Volume 1, the Story: Social Spending and Economic Growth Since the Eighteenth Century, Vol. 1. Cambridge: Cambridge University Press.

Liow, Eugene D. (2012). The neoliberal-developmental state: Singapore as case study. *Critical Sociology*, 38: 241–264.

Lipset, Seymour M. (March 1959). Some social requisites of democracy: Economic development and political legitimacy. *American Political Science Review*, 53(1): 69–105.

Liu, Elliot (2016). Maoism and the Chinese Revolution: A Critical Introduction. Oakland: PM Press.

Liu, Li (2009). Academic freedom, political correctness, and early civilisation in Chinese archaeology: The debate on Xia-Erlitou relations. *Antiquity*, 83: 831–843.

Liu, Mingfu (2010). *Zhongguo meng: ZhongMei shiji duijue, junren yao fayan* [The China Dream: Soldiers Must Speak Out on the Coming Sino-American Showdown]. Hong Kong: Zhonghua shujiu.

Liu, Mingfu (2015). The China Dream: Great Power Thinking and Strategic Posture in the Post-American Era. New York: CN Times.

Liu, William Guanglin (2015). The making of a fiscal state in Song China, 960–1279. *Economic History Review*, 68(1): 48–78.

Lu, Lachang and Yehua D. Wei. (2007). Domesticating Globalisation, New Economic Spaces and Regional Polarisation in Guangdong Province, China. *Tijdschrift Voor Economische en Sociale Geografie* 98(2): 225–244.

Luttwak, Edward N. (2011). *The Rise of China vs. the Logic of Strategy*. Cambridge, MA: Harvard University Press.

Lynch, Daniel (2015). China's Futures: PRC Elites Debate Economics, Politics, and Foreign Policy. Stanford: Stanford University Press.

Lyons, Thomas P. (1986). Explaining economic fragmentation in China: A systems approach. *Journal of Comparative Economics*, 10(3): 209–236.

Ma, L. J. (2005). Urban Administrative Restructuring, Changing Scale Relations and Local Economic Development in China. *Political Geography* 24(4): 477–497.

Ma, Yufeng (2006a). *Zoujin Xinjiapo 1* [Entering Singapore 1]. Singapore: Candid Creation Publishing.

Ma, Yufeng (2006b). *Zoujin Xinjiapo 2* [Entering Singapore 2]. Singapore: Candid Creation Publishing.

Makeham, John (2008). Lost Soul: 'Confucianism' in Contemporary Chinese Academic Discourse. Cambridge, MA: Harvard University Press.

Mao, Tse-tung. (1977). *Selected Works*, Vol. 5. Beijing: Foreign Languages Press.

Mao, Zedong (1999). *Mao Zedong Wenji* Vol. 7. Beijing: Renmin Chubanshe.

Mao, Zedong (1958). Concerning Economic Problems Of Socialism In The USSR. November. Available at: https://www.marxists.org/reference/archive/mao/selected-works/volume-8/mswv8_65.htm

Massey, Doreen (1984[1995]). *Spatial Divisions of Labour*. London: Routledge.

McCarthy, Susan (2011). Communist Multiculturalism: Ethnic Revival in Southwest China. Seattle: University of Washington Press.

McKinnon, Ronald I. (2013). The Unloved Dollar Standard: From Bretton Woods to the Rise of China. Oxford: Oxford University Press.

Mearsheimer, John J. (2014). Can China rise peacefully. *The National Interest*, 25 October, http://nationalinterest.org/commentary/can-china-rise-peacefully-10204

Meisner, M. (1999) *Mao's China and After: A History of the People's Republic*, Third Edition. New York: The Free Press.

Meng, Xin, Nancy Qian and Pierre Yared (2015). The institutional causes of China's Great Famine, 1959–1961. *The Review of Economic Studies*, 82(4): 1568–1611.

Meyer, Susanne D. Schiller, and J.R. Diez. (2012). The Localization of Electronics Manufacturing in the Greater Pearl River Delta, China: Do Global Implants Put Down Local Roots? *Applied Geography* 32(1): 119–129.

Miao, Bo and Graeme Lang (2015). A tale of two eco-cities: Experimentation under hierarchy in Shanghai and Tianjin. *Urban Policy and Research*, 33(2): 247–263.

Mierzejewski, Dominik (2009). *Public Discourse on the 'Peaceful Rise' Concept in Mainland China*. Discussion Paper 42, China Policy Institute, University of Nottingham.

Ming Bao (2012). Hu Yaobang erzi pi Bo Xilai: Chongqing moshi shi wenge siwei. [Son of Hu Yaobang criticizes Bo Xilai: The Chongqing model is a line of thought of the Cultural Revolution]. 4 December.

Minns, J. (2001). Of miracles and models: The rise and decline of the developmental state in South Korea. *Third World Quarterly*, 22(6): 1025–1043.

Morley, J. W. (2015). Driven by Growth: Political Change in the Asia-Pacific Region. London: Routledge.

Morton, H. W. (1984). *The Contemporary Soviet City*. Armonk, N. Y.: M.E. Sharpe.

Mulvad, Andreas (2015). Competing Hegemonic Projects within China's Variegated Capitalism: 'Liberal' Guangdong vs.'Statist' Chongqing. *New Political Economy* 20 (2): 199–227.

Mukhopadhaya, Pundarik (2014). *Income Inequality in Singapore*. Oxon: Routledge.

Murphy, Emma (2009). Learning the right Lesson from Beijing: A model for the Arab world. In Robert Springbord (ed.), *Development Models in Muslim Contexts: Chinese, 'Islamic' and Neo-Liberal Alternatives*. Edinburgh: Edinburgh University Press, pp. 85–114.

Nanyang Technological University. 2012. "NTU launches the new Mayors' Programme for high-level Chinese officials," 11 April, http://media.ntu.edu.sg/Pages/newsdetail. aspx?news=7d670892-53db-4056-abea-f16764d7226c. Accessed 20 September 2016

Nathan, Andrew (2015). China's challenge. *Journal of Democracy*, 26(1): 156–170.

National Bureau of Statistics. (2014). *China Statistical Yearbook 2013*. Beijing: China Statistics Press.

Naughton, Barry (1988). The third front: Defence industrialization in the Chinese interior. *China Quarterly*, 115: 351–386.

Naughton, Barry (1995). *Growing Out of the Plan*. Cambridge: Cambridge University Press, pp. 38–55.

Naughton, Barry (2007). *The Chinese Economy: Transition and Growth*. Cambridge, MA: MIT Press.

Naughton, Barry (2010). China's distinctive system: Can it be a model for others? *Journal of Contemporary China*, 19(65): 437–460.

Nee, Victor, Sonja Opper and Sonia Wong (2007). Developmental state and corporate governance in China. *Management and Organization Review*, 3(1): 19–53.

Nivison, David S. (1959). Ho-shen and his accusers: Ideology and political behaviour in the eighteenth century. In idem. and Arthur F. Wright (eds.), *Confucianism in Action*. Stanford: Stanford University Press, pp. 209–243.

Nolan, Peter (2008). Capitalism and Freedom: The Contradictory Character of Globalisation. Cambridge: Anthem Press.

Nolan, Peter (2012). *Is China Buying the World?* Cambridge: Polity.

Oh, Eun Young (2011). Is financial repression really bad? *International Journal of Economics and Finance Studies*, 3: 75–84.

Oi, Jean C. (1992). Fiscal reform and the economic foundations of local state corporatism in China. *World Politics*, 45(1): 99–126.

Oi, Jean C. (1999). Rural China Takes Off: Institutional Foundations of Economic Reform. Berkeley: University of California Press.

Olds, Kris and H. W.-C. Yeung. (2004). Pathways to global city formation: a view from the developmental city-state of Singapore. *Review of International Political Economy,* 11(3): 489–521.

Ong, Aihwa (2004). The Chinese axis: Zoning technologies and variegated sovereignty. *Journal of East Asian Studies,* 4: 69–96.

Ong, Weichong (2015). Malaysia's Defeat of Armed Communism: The Second Emergency, 1968–1989. Abingdon: Routledge.

Öniş, Ziya (1991). The logic of the developmental state. *Comparative Politics,* 24(1): 109–126.

Ortmann, Stephan (2012). The 'Beijing consensus' and the 'Singapore model': Unmasking the myth of an alternative authoritarian state-capitalist model. *Journal of Chinese Economic and Business Studies,* 10(4): 337–359.

Ortmann, Stephan and Mark Thompson (2014). China's obsession with Singapore: Learning authoritarian modernity. *The Pacific Review,* 27(3): 433–455.

Pak, Hyobom (1974). China and the West: Myths and Realities in History. Leiden: Brill.

Palmer, Michael J. E. (1987). The surface-subsoil form of divided ownership in late imperial China: Some examples from the new territories of Hong Kong. *Modern Asian Studies,* 21(1): 1–119.

Pan, Wei (2007). *The Chinese Model of Development*. Working Paper, 11 October, posted by The Independent, London-based think-tank, the Foreign Policy Centre.

Pan, Wei (2009). Dangdai Zhonghua tizhi – Zhongguo moshi de jingji, zhengzhi, shehui jiexi [The contemporary Chinese system: An analysis of the Chines emodel of economics, politics and social order]. In idem. (ed.), *Zhongguo Moshi* [The China Model]. Beijing: Zhongyang bianyi chubanshe, pp. 3–85.

Pantsov, Alexander V. and Steven Levin (2015). *Deng Xiaoping: A Revolutionary Life*. New York: Oxford University Press.

Park, Sang Young (2010). Crafting and dismantling the egalitarian social contract: The changing state-society relations in globalizing Korea. *The Pacific Review,* 23(5): 579–601.

Party Literature Research Office (1998). *Jianguo yilai Mao Zedong Wengao*, Vol. 13. Beijing: Zhongyang Wenxian Chubanshe.

Peck, Jamie (2002). Political economies of scale: Fast policy, interscalar relations, and neoliberal workfare. *Economic Geography,* 78(3): 331–360.

Peck, Jamie (2010). *Constructions of Neoliberal Reason*. Oxford: Oxford University Press.

Peck, Jamie and Nik Theodore (2007). Variegated capitalism. *Progress in Human Geography,* 31(6): 731–772.

Peck, Jamie and J. Zhang (2013). A variety of capitalism . . . with Chinese characteristics? *Journal of Economic Geography,* 13(3): 357–396.

Peerenboom, Randall (2007). *China Modernizes*. Oxford: Oxford University Press.

Pekkanen, Robert (2004). After the developmental state: Civil society in Japan. *Journal of East Asian Studies,* 4(3): 363–388.

Pereira, Alexius (2004). The Suzhou Industrial Park experiment: The case of China – Singapore governmental collaboration. *Journal of Contemporary China,* 13(38): 173–193.

Pereira, Alexius (2007). Transnational state entrepreneurship? Assessing Singapore's Suzhou Industrial Park project (1994–2004). *Asia Pacific Viewpoint,* 48(3): 287–298.

Pereira, Alexius (2008). Whither the developmental state? Explaining Singapore's continued developmentalism. *Third World Quarterly,* 29(6): 1189–1203.

Perkins, Dwight H. (2013). *East Asian Development*. Cambridge, MA: Harvard University Press.

Phoenix Weekly (2014). *Xinjiapo: Moshi bangyang weiji* [Singapore: Crisis of an exemplar model]. May.

Picketty, Thomas (2014). *Capital in the Twenty-First Century*. Cambridge, MA: Harvard University Press.

Pillsbury, Michael (2015). The Hundred-Year Marathon: China's Secret Strategy to Replace America as the Global Superpower. New York: Henry Holt.

Pines, Yuri (2005a). Beasts or humans: Pre-imperial origins of Sino-barbarian dichotomy. In Reuven Amitai and Michal Biran (eds.), *Mongols, Turks and Others: Eurasian Nomads and the Sedentary World.* Leiden: Brill, pp. 59–102.

Pines, Yuri (2005b). Disputers of abdication: Zhanguo Egalitarianism and the Sovereign's power. *T'oung Pao*, Second Series, 91(4–5): 243–300.

Pines, Yuri (2012). *The Everlasting Empire*. Princeton, NJ: Princeton University Press.

Pines, Yuri (2013). Between merit and pedigree: Evolution of the concept of 'elevating the worthy' in pre-imperial China. In Daniel A. Bell and Chenyang Li (eds.), *The East Asian Challenge for Democracy: Political Meritocracy in Comparative Perspective.* Cambridge: Cambridge University Press, pp. 161–202.

Poncet, S. (2005). A fragmented China: Measure and determinants of Chinese domestic market disintegration. *Review of International Economics*, 13(3): 409–430.

Pow, Choon Piew, and Harvey Neo (2013). Seeing red over green: Contesting urban sustainabilities in China. *Urban Studies*, 50(11): 2256–2274.

Puett, Michael (2015). Ghosts, gods, and the coming apocalypse: Empire and religion in early China and Ancient Rome. In Walter Scheidel (ed.), *State Power in Ancient China and Rome*. Oxford: Oxford University Press, pp. 230–259.

Puk, Wing-kin (2016). The Rise and Fall of a Public Debt Market in 16th-Century China: The Story of the Ming Salt Certificate. Boston: Brill.

Pye, Lucian W. (1995). Factions and the politics of guanxi: Paradoxes in Chinese administrative and political behaviour. *The China Journal*, 34: 35–53.

Qiu, Feng (2011). Huanying Guangdong moshi, Chongqing moshi de jingzheng [Welcoming the competition between the Guangdong and Chongqing models]. 10 June. Accessed 5 November 2015, http://view.qq.com/a/20110610/000038.htm

Qiushi (2014). The Chinese Path: An Answer to a Series of Problems Developing Countries Face in Modernization, vol. 6(3). July 1, http://english.qstheory.cn/2014-08/14/c_1111963549.htm

Radio Free Asia (2015). Li Guangyao de zhiguo linian (Yu Yingshi) [Lee Kuan Yew's principles and thoughts on government (Yu Yingshi)]. 8 April. Accessed 1 June, www.rfa.org/mandarin/pinglun/yuyingshi/yys-04082015143948.html

Rajaratnam, S. (1977). Non-communist subversion in Singapore. In Seah Chee Meow (ed.), *Trends in Singapore: Proceedings and Background Papers*. Singapore: Singapore University Press.

Ramakrishna, Kumar (2002). Emergency Propaganda: The Winning of Malayan Hearts and Minds, 1948–1958. Surrey: Curzon Press.

Ramo, Joshua Cooper (2004). *The Beijing Consensus*. London: Foreign Policy Centre.

Rapoport, Elizabeth (2014). Utopian visions and real estate dreams: The eco-city past, present and future. *Geography Compass*, 8(2): 137–149.

Rawski, Thomas G. (1995). Implications of China' Reform Experience. *The China Quarterly*, 144, 1150–1173.

Rowe, William T. (1990). Success stories: Lineage and elite status in Hangyang County, c. 1368–1949. In Joseph W. Esherick and Mary Backus Rankin (eds.), *Chinese Local Elites and Patters of Dominance*. Berkeley, CA: University of California Press, pp. 51–81.

Rowe, William T. (2010). *China's Last Empire: The Great Qing*. Cambridge, MA: Harvard University Press.

Rozman, Gilbert (2013). *Sino-Russian Relations and U.S. Alliances in Northeast Asia*. China Policy Institute Policy Paper.

Runciman, David (2013). *The Confidence Trap*. Princeton, NJ: Princeton University Press.

Saaler, Sven and Christopher W. Szpilman (2011). Introduction: The emergence of Pan-Asianism as an ideal of Asian identity and solidarity, 1850–2008. In idem. (eds.), *Pan Asianism: A Documentary History*, 2 vols. Lanham: Rowman & Littlefield, pp. 1–43.

Saich, Anthony (2010). *Governance and Politics of China*, Third Edition. Basingstoke: Palgrave MacMillan.

Sampson, Steven L. (1987). The second economy of the Soviet Union and Eastern Europe. The *Annals of the American Academy of Political and Social Science*, 493(1): 120–136.

Saunders, Phillip C. (2000). China's America watchers: Changing attitudes towards the United States. *The China Quarterly*, 161: 41–65.

Schenk, Catherine (2000). Another Asian financial crisis: Monetary links between Hong Kong and China 1945–50. *Modern Asian Studies*, 34(3): 739–764.

Schenk, Catherine (2002). Hong Kong as an International Financial Centre: Emergence and Development, 1945–1965. London: Routledge.

Schenk, Catherine. (2007). Economic and Financial Integration Between Hong Kong and Mainland China Before the Open Door Policy 1965–75. Working Paper, available at SSRN 1026322.

Schoppa, Leonard J. (1997). Bargaining With Japan: What American Pressure Can and Cannot Do. New York: Columbia University Press.

Schram, Stuart R. (1971). Mao Tse-tung and the Theory of the Permanent Revolution, 1958–69. *The China Quarterly*, 46, 221-244.

Schrecker, John E. (2004). *The Chinese Revolution in Historical Perspective*. Westport: Greenwood.

Schurmann, Franz (1964). China's 'new economic policy' – Transition or beginning. *The China Quarterly*, 17: 65–91.

Scobell, Andrew and Scott W. Harold (2013). An 'assertive' China? Insights from interviews. *Asian Security*, 9(2): 111–131.

Shambaugh, David (1991). *Beautiful Imperialists: China Perceives America, 1972–1990*. Princeton, NJ: Princeton University Press.

Shambaugh, David (2008). *China's Communist Party: Atrophy and Adaptation*. Berkeley, CA: University of California Press.

Shambaugh, David (2013). *China Goes Global: The Partial Power*. Oxford: Oxford University Press.

Shanghai Municipal People's Procuratorate (2003). *Shicheng fazhi guangan* [Perspectives on rule of law in Singapore]. Shanghai: Shanghai Municipal People's Procuratorate Political Department.

Shen, Simon (2011). 'Obamania' in China and Its yielding to nationalism: Quantitative responses from elitist Chinese students in Beijing toward the 2008 U.S. election and structural analysis. *China Review*, 11(2): 183–210.

Sheng, Yumin (2010). *Economic Openness and Territorial Politics in China*. New York, NY: Cambridge University Press.

Shi, Tianjian and Jie Lu (2010). The shadow of Confucianism. *Journal of Democracy*, 21(4): 123–130.

Shibata, Kuniko (2008). Neoliberalism, risk, and spatial governance in the developmental state: Japanese planning in the global economy. *Critical Planning*, 15: 92–118.

Shih, Victor C. (2008). *Factions and Finance in China*. Cambridge: Cambridge University Press.

Shih, Victor, Christopher Adolph and Mingxing Liu (2012). Getting ahead in the communist party: Explaining the advancement of central committee members in China. *American Political Science Review*, 106(1): 166–187.

Shiraev, Eric and Z. Yang (2014). The Gao-Rao affair: A case of character assassination in Chinese politics in the 1950s. In Martijn Icks and Eric Shiraev (eds.), *Character Assassination Throughout the Ages*. New York: Palgrave Macmillan, pp. 237–252.

Shirk, Susan L. (1993). *The Political Logic of Economic Reform in China*, Vol. 24. Berkeley, CA: University of California Press.

Shirk, Susan L. (1996). Internationalization and China's economic reforms. In R. Keohane (ed.), *Internationalization and Domestic Politics*. Cambridge: Cambridge University Press, pp. 186–206.

Shirk, Susan L. (2008). *China: Fragile Superpower*. New York: Oxford University Press.

Shirk, Susan L. (2010). Introduction. In idem. (ed.), *Changing Media, Changing China*. New York: Oxford University Press.

Sina Finance (2006). Yufu moshi: Guoqi gaige jiazhi yangban [Chongqing model of growing prosperous: Value template of reforming state-owned enterprises]. 17 March. Available at: http://finance.sina.com.cn/g/20060317/15492426932.shtml

Singapore Ministry of Culture (1965). Report on Mr. Lee Kuan Yew's speech at the 4th anniversary celebrations of Delta Community Centre on Sunday, 30th May.

Smith, Neil (1984). *Uneven Development: Nature. Capital, and the Production of Space*. Oxford: Blackwell.

Smith, Paul Jacov (2003). Introduction: Problematizing the Song-Yuan-Ming transition. In idem. and Richard Von Glahn (eds.), *The Song-Yuan-Ming Transition in Chinese History* Cambridge, MA: Harvard University Press.

So, Alvin Y. (2016). The post-socialist path of the developmental state in China. In Y. Chu (ed.), *The Asian Developmental State*. Basingstoke: Palgrave Macmillan, pp. 175–196.

Sohu Finance (2012). Zhuanfang Cui Zhiyuan: Kending Chongqing jingyan erfei Chongqing moshi. [Exclusive interview with Cui Zhiyuan: Affirming the Chongqing experience, not the Chongqing model]. 19 January.

Solé-Farràs, Jesús (2013). *New Confucianism in Twenty-First Century China: The Construction of a Discourse*. New York: Routledge.

Somers, Robert M. (1986). Time, space and structure in the consolidation of the T'ang Dynasty (A.D. 617–700). *Journal of Asian Studies*, 45(5): 971–994.

Song, Hongbing (2007) *Currency Wars (貨幣戰爭)*.Beijing: Zhongxin Chubanshe.

Song, Jaeyoon (2011). Redefining good government: Shifting paradigms in the Song Dynasty (960–1279) discourse on 'Fengjian'. *T'oung Pao*, 97: 301–343.

Song, Qiang Zhang Zangzang, Qiao Ben, Gu Qingsheng and Tang Zhengyu (1996)*Zhongguo Neng Shuo Bu [China Can Say No]*. Beijing: Zhonghua Gongshang Lianhe Chubanshe.

Song, Xiaojun, Wang, Xiaodong, Huang, Jisu, Song, Qiang and Liu, Yang (2009). *Unhappy China: The Great Era, Grand Objective, and Our Domestic Troubles and Foreign Calamities (中国不高兴：大时代, 大目标及我们的内忧外患)*. Nanjing: Jiangsu renmin chubanshe.

Sørensen, Camilla T. N. (2015). The significance of Xi Jinping's 'Chinese dream' for Chinese foreign policy: From 'Tao Guang Yang Hui' to 'Fen Fa You Wei'. *Journal of China and International Relations*, 3(1): 53.

South China Morning Post (1999). Singapore drops control of Suzhou park. June 29.

Spulber, Nicolas (1979). *Organizational Alternatives in Soviet-Type Economies*. Cambridge: Cambridge University Press.

Steinbock, Dan (2012). One growth model, many Chinas: Guangdong, Chongqing, and China's regional differences. *Roubini EconoMonitor*, 12 December. Accessed 3 November 2015, www.economonitor.com/blog/2012/12/one-growth-model-many-chinas-guang dong-chongqing-and-chinas-regional-differences/

Stockwell, Anthony (1993). A widespread and long-concocted plot to overthrow government in Malaya'? The origins of the Malayan emergency. *The Journal of Imperial and Commonwealth History*, 21(3): 66–88.

Stockwell, Anthony (2006). Chin Peng and the struggle for Malaya. *Journal of the Royal Asiatic Society of Great Britain & Ireland*, 16(3): 279–297.

Stubbs, Richard (2009). What ever happened to the East Asian developmental state? The unfolding debate. *The Pacific Review*, 22(1): 1–22.

Studwell, Joe (2013). How Asia Works: Success and Failure in the World's Most Dynamic Region. New York: Grove/Atlantic, Inc.

Studwell, Joe (2014). How Asia Works: Success and Failure in the World's Most Dynamic Region. London: Profile Books.

Su, Wei, Fan Yang and Shiwen Liu (2011). *Chongqing moshi* [The Chongqing Model]. Beijing: Zhongguo Jingji Chubanshe.

Suettinger, Robert L. (2004). The rise and descent of 'peaceful rise'. *China Leadership Monitor*, 12: 3–5.

Summers, Tim (2015). China's 'New Silk Roads': Sub-national regions and networks of global political economy. *Third World Quarterly*, 37(9): 1628–1643.

Summers, Tim (Forthcoming 2017). Rocking the boat? China's 'belt and road' and global order. In A. Ehteshami and N. Horesh (eds.), *China's One Belt, One Road Vision: Implications for the Middle East*. Abingdon: Routledge.

Tan, See Seng (2009). Riding the Chinese: Singapore's pragmatic relationship with China. In Jun Tsunekawa (ed.), *The Rise of China: Responses From Southeast Asia and Japan*. Tokyo: National Institute for Defense Studies, pp. 21–46.

Taylor, Romeyn (1990). Official and popular religion and the political organization of Chinese society in the Ming. In Kwang-Ching Liu (ed.), *Orthodoxy in Late Imperial China*. Berkeley, CA: University of California Press, pp. 126–157, p. 131.

Teiwes, Frederick C. (1990). Politics at Mao's Court: Gao Gang and Party Factionalism in the Early 1950s. Armonk, N.Y.: ME Sharpe Inc.

Temenos, Cristina, and Eugene McCann (2013). Geographies of policy mobilities. *Geography Compass*, 7(5): 344–357.

Teng, Su Ching. 1998. *The mountains are high and the emperor is far away: developing the Suzhou Industrial Park in China*. Case Study C9-98-1009.0, Public Policy Programme, National University of Singapore.

Ter Haar, Barend J. (2000). Rethinking violence in Chinese culture. In Jon Abink and Goran Aijmer (eds.), *The Meaning of Violence: A Cross-Cultural Perspective*. London: Bloomsbury, pp. 123–140.

Terrill, Ross (2009). The New Chinese Empire: And What It Means For The United States. New York: Basic Books, p. 56.

Thornton, Patricia (2007). *Disciplining the State: Virtue, Violence and State-Making in Modern China*. Cambridge, MA: Harvard University Press, Chaps. 2–3.

Thurbon, Elizabeth (2016). Developmental Mindset: The Revival of Financial Activism in South Korea. Ithaca: Cornell University Press.

Tiezzi, Shannon (2015). America's AIIB disaster: Are there lessons to be learned. *The Diplomat*, 18 March, http://thediplomat.com/2015/03/americas-aiib-disaster-are-there-lessons-to-be-learned/

Tin-Bor Hui, Victoria (2005). *War and State Formation in Ancient China and Early Modern Europe*. Cambridge: Cambridge university Press, p. 148.

To, Lee Lai (1981). Deng Xiaoping's ASEAN tour: A perspective on Sino-Southeast Asian relations. *Contemporary Southeast Asia*, 3(1): 58–75.

Tracy, Noel and Constance Lever-Tracy (2004). China's local industries and the Chinese diaspora. In T. Menkhoff and S. Gerke (eds.) *Chinese Entrepreneurship and Asian Business Networks*, London: Routledge, pp. 65–83.

Tsang, Steve (1988). *Democracy Shelved: Great Britain, China, and Attempts at Constitutional Reform in Hong Kong, 1945–1952*. Hong Kong: Oxford University Press.

Tsang, Steve (2007). *A Modern History of Hong Kong*. London: I.B. Tauris.

Tsui, Kai Yuen (1991). China's regional inequality, 1952–1985. *Journal of Comparative Economics*, 15(1): 1–21.

Twichett, Denis (1959). The Fan Clan's charitable estate, 1050–1760. In David S. Nivison and Arthur F. Wright (eds.), *Confucianism in Action*. Stanford: Stanford University Press.

Twitchett, Denis (1995). *Financial Administration Under the T'ang Dynasty*. Cambridge: Cambridge University Press.

van de Ven, Hans J. (1992). *From Friend to Comrade: The Founding of the Chinese Communist Party, 1920–1927*. Berkeley, CA: University of California Press.

van der Kroef, Justus (1964). Nanyang University and the dilemmas of overseas Chinese education. *The China Quarterly*, 20: 96–127.

van der Kroef, Justus (1967). *Communism in Malaysia and Singapore: A Contemporary Survey*. The Hague: Martin Nijhoff.

Van Ness, Peter (1970). *Revolution and Chinese Foreign Policy: Peking's Support for Wars of National Liberation*. Berkeley: University of California Press.

Viola, Lynne (2007). *The Unknown Gulag: The Lost World of Stalin's Special Settlements*. Oxford: Oxford University Press.

Vogel, Ezra F. (1981). *Japan as Number One: Lessons for America*. Cambridge, MA: Harvard University Press.

Vogel, Ezra F. (2011). *Deng Xiaoping and the Transformation of China*. Cambridge, MA: Harvard University Press.

Von Glahn, Richard (2004). *Sinister Way: The Divine and the Demonic in Chinese Religious Culture*. Berkeley: University of California Press.

Wade, Robert (1990[2003]). *Governing the Market: Economic Theory and the Role of Government in East Asian Industrialization*. Princeton, NJ: Princeton University Press.

Walder, A. G. (2015). *China Under Mao*. Cambridge, MA: Harvard University Press.

Wall Street Journal (2008). Lin urges flexibility in fighting poverty. 29 February. Accessed 31 March 2016, http://online.wsj.com/news/articles/SB120422296784800317

Walter, C., and F. Howie (2011). *Red Capitalism: The Fragile Financial Foundation of China's Extraordinary Rise*. Singapore: Wiley.

Wan, Ming (2014). *The China Model and Global Political Economy: Comparison, Impact, and Interaction*. Abingdon: Routledge.

Wang, Gungwu (1970). Chinese politics in Malaya. *The China Quarterly*, 43, 1–30.

Wang, Gungwu, and Weichong Ong (eds.) (2009). *Voice of Malayan Revolution: The CPM Radio War Against Singapore and Malaysia 1969–1981*. Singapore: Select Books.

Wang, Gungwu and Zheng Yongnian (2008). Introduction. In idem. (eds.), *China and the New International Order*. Abingdon: Routledge.

Wang, Hui (2011). *The End of the Revolution: China and the Limits of Modernity*. London: Verso.

Wang, Huning (1991). *Meiguo fandui Meiguo*. Beijing: Xinhua.

Wang, Jianwei (2000). *Limited Adversaries: Post-Cold War Sino-American Mutual Images.* Oxford: Oxford University Press.

Wang, S., and A. Hu (1999). *The Political Economy of Uneven Development: The Case of China.* Armonk, NY: ME Sharpe.

Wang, Yi (2014). Peaceful development and the Chinese dream of national rejuvenation. *China Institute of International Studies,* 11 March, www.ciis.org.cn/english/2014-03/11/content_6733151.htm

Wang, Yigui (2011). Transcend peaceful rise – The necessity and possibility of China's implementation of strategy of tolerant rise. *World Economics and Politics,* 8(2011): 150.

Wang, Yuan-kang (2010). *Harmony and War: Confucian Culture and Chinese Power Politics.* New York: Columbia University Press.

Wang, Zhiying, and Chao Ren (2008). Dui Xinjiapo shehui baozhang zhidu de pingjia yu jiejian. [Evaluating and learning from Singapore's social welfare institution]. *Social Sciences Journal of Colleges of Shanxi,* 19(12): 30–33.

Webber, Michael M. Wang, and Z. Ying, eds. (2002). *China's Transition to a Global Economy.* Basingstoke: Palgrave MacMillan.

Wechsler, Howard J. (1979) T'ai-tsung (reign 626–49) the consolidator. In Denis Twitchett (ed.), *Cambridge History of China,* vol. 3, Part I, Cambridge: Cambridge University Press, pp. 188–241.

Wei, Yehua (1996). Fiscal systems and uneven regional development in China, 1978–1991. *Geoforum,* 27(3): 329–344.

Weiss, Jessica C. (2014). *Powerful Patriot: Nationalist Protest in China's Foreign Relations.* Oxford: Oxford University Press.

Wemheuer, Felix (2014). The Chinese revolution and 'liberation': Whose tragedy? *China Quarterly,* 219: 849–863.

Wested, Odd Arne (2005). The Global Cold War: Third World Interventions and the Making of Our Times. Cambridge: Cambridge University Press.

Whyte, Martin K. (2010). The paradoxes of rural-urban inequality in contemporary China. In idem. (ed.), *One Country, Two Societies: Rural-urban Inequality in Contemporary China.* Cambridge, MA: Harvard University Press.

Whyte, Martin K. (2012). China's post-socialist inequality. *Current History,* 111: 229–234.

Whyte, Martin K. (2016). China's dormant and active social volcanos. *The China Journal,* 75: 9–37.

Whyte, Martin K. and Dong-kyun Im (2014). Is the social volcano still dormant? Trends in Chinese attitudes toward inequality. *Social Science Research,* 48: 62–76.

Will, Pierre-Étienne and Roy Bin Wong (1991). *Nourish the People: The State Civilian Granary System in China, 1650–1850.* Ann Arbor: University of Michigan Press.

Wong, Joseph (2004). The adaptive developmental state in East Asia. *Journal of East Asian Studies,* 4(3): 345–362.

Wong, J. (2006). *Healthy Democracies: Welfare Politics in Taiwan and South Korea.* Ithaca: Cornell University Press.

Woodside, Alexander (2006). Lost Modernities: China, Vietnam, Korea, and the Hazards of World History. Cambridge, MA: Harvard University Press.

Wu, Fulong (2010). How neoliberal is China's reform? The origins of change during transition. *Eurasian Geography and Economics,* 51(5): 619–631.

Wu, Junqing (2014). *State and Heretics: The Construction of 'Heresy' in Chinese State Discourse.* Unpublished PhD Dissertation, University of Nottingham.

Wu, Yuanhua (2014). *Xinjiapo liangzhi* zhidao [The Path of Benevolent Governance in Singapore]. Beijing: China Social Sciences Press.

Wyatt, Don J. (2012). *The Blacks of Premodern China*. Philadelphia: University of Pennsylvania Press.

Xia, Yulong and Z. Feng. (1982). Tidu Lilun yu Quyu Jingji [Ladder-Step Theory and Regional Economies]. *Shanghai Kexue Yanjiusuo Qikan (Yanjiu yu Jianyi)*, 8: 21–24.

Xie, Shiqing (2009). Chengshi jichu sheshi de tourongzi tizhi chuangxin: 'Chongqing moshi'. [Institutional innovation in the financing of basic urban infrastructure: 'Chongqing model']. *Guoji Jingji Pinglun*, 7–8: 59–63.

Xu, Chenggang (2011). The fundamental institutions of China's reforms and development. *Journal of Economic Literature*, 49(4): 1076–1151.

Xu, Youyu (2013). Chongqing moshi he wenge yinghun [The Chongqing model and the lingering spirit of the Cultural Revolution]. *Yangguang Shiwu Zhoukan*, 38: 89–90.

Yan, Xuetong (2004). Peaceful rise: Divergences, meaning and tactics. *Social Sciences in China*, 5: 52.

Yan, Xuetong (2011). *Ancient Chinese Thought, Modern Chinese Power*. Princeton, NJ: Princeton University Press.

Yan, Xuetong (2014). From Keeping a Low Profile to Striving for Achievement, *The Chinese Journal of International Politics*, 7(2): 153–184.

Yang, Chun (2014). Market rebalancing of global production networks in the Post-Washington Consensus globalizing era: Transformation of export-oriented development in China. *Review of International Political Economy*, 21(1): 130–156.

Yang, Jianxue (2009). Xinjiapo fazhi moshi chutan [Preliminary exploration of Singapore's rule-of-law model]. *Around Southeast Asia*, 6: 29–32.

Yang, Jiechi (2013). Implementing the Chinese dream. *The National Interest*, 10 September, http://nationalinterest.org/commentary/implementing-the-chinese-dream-9026

Yang, Mu and Liang Fook Lye (2009). Sino-Singapore Tianjin Eco-city: Features of a model of sustainable living. In Swee-Hock Saw and John Wong (eds.), *Regional Economic Development in China*. Singapore: ISEAS-Yusof Ishak Institute, pp. 235–259.

Yao, Souchou (2008). All quiet on Jurong Road: Nanyang University and radical vision in Singapore. In Carl Trocki and Michael Barr (eds.), *Paths Not Taken: Political Pluralism in Post-War Singapore*. Singapore: NUS Press, pp. 170–187.

Yeung, Henry W. C. (2014). Governing the market in a globalizing era: Developmental states, global production networks and inter-firm dynamics in East Asia. *Review of International Political Economy*, 21(1): 70–101.

Yeung, Henry W. C. (2016). *Strategic Coupling: East Asian Industrial Transformation in the New Global Economy*. Ithaca: Cornell University Press.

You, Yu and Yanhong Lei (2013). Chongqing moshi de jingji weidu. [The economic dimension of the Chongqing model]. *Ershiyi Shiji Pinglun*, 135: 50–58.

Yu, Hong (2015). *Chinese Regions in Change: Industrial Upgrading and Regional Development Strategies*. London: Routledge.

Yu, Maochun (1996). *OSS in China: Prelude to Cold War*. New Haven: Yale University Press.

Yu, Wenxuan, Marilyn Rubin and Wei Wu (2012). An executive MPA program for China: Lessons from the field. *Journal of Public Affairs Education*, 18(3): 545–564.

Yü, Ying-shih (1994). Intellectual breakthroughs in the T'ang-Sung Transition. In Willard J. Peterson, Andrew H. Plaks and idem. (eds.), *The Power of Culture: Studies in Chinese Cultural History*. Hong Kong: The Chinese University Press, pp. 158–171.

Yu, Ying-shih (2000). *Democracy, Human Rights and Confucian Culture*. Oxford: St Anthony's College.

Yu, Ying-shih (2010). *Zhongguo wenhua tongshi*. Hong Kong: Oxford University Press.

Yusuf, Shahid (2014). There was once a Korean model. *Asian-Pacific Economic Literature*, 28(2): 88–96.

Zahari, Said (2007). *The Long Nightmare: My 17 Years as a Political Prisoner*. Kuala Lumpur: Utusan Publications.

Zeng, Jinghan (2013). What matters most in selecting top Chinese leaders? A qualitative comparative analysis. *Journal of Chinese Political Science*, 18: 223–239.

Zhang, Biwu (2012). Chinese Perceptions of the US: An Exploration of China's Foreign Policy Motivations. Lanham: Lexington Books.

Zhang, Feng (2012). Rethinking China's grand strategy: Beijing's evolving national interests and strategic ideas in the reform era. *International Politics*, 49(3): 318–345.

Zhang, Feng (2013). The rise of Chinese exceptionalism in international relations. *European Journal of International Relations*, 19(2): 310–314.

Zhang, Jun (2012). From Hong Kong's capitalist fundamentals to Singapore's authoritarian governance: The policy mobility of neo-liberalising Shenzhen, China. *Urban Studies*, 49(13): 2853–2871.

Zhang, Jun and Jamie Peck (2015). Variegated capitalism, Chinese style: Regional models, multi-scalar constructions. *Regional Studies*, 50(1): 52–78.

Zhang, Jian (2015). China's new foreign policy under Xi Jinping: Towards 'Peaceful Rise 2.0'. *Global Change, Peace & Security*, 27(1): 9–11.

Zhang, Jun (2012). From Hong Kong's capitalist fundamentals to Singapore's authoritarian governance: The policy mobility of neo-liberalising Shenzhen, China. *Urban Studies*, 49(13): 2853–2871.

Zhang, Shengjiang and Weining Hu (2010). <中国睦邻外交传统的文化底蕴> [The underlying essence of China's traditional good-neigbourly relations]. *Nanjing zhengzhi xueyuan xuebao* 南京政治学院学报 , 5: 69–71.

Zhang, Weiwei (2012). *The China Wave: Rise of a Civilizational State*. Singapore: World Scientific.

Zhao, Suisheng (2015). Rethinking the Chinese world order: The imperial cycle and the rise of China. *Journal of Contemporary China*, 24(96): 961–982.

Zhao, Tingyang (2005). 赵汀阳, 天下体系: *世界制度哲学导论* [The Tianxia System: A Philosophical Introduction] Nanjing: Jiangsu jiaoyu chubanshe, pp. 14–15, 154–160.

Zhao, Yuezhi (2012). The struggle for socialism in China: The Bo Xilai saga and beyond. *Monthly Review*, 64(5): 1–17.

Zhao, Ziyang (2009). *Prisoner of the State: The Secret Journal of Premier Zhao Ziyang*. New York, NY: Simon and Schuster.

Zheng, Bijian (2011). China's Road to Peaceful Rise: Observations on Its Causes, Basis, Connotations and Prospects. London and New York: Routledge.

Zheng, Bijian (2014). Sino-American cooperation is the core, common development in the Asian Pacific Region. *China Institute for Innovation & Development Strategy*, 20 June, www.ciids.cn/content/2015-10/14/content_11707792.htm

Zheng, Shiping (1997). *Party vs. State in Post-1949 China: The Institutional Dilemma*. Cambridge: Cambridge University Press.

Zheng, Yushuo (1998). *The Guangdong Development Model and Its Challenges*. Hong Kong: City University of Hong Kong Press.

Zheng, Yongnian (1994). Perforated sovereignty: Provincial dynamism and China's foreign trade. *The Pacific Review*, 7(3): 309–321.

Zheng, Yongnian (2013). China in 2012: Troubled elite, frustrated society. *Asian Survey*, 53(1): 162–175.

Zheng, Yongnian (2009). The Chinese Communist Party as Organisational Emperor. Abingdon: Routledge.

Zheng, Yongnian (2011). *Zhongguo moshi: jingyan yu kunju.* Beijing: Yangzhi wenhua.

Zheng, Yongnian and John Wong (eds.). (2013). *Goh Keng Swee on China: Selected Essays.* Singapore: World Scientific.

Zhou, Tianyong (2013). *The China Dream and the China Path.* Singapore: World Scientific.

Zhu, Houlun (2004). *Zhongguo Quyu Jingji Fazhan Zhanlüe [Regional economic development strategy of China].* Beijing: Shehui Kexue Wenxian Chubanshe.

Zhu, Jieming (2004). Local developmental state and order in China's urban development during transition. *International Journal of Urban and Regional Research,* 28(2): 424–447.

Zürcher, Erik (1972). *The Buddhist Conquest of China.* Leiden: Brill.

Zweig, David (2001). China's stalled 'fifth wave': Zhu Rongji's reform package of 1998–2000. *Asian Survey,* 41(2): 231–247.

Index